*This study has been accomplished
in part as a result of grants from
the National Trust for Historic Preservation,
the National Park Service, the Clark Foundation,
and the S.S. Johnson Foundation.*

VIRGINIA GUEST FERRIDAY

LAST OF THE
HANDMADE BUILDINGS

Glazed Terra Cotta in Downtown Portland

MARK PUBLISHING COMPANY

Portland, Oregon 1984

To Professor Marion Dean Ross,
who introduced me to terra cotta.

CONTENTS

ACKNOWLEDGEMENTS

Research on Portland's glazed terra-cotta buildings began in 1975 as the author's volunteer project for the Portland Junior League, and throughout the course of this study the League has been a mainstay. In 1979, the Junior League mounted an exhibit (also titled "Last of the Handmade Buildings") in its Architectural Preservation Gallery. The exhibit was devoted entirely to glazed terra-cotta buildings in Portland. Research conducted by the exhibit committee greatly enriched this study. Members of the exhibit committee were Marge Johnson (Gallery Chairman), Janet Charlton (Exhibit Coordinator), Claudia Ainsworth, Judy Daigle, Susan Hartwell, Paula Madden, Anne Murphy, Marcia Olson, Susan Redding, and Jean White. A second Junior League committee, researching individual buildings for the Portland Historical Landmarks Commission, also provided valuable information. Its members were Sharley Bryce, Ann Williams Hendrickson, Shirley Kuse, Jean Lofgren, Pat Roduner, and Bonnie Schlieman. In addition, the Junior League acted as the "umbrella" agency for the study, administering its grant funds.

As work on the project continued over the years (intermittently, to be sure), other individuals were of assistance. Al Edelman took dozens of excellent photographs, several of which are reproduced in this publication. The author consulted frequently with a number of experts. Of these unofficial advisors, the following read and commented on various portions of the manuscript: Tom Crawford, Steve Dotterer, Richard Engeman, Michael Harrison, James Hamrick, David Look, Lewis McArthur, George McMath, Rod O'Hiser, Elisabeth Potter, Tom Sawyer, Arthur C. Spencer III, Al Staehli, David Talbot, Robert Weil, and Leo Dean Williams.

Jane Hofmann edited the manuscript. Her ability to focus on details without losing sight of the whole was a blessing for the final product.

Staffs of the Oregon Historical Society and the City of Portland Bureau of Buildings were unusually helpful in locating photographs, plans, and specifications. Employees of Gladding, McBean & Co. were also generous with their time.

Finally, the author would like to acknowledge the work being done by the Friends of Terra Cotta. This organization, which has been largely responsible for the increased interest in terra cotta over the past few years, provides an invaluable network for the dissemination of information on the production, installation, maintenance, and restoration of terra cotta.

Virginia Guest Ferriday
September, 1984

INTRODUCTION

The complex nature of architecture allows for many different approaches to the writing of its history. Some architectural historians, fascinated by the role of an individual designer, choose to document one person's work, tracing its development and influences. Other historians select particular types of buildings (such as theaters, depots, or courthouses) or buildings of a particular architectural style. Still others concentrate on groups of buildings constructed of particular materials. The choice of glazed terra cotta as the theme for this study follows the latter approach and continues a tradition that includes research of log construction and cast iron. By further limiting this investigation to the use of glazed terra cotta in a specific downtown area, it has been possible to present not only a detailed discussion of a particular building material, but also, as sub-themes, analyses of a downtown business district in a distinct phase of its development and the types of structures found there.

Terra cotta, which can be translated literally as "burnt earth," is a hard-baked, fine-grained clay. It is similar to brick, but made of a better grade of clay and fired at a higher temperature. This study concerns itself with a specific type of terra cotta, called architectural terra cotta — hollow blocks, approximately 4-inches deep, with faces typically about 12 inches by 18 inches, applied to building exteriors. Architectural terra cotta is different from terra-cotta pots, statuary, and garden furniture, as well as structural terra cotta, which was used in the construction of interior partitions, column enclosures, and floor slabs. This study is also limited to *handmade* architectural terra cotta — that is, terra-cotta blocks formed by hand-pressing clay into plaster molds — and does not deal with ceramic veneer, a 1-1/2-inch thick, machine-extruded, architectural terra cotta developed in the 1930s.

While the use of baked-clay ware in the form of brick, tile, and pottery has evidently continued without interruption from earliest times, the use of architectural terra cotta (henceforth, referred to simply as "terra cotta") has been sporadic. Ornamental portions of Greek and Roman masonry structures were of terra cotta, as were many buildings of the Italian Renaissance. During the mid-1800s, its use in Europe expanded, and interest soon spread to the United States. By 1870, cornices and window frames of terra cotta were being produced in Chicago. In 1871, a paper entitled "Terra Cotta and its Uses" was presented at an American Institute of Architects convention. The first use in the United States of terra cotta for the overall facing, as well as individual decorative elements, of a large commercial building occurred in Chicago in the 1890s. By the late 1890s, terra cotta adorned commercial structures throughout the United States.

The rise in popularity of terra cotta around the turn of the century was aided by three technological developments that changed the size and shape of commercial buildings: the electric streetcar, the elevator, and the steel frame. The electric streetcar, because it could transport large numbers of people to shop and work in the central business district, created a demand there for dense development. The elevator made tall buildings usable, and the steel frame made them structurally feasible. Steel frames required protection from fire and weather, and the large size of commercial buildings demanded protective facings that were both lightweight and economical. Terra cotta answered these needs. Exterior walls faced with terra cotta weighed much less than walls faced with stone. Because the plaster molds for terra cotta were reusable, repetitive ornament could be economically produced.

Terra cotta can be unglazed, have a vitrified coating of pure clay (slip), or be fully glazed. Unglazed terra cotta is composed of the same material throughout and either derives its color from the material itself or is painted. Because the finish of any unglazed clay product will fuse through firing and become harder and denser than the main body, neither vitrified slips nor full glazes are necessary to protect terra-cotta blocks. They are applied, rather, to obtain a wide variety of permanent colors or a high gloss. Most Greek, Roman, and Italian Renaissance terra cotta was unglazed and painted. In Italy, the use of glazes was generally limited to small-scale works of art, such as those of the Della Robbia family.

Around 1885, technological developments in the terra-cotta industry made possible the production of a glazed terra cotta suitable for facing whole building exteriors. Extensive utilization of glazes had to wait a few years, however, for the change in architectural taste that followed the 1893 Columbian Exposition in Chicago. In contrast to the dark red and brown Richardsonian Romanesque buildings, which were popular prior to the time of the fair, Exposition buildings were, in conformance with their classical style, very light in color. Light-colored, classical-style buildings were soon being built across the United States.

The popularity of the classical styles, of light colors and of the glaze necessary to achieve these light colors on terra cotta remained strong to about 1920. During the 1920s, architectural tastes shifted again, to the Art Deco blacks, golds, greens, and peach colors, which also required glazes on terra cotta. This burst of color came at a point, however, when more and more ornament was being made of cast stone rather than terra cotta. Because it did not require firing, cast stone was cheaper to produce than terra cotta. It had one major disadvantage, however: it could not be glazed, so its color was limited to what could be added to the cement mixture itself.

During the 1930s, ceramic veneer, which was lighter in weight than traditional terra cotta (15 pounds per square foot versus 70 pounds per square foot) and cheaper to produce (30%-40% less), gained in popularity over terra-cotta blocks. However, ceramic veneer had a serious drawback: as an extruded product, its decoration was limited to designs with all lines parallel to the extrusion axis.

The use of glazed and unglazed terra cotta in Portland closely paralleled that in other cities of the United States. Portland's Richardsonian Romanesque commercial buildings of the late 1880s and 1890s have unglazed terra-cotta ornamentation. The effects of the 1893 Columbian Exposition were seen immediately in Portland with the construction of yellow-brick office structures with classical decorations in terra cotta, either painted off-white or with an off-white slip. Full-glazed terra cotta came into use around 1907. Classical ornament and off-white or buff-colored full glazes remained popular in Portland through the late 1920s. There is only one Art Deco glazed terra-cotta building in the downtown area — a black-and-gold façade installed in 1930.

Portland, in the first decades of this century (as now), had the reputation of being a conservative city; its classical buildings symbolized well the beliefs and aspirations of its business leaders. Clients responsible for construction of the downtown glazed terra-cotta buildings were of diverse backgrounds, having migrated from many parts of the United States, Canada, and Europe. Most, however, were middle-aged or older, and their investment in downtown real estate followed success in other fields — retailing, banking, and lumbering. As a result, they were undoubtedly more concerned with stability than with innovation. Their architects were generally younger, but most had either studied at the École des Beaux Arts or traveled in Europe — both prerequisites for producing correct classical designs.

Europe also provided the third and also essential group in the building process: craftsmen-artisans. On the West Coast, as in other parts of the United States, there were many immigrants who had been trained in Europe, not only in the technical aspects of their trades, but also in classical form, scale, and proportion. Architects depended on these men to correctly interpret their architectural drawings.

There is no evidence that Portland's own small version of the Columbian Exposition — the Lewis and Clark Fair of 1905 — had any measurable influence on local architectural styles. It did, however, mark the beginning of a period of rapid development, and it was this post-1905 growth spurt that produced the downtown group of glazed terra-cotta buildings. This period of accelerated development went hand in hand with the expansion of Portland's streetcar system; the glazed terra-cotta buildings are concentrated along what were at that time the major downtown carlines. This clustering of glazed terra-cotta buildings along the carlines is typical of other West Coast cities. It is in contrast to the scattering that occurred in East Coast and Midwest cities, where development of downtown cores preceded by some years the popularity of glazed terra cotta.

In Portland, as elsewhere in the United States, development slowed to a near halt during the 1930s. By the time construction resumed after World War II, classical styles had been abandoned entirely in favor of modern architecture. The first major commercial building constructed in Portland after the war — Pietro Belluschi's Equitable Building of 1948 — was sheathed in aluminum and glass.

Because the years 1905-1930 neatly encompass Portland's use of glazed terra cotta, its heyday of classical ornament, and its era of streetcar-oriented development, they have been chosen to delineate this study.

The study itself is divided into three parts. Part I traces the development of the district in which the glazed terra-cotta buildings are located, analyzes the basic building types on which terra cotta was placed, explains the production and installation of glazed terra cotta, and identifies other materials used in conjunction with the medium. Part II deals with preservation and restoration of the district, of the buildings, and of glazed terra cotta and other building materials. Part III contains a photograph and basic facts for each of the surviving downtown glazed terra-cotta buildings. Building names used throughout are the original names. An alphabetical list of original names with present-day names can be found in Part III.

Depending on a person's particular involvement with planning, architecture, or construction, different portions of this study will be of greater or lesser interest. It is the author's hope, however, to increase all readers' enjoyment of a highly significant urban resource.

PART I

HISTORY

DISTRICT DEVELOPMENT

Cities of the American West Coast tell the history of urban development in condensed form. In cities such as Los Angeles, Seattle, and Portland, the streetcar era followed the pedestrian era and the automobile the streetcar in rapid succession, each leaving clearly identifiable districts. Portland's glazed terra-cotta district remains today a nearly-unaltered artifact of the streetcar era, an artifact that at the same time reveals certain lasting patterns of the earlier pedestrian city.

PORTLAND'S PEDESTRIAN ERA (1850s-70s)

Incorporated in 1851, Portland was, by 1853, the principal port in Oregon, with a variety of commercial establishments along the west bank of the Willamette River. Its original 1845 street grid had been oriented to the river, rather than to the points of the compass, with streets perpendicular to the river terminating in wharves. This 1845 plat extended eight blocks along the river and was only two blocks deep. The northernmost and southernmost streets were extensions of the two principal roads leading to Portland from the rich agricultural lands to the west: Barnes Road, which ran directly into Washington Street, and Canyon Road, which ran into Jefferson Street.

In 1846, another row of eight blocks was platted to the west, and, in 1850, two more rows. Subsequent increments carried the grid, maintaining its original orientation, several blocks north and south, and westward to the base of the line of hills known as "the West Hills."

The street grid of Couch's Addition, platted in 1865 north of the original plat, followed a true north-south/east-west orientation, thereby creating a mismatch where it met the older grid. This second street system was also eventually extended to the base of the West Hills.

In 1852, two major sets of blocks were deeded for park use — the two Plaza (Courthouse) Blocks, between Third and Fourth Avenues and Salmon and Madison Streets, and the South Park Blocks, between Eighth and Ninth Avenues. The South Park Blocks were originally to have extended north to Washington, but the blocks north of Salmon were never firmly secured for park use and were eventually subdivided and developed. The Couch's Addition plat also included a row of blocks dedicated to park use between Eighth and Ninth, known as the North Park Blocks.

Transportation in the little river port was predominantly either by water or on foot, with handcarts and wagons serving primarily for the movement of goods. A ferry to the as-yet-undeveloped east side of the river began operation at Stark Street in 1855.

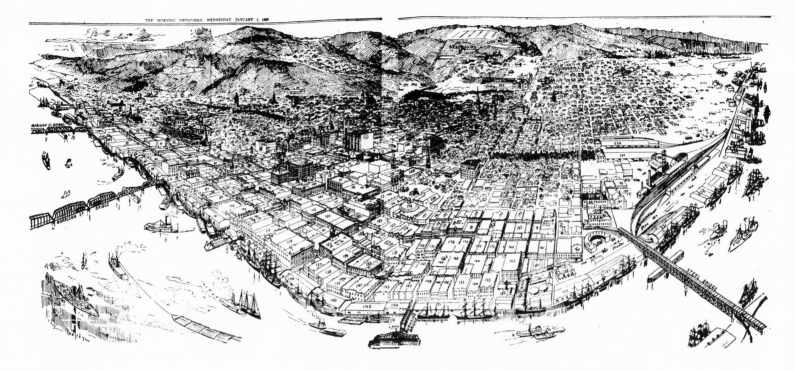

Fig. I-1. Bird's-eye view of downtown Portland looking southwest, 1896. The building in the center with the clock tower marks the nucleus of the newly-emerging streetcar commercial core.

STREETCARS AND BRIDGES (1870s-90s)

In 1872, a little "bobtail horsecar drawn by a Cayuse with a bell dangling from his collar"[1] began making occasional trips up and down First Avenue. Two more horsedrawn lines were established by 1882, and they continued to operate until they were retired in 1894. Steam-powered streetcar lines were running on Washington in 1889. By 1890, electricity was the major source of power for the streetcar system.

The Washington electric line was extended west and north to the new residential development of Willamette Heights in 1891. An 1890 cable-car line serving another West Hills residential area, Portland Heights, was later replaced by a streetcar line that also entered downtown on Washington. Thus, Washington very early became the major streetcar route from the west.

The first bridge across the Willamette, the 1887 Morrison Street Bridge, was followed by the Steel Bridge (1888), Madison Bridge (1891), and Burnside Bridge (1894). Because of the City's complicated franchises, streetcars often met at, rather than crossed, the bridges. Some streetcar lines from the bridges turned onto north-south streets in the riverfront commercial area. Still, the bridges tended to reinforce the importance of the downtown streets of which they were extensions. Notable exceptions were Madison and Burnside Streets. All cars from the Burnside Bridge turned either on First or Fifth Avenue, leaving the stretch of Burnside west of Fifth to Sixteenth Avenue (where Washington joined Burnside) devoid of service. Cars from Madison turned at Second Avenue. This left Glisan Street (at the Steel Bridge) and Morrison as the main beneficiaries of streetcar traffic from the, by 1900, rapidly developing East Side.

A bird's-eye view of Portland's downtown, which ran in the *Morning Oregonian* 1896 New Year's edition, shows clearly the incipient effects of these bridges and streetcar lines on the commercial core. (Fig. I-1.) The riverfront is lined with wharves and warehouses, with the Stark Street ferry still occupying a prominent position. The blocks between the river and Third are densely packed with three- and four-story buildings from Madison at the south to the Steel Bridge at Glisan on the north. But approximately five blocks west of the river along Morrison and Washington, a cluster of taller buildings has sprung up. These mostly Richardsonian Romanesque office buildings were the vanguard of the new streetcar-oriented downtown commercial core.

[1] Al J. Plamendon, compiler, "The Plamendon Scrapbooks."

LOCATION OF STREETCAR-ERA COMMERCIAL CORE

Though it now seems inevitable that the new commercial core would develop between Washington and Morrison west of Third, the degree to which this location was determined, not only by streetcar routes, but also by pre-existing land uses, is not generally perceived.

Any large new commercial buildings constructed after about 1900 would logically replace frame structures to the west rather than still-valuable masonry buildings in the riverfront commercial district. A westward movement was also logical because of flooding that periodically spread several blocks westward from the river. It was, in addition, assumed at the time that new development would leap over the blocks between Second and Third, which had, by 1890, when Portland's Chinese residents numbered about 20,000, become predominantly Chinese.

If Portland's residential areas had (like Seattle's, for example) lain north and south on an axis with its waterfront commercial district, the new streetcar-era downtown would (like Seattle's) have been located along car lines running parallel to the river. Portland's residential development was, however, taking place primarily on the east side of the river, in the West Hills, and within the near Northwest. Thus, streetcar lines that served these residential areas would enter downtown perpendicular to the old riverfront commercial district and establish a new district at right angles rather than parallel to it.

With Glisan, Washington, and Morrison as major streetcar routes and lines also operating on Burnside, Madison, and Jefferson, the new commercial district could

Fig. I-2. Bird's-eye view of downtown Portland looking southwest, 1928. With all but two glazed terracotta buildings in place, the new streetcar-era commercial core is nearly complete.

Fig. I-3. Map of downtown Portland, ca. 1900, showing streetcar lines and new westward bulge of commercial core. Dots indicate major commercial buildings constructed during the 1890s.

conceivably have located anywhere along the 17 blocks between Glisan and Jefferson. Circa-1900 land uses along these six east-west streets were, however, quite different, greatly influencing subsequent development. (Fig. I-3.)

Portland's 1890 Union Station had been built just two blocks north of Glisan and, as a result, the area along Glisan was soon dominated by railroad-related uses: warehousing, manufacturing, and lodging.

At the other extreme, the areas along Jefferson and Madison to the south were primarily residential and institutional, a consequence of dedicated uses adjacent to park blocks. The Plaza Blocks had been designated as courthouse squares, and the first county courthouse was built on the block adjacent to the northern block, on the site of the present courthouse. Portland's 1895 City Hall was located on the block cater-corner to (southwest of) the south Plaza Block. Numerous lots bordering the South Park Blocks had been deeded in 1853 to churches and fraternal organizations. There had thus been created, very early, an area of institutional uses along the southwest edge of downtown. Intermingling with the institutions were single-family and rental houses (as well as some tenements), all attracted no doubt by the park blocks.

Fig. I-4. Downtown Portland, ca. 1930, showing streetcar lines and fully-developed streetcar-oriented commercial core. Dots indicate glazed terra-cotta buildings, both remaining and demolished.

In 1869, the federal (Pioneer) courthouse was built between Morrison and Yamhill Street on the edge of the residential-institutional area. The courthouse was evidently a very busy place as it soon established a pattern of pedestrian movement up Morrison from the riverfront commercial area. In recognition of this new pattern, a streetcar loop along Morrison and Yamhill, between Front and Eleventh Avenues, was constructed in 1886. The Portland Hotel (demolished in 1951) was completed on the block west of the federal courthouse in 1890, and, in 1891, the Olds, Wortman & King department store relocated two blocks north at Fifth and Washington. The Meier & Frank Co. department store followed in 1898, constructing a half-block building (later demolished to make way for the present glazed terra-cotta structure) along Fifth on the block directly north of the courthouse.

By 1900, then, it was clear both from streetcar routes and from prevailing land uses that the new downtown commercial core would locate along Morrison. It was Washington, however, rather than Yamhill that became the second major east-west commercial street. Washington's advantage over Yamhill was due to one factor — that it, not Yamhill, carried the major streetcar lines serving westside residential areas.

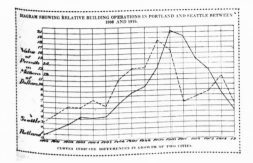

DIAGRAM SHOWING RELATIVE BUILDING OPERATIONS IN PORTLAND AND SEATTLE BETWEEN 1900 AND 1916.

CURVES INDICATE DIFFERENCES IN GROWTH OF TWO CITIES.

Fig. I-5. Graph from the *Morning Oregonian,* Jan. 1, 1916, showing building activity in Portland and its rival city, Seattle. Both cities had experienced dramatic increases in population during the years 1900 to 1910 — Seattle from 80,671 to 237,194 and Portland from 90,426 to 207,214. In Portland construction of glazed terra-cotta buildings peaked about three years after general construction.

LOCATION OF GLAZED TERRA-COTTA BUILDINGS

Surprisingly, one of the first glazed terra-cotta buildings built downtown and Portland's first "skyscraper," the 1907 Wells Fargo Building, was not located in the newly-developing commercial core, but rather to the north at the southwest corner of Sixth Avenue and Oak Street. Selection of the Wells Fargo Building site was, however, evidently a cost-saving measure as, according to a newspaper article of the time, the first choice site, at Fifth and Alder Street, was eliminated because the price was too high. Also, because the Wells Fargo Building was to be occupied by the three large companies responsible for building it, rather than rented to numerous small firms and professionals, accessibility was probably not as important a consideration as it would have been had there been the need to attract tenants.

Following 1907, however, construction of glazed terra-cotta buildings was concentrated in the new commercial core (in some cases, replacing earlier Richardsonian Romanesque structures). (Fig. I-4.) With their greater height and lighter-colored exteriors, the group of glazed terra-cotta buildings dominated the older riverfront district structures, clearly marking the new center of downtown and the rapidly expanding metropolitan area. (Fig. I-2.)

BUILDING ACTIVITY

Construction of glazed terra-cotta buildings in Portland's downtown did not occur at a steady pace. There was, instead, a sharp peak around 1913, one year after what was (according to historian John T. Labbe) probably the high point of Portland's electric streetcar system.[2] (Fig. I-5.) Three major glazed terra-cotta buildings were completed in 1912, four in 1913, and three in 1914. Then, with the demand for downtown office space temporarily satisfied, construction fell off rapidly.

While downtown glazed terra-cotta buildings of the 1900s and 1910s were predominantly office and retail structures, a full third built in the 1920s were residential or institutional.

Because most large commercial structures built in Portland's downtown between 1907 and 1920 were of glazed terra cotta, their numbers and types are representative of downtown construction in general during those years. During the 1920s, however, glazed terra cotta was losing relative favor and its use was no longer indicative of general downtown building activity.

SUBDISTRICTS

Clustered in and around the principal streetcar-era, downtown commercial district were several subdistricts. After 1905, a real-estate-oriented district began to develop around the intersection of Fourth and Oak with a builders' exchange, title insurance companies, and contractors' and architects' offices. A crescent-shaped hotel district grew up gradually between Park Avenue and Ninth and Washington and Oak Streets. By the late 1920s, banks were assembled along Stark between Fifth and Seventh.

In the office-retail core itself, neither Morrison nor Washington ever became *the* retail street. Each street specialized instead, with ladies' shops predominating on Morrison and men's shops on Washington. Because there were no alleys in the downtown area, the intervening street, Alder, became the service street for the Meier & Frank Co. and Lipman, Wolfe & Co. department stores, with loading docks between Fifth and Sixth.

How far west retail activity would extend was not determined by either streetcar routes or established land uses. Even though the federal courthouse and Portland Hotel created a retail void along the south side of Morrison, there were retail establishments west of Seventh and, in 1910, Portland's first full-block department store was built for Olds, Wortman & King between Morrison and Alder and Ninth and Tenth Avenue. In spite of this

[2]John T. Labbe, *Fares, Please! Those Portland Trolley Years,* p. 131.

Fig. I-6. Downtown pedestrian counts Thursday, Oct. 25, 1928. Upper figures in brackets are for 11:00 to 11:30 a.m., lower figures for 2:30 to 3:00 p.m. Fifty-two years later the center of activity had shifted only one block, to Fifth between Morrison and Alder. There was, however, a slight decline in volume compared to 1928.

relatively far-flung magnet, the highest pedestrian count remained on Fifth between Alder and Washington by the Lipman, Wolfe & Co. department store. (Fig. I-6.)

POST-1900 BRIDGES AND STREETCARS

Although construction in 1913 of the Broadway Bridge certainly had a tremendous effect on downtown development and, after its completion, some streetcar lines were shifted onto it from the Burnside and Steel Bridges, no long-term effect on the location of glazed terra-cotta buildings is apparent. Three of the four glazed terra-cotta buildings constructed in 1913 were on Seventh (renamed Broadway that year); but, of the large glazed terra-cotta buildings constructed between 1914 and 1930, not one was located on Broadway. Most of these later glazed terra-cotta buildings were sited on the fringes of the commercial core, a consequence in part of the high proportion of institutional structures.

DISTRICT CHARACTER

The new downtown commercial district, which developed between 1905 and 1930, had a particular character. Buildings were an average of nine stories tall and built to the property line, creating an almost canyon-like street space. Deep overhanging cornices provided a hint of overhead enclosure. Before the streets became clogged with automobiles, they were used somewhat as plazas, with pedestrians crossing at will, even at mid-block.

At the sidewalk level, building façades were filled with windows. There were elaborate metal-and-glass canopies (consistently referred to as *marquise* at the time) at main entrances and retractable awnings at storefronts. Awnings were also often placed at the office windows above. (Fig. I-7.)

The glazed terra-cotta building surfaces were quite light, richly fenestrated, and highly

Fig. I-7. Fifth looking north, with the Meier & Frank Co. department store building to the left and the Lipman, Wolfe & Co. department store building just beyond.

Fig. I-8. The Journal Building at night. Many buildings constructed between 1905 and 1930 were similarly lit.

reflective. Individual light bulbs outlined buildings, marquees, and signs. Pedestrian-level signs were either run along the fascia above storefronts or projected over sidewalks. Many buildings had roof signs composed of lighted individual letters on open trusswork. Almost every building had a flagpole on the roof, usually topped by a gilded ball. The overall atmosphere was reminiscent of the 1893 Chicago World's Fair and Portland's 1905 Lewis and Clark Exposition: light-colored buildings gleaming by day and sparkling with thousands of tiny lights at night. (Fig. I-8.)

Although very few 1905-30 buildings in the district have been demolished, ground floors have been drastically remodeled and many of the characteristic features, such as lights and marquees, removed. Today, only in looking up do we fully sense the downtown created by streetcars.

BUILDING TYPES

Portland's downtown buildings of the glazed terra-cotta era exhibit numerous common characteristics that distinguish them from pre-1905 or post-1930 buildings. Their plans, heights, façade treatment, and circulation systems are all surprisingly uniform. Some of these consistencies are typical of buildings of the same era in other cities, but other characteristics are peculiar to Portland.

LOT SIZE

Portland's 200 x 200 foot downtown blocks were originally platted with eight 50 x 100 foot lots fronting on north-south streets and the early commercial buildings were 50 feet (or occasionally only 25 feet) wide. Some cast-iron buildings of the 1870s and 1880s and most Richardsonian Romanesque buildings of the 1890s were quarter-block (100 x 100 feet) buildings. During the glazed terra-cotta era, though the quarter-block building remained the norm, many half-block, and even a few full-block, buildings were also constructed. (That the typical building so early occupied such a large proportion of a block is not, of course, due to Portland having unusually large buildings for the time, but rather to its having unusually small blocks.)

BUILDING LINES

Virtually all glazed terra-cotta buildings in the downtown area were built to the property line on each street frontage. This was true not only for retail and office structures, but also for hotels, club buildings, and even for the courthouse and church. On all but three terra-cotta buildings, street façades rise straight up to the roof cornice without setbacks of any kind. Exceptions are the Journal Building, (Fig. III-17), Pittock Block (Fig. III-23), and Public Service Building (Fig. III-39). The Public Service Building was designed to have its two wings increased to twelve stories (which they later were), leaving it finally with only a hint of a setback where the central mass now rises three stories above the wings. The setback on the Pittock Block resulted from placement of one of its light courts at the street façade rather than in the interior of the block. The Journal Building's free-standing corner tower conformed to the practice of giving newspaper buildings distinctive forms, symbolizing their roles as important institutions. The Portland Telegram Building also followed this custom. (Figs. III-17 and III-32.)

STRUCTURAL SYSTEMS

Most of Portland's glazed terra-cotta buildings have a riveted steel skeleton with a ribbed-concrete floor system. (Fig. I-9.) Structural bay sizes range from about 13 x 13 feet to 20 x 20 feet. Concrete ribs were formed by laying terra-cotta tiles (structural terra cotta similar to that used for office building partitions) on the formwork. The flat-arch tile-system, which was popular in Chicago at the time its terra-cotta buildings were built, was apparently never used in Portland.

Reinforced concrete came into use in Portland around 1906, but, as a relatively untried material, it was slow to gain acceptance for major buildings. Some examples of glazed terra-cotta buildings with reinforced concrete frames are the 1910 Arlington Club, 1914-23 Pittock Block, and 1926 Pacific Building.

Even as late as the 1920s, commercial buildings were being constructed in downtown Portland with wood-joist floor systems. The 1909 Seward Hotel has cast-iron columns and a wood-joist floor system. The 1909 Henry Building and 1922 Fitzpatrick Building also have wood-joist floor systems.

Fig. I-9. Erection of a riveted steel-frame building, 1907. Rivets were fabricated with one rounded cap. The other end was struck sideways and then hammered into a flattened, rounded shape after placement. Hoist was steam powered.

HEIGHTS

Prior to about 1920, any building in Portland more than eight-stories tall was considered a "skyscraper." Glazed terra-cotta building heights varied from a two-story church to a 16-story office building. Office buildings were typically twelve-stories high, but they ranged as low as three stories. Buildings given over entirely to retail ranged from three stories to twelve, with seven stories the average. Hotels were around nine stories.

Prior to 1913, heights of glazed terra-cotta buildings conformed to limits imposed by local ordinances. From 1913 on, there were a few exceptions to code requirements.

Building-height restrictions in Portland's downtown were initially intended for fire safety and were contained in a building code rather than a zoning code. Portland's first building code was adopted in 1904. Its first zoning code, which was not adopted until 1924, regulated only uses; height restrictions remained in the building code. The 1904 building code limited "fireproof" buildings (steel frame structures built completely of non-inflammable materials — except for wood window and door frames, floor finishes, and trim) to 201 feet (equivalent to approximately 15 stories). Non-steel-frame buildings, with all exterior surfaces other than masonry covered with non-inflammable materials and with metal lath and plaster partitions, were limited to 100 feet.

The 1904 code made no provision at all for reinforced-concrete structures. In 1906, an amendment allowed reinforced concrete for the structural frames of buildings up to 100 feet tall. In 1908, the code was liberalized to allow reinforced-concrete buildings with a minimum ground plan dimension of 100 feet to be 150 feet tall (but not to exceed twelve stories).

A completely revised code took effect on Jan. 1, 1911, limiting both "absolutely fireproof" (like the 1904 "fireproof," but with no wood at all) and "fireproof" (same as the 1904 "fireproof") to 160 feet, not to exceed twelve stories. This 1911 code remained in effect until 1918.

Six of the eight glazed terra-cotta office buildings constructed prior to 1913 were twelve stories tall. The 1911 Yeon Building was 15 stories tall, in conformance with the code in effect in 1910 when its permit was issued. The six-story Henry Building, because of its wood floor system, was limited to 100 feet. One building constructed in 1913 exceeded the height limit: the 14-story Northwestern National Bank Building.

After New York City passed the Nation's first zoning code in 1916, many other municipalities across the United States adopted building-height and bulk limitations similar to New York's. Portland's building code was revised in 1918 to include a setback provision very much like one in the New York code. The allowable building height at the street façade was reduced to 110 feet (or 8 stories), but a provision permitted the height of setback portions to be increased four feet for every one foot of setback. This same setback ratio had been applied to the Grand Central area in New York City, but starting from a higher allowable street façade height based on street widths. The purpose of setbacks in New York City was to safeguard access of light and air. This must have been the intention of the Portland ordinance also, though, with the number of low buildings remaining at the time in downtown, the possibility of deep, dark street spaces was exceedingly remote.

The 1918 code stipulated that City Council could grant special permission for heights over the limit. No conditions for approval were specified, only that the Council must hold a public hearing. The Pacific Building's 144-foot street façade height and the Public Service Building's 207-foot, 6-inch street façade height were permitted by Council in 1925 and 1926 with no reasons stated in the ordinances.

FAÇADES

Ground floors of glazed terra-cotta buildings were typically given over to retail uses. This was true for some hotel and institutional structures, as well as for office buildings, and even for some buildings far out of the retail core. Optimum display of retail goods to pedestrians called for maximum glass area and led to what is usually referred to as the "glass retail base.'

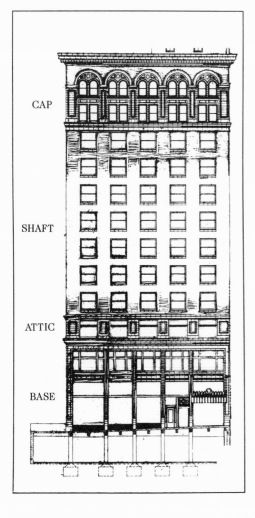

CAP

SHAFT

ATTIC

BASE

Fig. I-10. Selling Building façade showing typical composition of base, attic, shaft, and cap.

Twenty-six of the 40 glazed terra-cotta buildings included in this study have a glass retail base. Of the remaining 14, one is a church, one a courthouse, one a private club, two are hotels, one was a newspaper office, and four had their ground floors almost entirely given over to public banking rooms.

The design for almost all of Portland's glazed terra-cotta building façades followed design principles taught in the Beaux-Arts system. Application of these principles to twelve-story buildings with glass retail bases presented challenges not encountered by architects of the Greek and Roman buildings that served as models in Beaux-Arts instruction. Architect T. E. Tallmadge, writing in the 1920s, explained the difficulties encountered by architects of the early tall commercial buildings, as follows:

"The formulas by which [classic] buildings were designed were based on the assumption that for proper proportion a building must have a base, shaft and cap. In the skyscraper, unfortunately, the base which was the ground story, was occupied usually by shops which required the maximum amount of glass and the minimum amount of pier, while the architect according to the rules which for two thousand years had been unquestioned should demand at this portion the minimum amount of glass and the maximum amount of pier...This [skyscraper] base usually ran through two stories, so the third floor was treated as a different feature — an attic to the base, a kind of transition to the shaft...the upper two stories and attic were left for the cap. Often here a row of attached columns or pilasters formed a grandiose termination which in its festive appearance seemed to indicate for this portion of the design the harboring of a great banquet hall or *salle des fêtes*...

"The cornice was as big a puzzle to the...architect as the base. If it were proportioned to the entire height of the building it would have to be some fifteen feet or more in height and project an equal distance — obviously impossible. On the other hand, if the...designer proportioned it to the upper order, then it would be so small that it could hardly be seen from the street."[1]

Façades for almost all of Portland's glazed terra-cotta commercial buildings followed the scheme of base, attic, shaft, and cap with the base usually primarily of glass. This composition is clearly stated in the façade of the Selling Building. (Fig. I-10.) Almost all also featured large overhanging roof cornices of a size somewhere between what would be appropriate for the upper order and for the entire façade. This base-attic-shaft-cap façade is, of course, not peculiar to Portland, but is found nationwide. As a type, it did, however, remain *de rigeur* in Portland much later than in other cities. This was perhaps due to the preponderance of buildings designed by architect A. E. Doyle, a classicist to the end, who once wrote: "All of my training...has been in offices doing classical things, with a strong leaning toward the Greek...and I believe...that there is not much good that is not in some way based on something old that is good."[2]

PARTY WALLS

One feature of early 20th-century commercial buildings, which Portland's Beaux-Arts-trained architects apparently never grappled with at all, was the totally unadorned wall along the property line in the interior of a city block (party wall). This neglect was probably based on the assumption that buildings of like height would be constructed on adjacent lots, but this seldom occurred. In a city with larger rectangular blocks, views of party walls would in most cases be blocked by other tall buildings on the block. On one of Portland's 200 x 200-foot blocks, the party wall of a tall quarter-block building with a lower quarter-block neighboring building is very much in evidence. As a result, many blocks in downtown have a somewhat unfinished, unbalanced look. (Fig. I-11.) The concentration of all embellishment on the street façades, in conjunction with the break in height and fenestration at mid-block, does, however, have the interesting effect of focusing attention on street intersections.

[1]Thomas E. Tallmadge, *The Story of Architecture in America* (New York, 1927) pp. 253-254.

[2]Felicity Musick, "The Development of the Pacific Building and the Public Service Building" (Unpublished thesis, Oregon Historical Society, 1976).

Office Building Plans

A close look at plans for glazed terra-cotta office buildings explains why all street façades for office buildings were built on the property lines and also reveals prototypical layouts for each size building lot.

Conformance to street building lines resulted from dependence on natural light and ventilation. Although incandescent lighting was the prevailing light source during the years 1905-30, electricity was not always dependable during the early years and, even when electricity was consistently available, the levels of light provided by incandescent fixtures were very low. (In 1919, the suggested level at office desks was five foot-candles, compared to 75-150 foot-candles in 1970.) Few of the glazed terra-cotta office buildings had mechanical ventilating systems of any kind. It was, therefore, essential that each individual office have access to natural light and ventilation.

The maximum distance for penetration of natural light was generally accepted at the time to be 16 feet. Two 16-foot offices with a corridor between established the basic office module of approximately 40 feet. Though arrangement of this module varied according to whether the lot was eighth-block, quarter-block, half-block, or full-block, one factor remained constant: the necessity of facing some offices onto interior light courts.

Given the need for light courts, it is obvious that their size would be maximized and that maximizing their size would push street façades to the property lines. It was only after fluorescent lighting and mechanical ventilation for offices became widespread that office depths increased, office buildings no longer included light courts, and façades pulled back from street property lines. The distance from window wall to window wall in present-day office towers is 110 feet, or more, a far cry from the standard 40 feet of glazed terra-cotta buildings.

For glazed terra-cotta office buildings on an eighth-block (50 x 100 foot) corner lot, the 40-foot module would run along the long façade, leaving a light court ten feet in width. (Fig. I-12.) On a quarter-block lot, there would either be two parallel office modules and two parallel light courts or one wider light court with a 40-foot office module on one side and a half-module combined with building service spaces at the party wall. (Fig. I-13.) A half-block lot provided greater flexibility and, consequently, more variety in office layouts, with office reception and waiting rooms added between the 16-foot office and corridor, and, typically, two light courts. (Fig. I-14.) A full-block site (Fig. I-15.) allowed for opening up one light court to the street (with some loss of rentable space, to be sure) and, most importantly, the designation of offices facing this light court as "outside offices." (Offices facing interior light courts were naturally considered inferior to those facing the street, and to say that a person had an "inside" office was decidedly a slur.)

Offices had full-height partitions and were rented as suites of separate rooms. In order to maximize diffusion of natural light from room to room and to corridors, approximately

Fig. I-11. Yeon Building party wall. Street façades are faced with glazed terra cotta; party walls are of painted concrete. Running the cornice around the party wall was not usual; most cornices ended just past the corner.

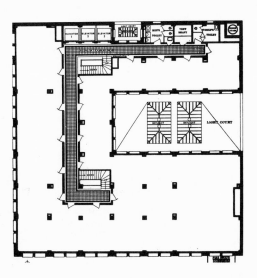

Fig. I-12. Typical plan for upper floors of eighth-block Wilcox Building.

Fig. I-13. Floor plan for upper floors of quarter-block Spalding Building. According to the promotional brochure in which this plan appeared, interior rooms opened "...upon the large uninterrupted space above the glass roof and extending to limit of property."

Fig. I-14. Typical plan for upper floors of half-block Morgan Building. This building was occupied primarily by physicians, and, therefore, had more complicated layouts with many more ante-rooms than the usual office building of the time.

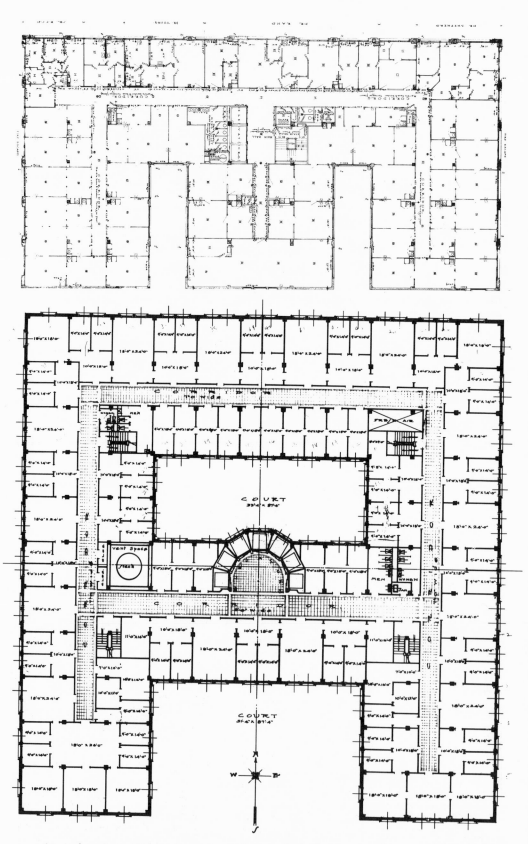

Fig. I-15. Typical plan for upper floors of Pittock Block, the only glazed terra-cotta office building in Portland occupying a full block and the only one with a light court open to the street.

one-third of each partition was made of glass (re-lights). Obscure glass or roll-up shades (sometimes in the form of large maps) allowed for privacy. Operable transoms above each interior door provided for cross ventilation. (Fig. I-16.)

Even a half-block office building might have only one interior stair. Exterior wrought-iron fire escapes, with access through rented office space, served both as an alternate means of emergency egress and as entrances for firemen. Interior stairs, as well as

Fig. I-16. Early office interior of the glazed terra-cotta era. The ceiling is higher and the area larger than was usual, but the glass-filled partition is typical. Note "task lighting."

elevators and toilet rooms, were generally located in the windowless areas at the corners of the light courts. This location for stairs, even when there was more than one, created long dead-end corridors.

Light courts did not extend to the ground, but generally terminated above the second floor level in a decorative skylight. Below this skylight was some sort of public space.

If ground-floor retail space in a corner building were rented to a single tenant, the tenant's principal entrance would be on one façade and the building lobby entrance on the other façade. If there were multiple retail tenants, each with his own entrance, the corner tenant might have a recessed corner entrance. There was no distinct pattern of either north-south or east-west orientation for either retail or building lobby entrances; locations were determined by each building's ground floor rental mix and by surrounding foot-traffic volumes.

Because elevator lobbies generally ran perpendicular to the street façade at mid- or quarter-block, they tended to be relatively dark spaces. Architects capitalized on the almost cave-like quality of these spaces by ornamenting them with deeply-modeled, cast-plaster ornament, highlighted by light from widely-spaced incandescent light fixtures. Light from these fixtures was also reflected off sharply-modeled, cast-bronze grilles, elevator doors, and hardware, as well as the cast-bronze light fixtures themselves.

Office building basements were often rented, usually to barbershops. Basements were reached by ornamental cast-iron stairs located in the elevator lobby.

Upper-level retail space was generally limited to a mezzanine over a maximum of one-third of the ground floor area located at the rear of the building. This mezzanine arrangement allowed for penetration of natural light far into the store interior. To further maximize this penetration, store-front transoms were often filled with prism glass (pressed glass with prismatic ridges on its inside face) to deflect light up and into the interior of the store. Awnings were hung below rather than above transom windows to allow light to pass through.

STORE BUILDING PLANS

Of the seven glazed terra-cotta buildings given over entirely to retail use, only one — Olds, Wortman & King — was originally built as a full-block building and could, as a result, utilize the large central skylighted court typical of department stores of the era. The Meier & Frank Co. department store, though eventually a full block, was built in three stages, with no apparent thought of a central light court. Portland's smaller glazed terra-cotta store buildings typically had no light courts of any size. Except for the ubiquitous main floor mezzanine, their sites were totally covered from the ground floor to the roof.

Entrances to store buildings were placed on the centers of their façades. Elevators and enclosed stairs were located at a party wall or, in the case of Olds, Wortman & King, on an exterior wall. Most stores also had grand staircases leading to the mezzanine (or, in the case of Olds, Wortman & King, to the second floor). (Fig. I-17.) Lipman, Wolfe & Co. also had a grand stair to its basement retail space.

HOTEL BUILDING PLANS

Layouts for hotels were similar to those of office buildings: double-loaded corridors with some rooms facing the street and others a light court. The quarter-block Imperial Hotel, a comparatively luxurious hotel for its time, had only one large light court, while the quarter-block Seward hotel had two. Neither had private baths. The Imperial had connecting baths; the Seward had connecting baths for outside rooms and baths "down the hall" for inside rooms.

Ground floors of both the Oregon and the Imperial were given over to public rooms; the Seward's ground floor was partially retail. The Oregon's lobby featured a mezzanine and the Imperial's a decorative skylight.

Two later residential hotels, the Roosevelt and Sovereign, did not depart significantly from the basic pattern of the earlier hotels.

Fig. I-17. Main-floor retail space of Woodard, Clarke & Co. in the Woodlark Building. Mezzanine with grand stair and cast-iron railing, dark-stained casework, and hex-tile floor were typical for ground-floor interiors.

BANKS

The long-standing tradition of temple forms for bank buildings continued well into Portland's glazed terra-cotta era, with the United States National Bank building a prime example. This elegant Roman temple is decorated with one of Portland's best examples of glazed terra-cotta ornament and also boasts what many people consider to be the loveliest interior space in the downtown area. (Figs. III-26 and I-44.)

Two office buildings with banks occupying their ground floors retained vestiges of the temple form on their ground floor façades: the Spalding Building and Northwestern Bank Building. (Figs. III-8 and III-20.) Combining a full-temple form with an office tower was a formidable design problem, as evidenced by architect A. E. Doyle's sketch showing the never-built United States National Bank tower. (Fig. I-18.)

By 1925, when the Bank of California was designed, architects were experimenting with other styles for bank buildings and Doyle gave it the look of an Italian palazzo. (Fig. III-35.)

INSTITUTIONAL BUILDINGS

The single-glazed terra-cotta church, the First Christian Church, is a central-plan building with corner entrance stairway spilling out toward the South Park Blocks. (Fig III-31.)

Homes for the three men's clubs were as varied as their memberships: the 1910 Arlington Club, an unobtrusively dignified Georgian block (Fig. III-7.); the Odd Fellows Building, a mysterious assemblage of Gothic forms above a glass retail base (Fig. III-29.); and the Elks Temple, a derivation of the Farnese Palace with hints of naughtiness throughout its interior. (Fig. III-27.) These buildings are in categories by themselves, a reminder that for Portland's glazed terra-cotta era, as in any other era, the singular had its place along with the typical.

Fig. I-18. Architect A. E. Doyle's sketch for an office tower atop the United States National Bank. Planned as part of the 1923 addition, but not constructed because of economics, this would have been Portland's only glazed terra-cotta office tower set back on all sides from the street.

GLAZED TERRA-COTTA ORNAMENT

In a fascinating book, *Architecture and Democracy,* published in 1926, author Claude Fayette Bragdon grappled with the meanings of ornament to 20th-century man. After stating that the ornament then in common use had been gathered from the "dust bin of the ages," he went on to justify the use and meaning of ornament by identifying archetypal forms and expressions of cosmic truths in various motifs and by showing how ornament could be scientifically derived from number and color theory.[1] Bragdon was, of course, not the only theorist analyzing the role of ornament during the glazed terra-cotta era. The majority were, however, like Bragdon, questioning only the form ornament should take and not the need for ornament *per se.* Ornament was as essential a component of a building as its structure or enclosure.

However essential, ornament's role was a subservient one: to augment the architectural design. It also had to be economically produced. Production of ornament that was both harmonious and economical was possible because there existed a standard vocabulary of motifs with which both designers and craftsmen were intimately familiar and which was applied, according to accepted rules, to the few basic building types.

TYPES OF ORNAMENT

Ornament of the glazed terra-cotta era can usefully be classified into five types: supports (columns and pilasters); bands (friezes, cornices, etc.); panels; diapers (overall patterns); and free ornaments (rosettes, finials, cartouches, etc.). Each type of ornament occurred at specific places: supports, at the building base, cap, and, sometimes, corners; bands, between major horizontal divisions (base, attic, shaft, and cap) and at the roof line; panels, between windows; diapers, on floors; and free ornaments, as accents at the roof line, corners, and intersections of major compositional lines.[2]

Wall surfaces between these glazed terra-cotta decorative elements were generally of brick. Structures given over predominantly to retail uses were, however, almost always faced entirely with glazed terra cotta, presumably because of their special need to "shine."

Economy of production of glazed terra cotta was achieved through repetition of ornamental motifs. Only at major entrances did singular pieces occur.

CLASSICISM

Each architectural style in use during the years 1905-30 had its own particular set of motifs for each type of ornament. The classical motifs found on most of Portland's glazed

[1]Claude Fayette Bragdon, *Architecture and Democracy,* p. 62.

[2]Franz Sales Meyer, *A Handbook of Ornament.*

terra-cotta buildings were similar to those popular in New York City and in other cities where architects were influenced by the highly-regarded New York firm, McKim, Mead & White. Three of the buildings in this study were designed by architects whose offices were located in New York City: the 1907 Wells Fargo Building by Benjamin Wistar Morris, the 1910 Spalding Building by Cass Gilbert, and the 1925 Bedell Building by G. A. Schonewald. William M. Whidden, of the firm Whidden & Lewis, architects for seven of the buildings in this study, first came to Portland as an employee of McKim, Mead & White, sent by them to supervise construction of the Portland Hotel. A. E. Doyle, whose firm was responsible for a dozen of the glazed terra-cotta buildings, was an apprentice for twelve years in the Whidden & Lewis office and, like so many of his contemporaries in Portland, spent time working in an architectural office in New York[3]. Doyle's early glazed terra-cotta buildings differ little from those designed by Whidden & Lewis. (Fig. I-19, I-20.)

Fig. I-19. Glazed terra-cotta ornament at the upper floors of the 1911 Wilcox Building. Antefixae, lions' heads, egg-and-dart, block modillions, dentils, urns, putti, scrolls, and rosettes were all often-used classical motifs.

Fig. I-20. Glazed terra-cotta ornament above the main entrance to the 1913 Morgan Building by Doyle & Patterson.

NON-CLASSICAL ECLECTICISM

Not all of Portland's glazed terra-cotta buildings featured classical ornament. Exceptions followed the accepted principle that architectural style should correspond to building function. While classical styles with their associations to temples and basilicas were appropriate when it was important to convey a sense of civic responsibility and tradition, the Gothic Style was a natural choice for a religious building and Georgian for a

[3]Felicity Musick, "The Development of the Pacific Building and the Public Service Building," p. 8.

clubhouse. Thus, we have the Gothic decoration on the lodge building constructed for the Odd Fellows, an organization whose work was based on the Bible, and the Georgian Arlington Club, home-away-from-home for Portland's men of influence. (Fig. I-21, III-7.)

MODERNE

Practicing at the same time as A. E. Doyle in Portland was a truly unconventional architect, William C. Knighton. Born in Indianapolis, Indiana in 1866 and trained in Birmingham, Alabama, and Chicago, Knighton moved first to Salem, Oregon where he practiced from 1893 to 1896. By 1902, he was in Portland, having spent several of the intervening years in Birmingham[4]. The glazed terra-cotta decoration on his 1908 Seward Hotel owes nothing to the classic traditions. Its forms are similar to those developed by

Fig. I-21. Glazed terra-cotta Gothic ornament on the 1922 Odd Fellows Building. Decorative lighting was provided by bulbs inside each canopy.

Fig. I-22. Glazed terra-cotta ornament on William C. Knighton's 1909 Seward Hotel. The trapezoidal-like shape occurring throughout the building, both inside and out, became Knighton's trademark.

avant-garde designers in Vienna, starting around 1903. In fact, one recurring motif, a sort of trapezoidal shape that became Knighton's trademark, is frequently found on household objects designed by members of the Wiener Werkstätte. (Fig. I-22.) How Knighton happened to design such abstract ornament at such an early date has yet to be determined. According to Fred C. Baker, designer and producer of lighting fixtures for many glazed terra-cotta buildings, Knighton was a "rebel" and the Seward was considered "far out" at the time it was built. Baker's own opinion was that Knighton "went a little bit overboard on the outside of the Seward."[5]

Portland's only other example of glazed terra-cotta *Moderne,* the 1930 Charles F. Berg façade, could more exactly be termed *Art Deco.* It is of interest, not only because of its

[4]David C. Duniway, "National Register of Historic Places Inventory — Nomination Form for Bayne Building, Salem, Oregon," 1982.

[5]Fred C. Baker, Recorded interview by Janet Charlton, George McMath, and Anne Murphy, 1978. Notes in author's collection.

elegant black, gold, cream, and greenish-blue glazes, but also because it is the only glazed terra-cotta façade on which verticality rather than horizontal layering is emphasized. Between the streamlined pilasters are panels decorated with zig-zags, spirals, rain clouds, sunbursts, and peacocks. (Fig. I-23.) As the newspaper account of its opening explained, it departed "…from the convention of classic art and [took] nothing from earlier schools of art and architecture but the basic principles that are common to all."[6] It is ironic that such a splendid example of glazed terra-cotta decoration should have been designed by the Grand Rapids Store Equipment Company as part of the remodel and interior refurbishing of an existing structure. (It has been suggested, but not documented, that the design was done by German-born, California-based Kem Weber. Weber, who had a national reputation, is known to have been designing furniture for the Grand Rapids Chair Company at the time. His work is, however, stylistically dissimilar to the Berg Building.)

Fig. I-23. Polychrome glazed terra cotta on the 1930 Charles F. Berg building. Black with vertical bands of gold at pilasters and mullions. Lighter, decorative spandrel panels are cream-colored. Upper decorative panels are dark greenish-blue.

GLAZED TERRA-COTTA FIRMS

Architects were only the first of a series of persons involved in the design and production of glazed terra-cotta ornament. Interpretation of the architects' working drawings rested with employees of the firms producing glazed terra cotta. Most ornament for Portland buildings was produced by Gladding, McBean & Co. Other firms responsible for local work were N. Clark & Son and Washington Brick, Lime & Sewer Pipe Company.

Gladding, McBean & Co. was established in Lincoln, California after Charles Gladding, visiting there from Chicago, took clay samples back to Peter McGill McBean and George Chambers and, on the quality of the clay, persuaded them to build a plant at Lincoln for manufacturing clay sewer pipe.[7] Company job records show production of architectural terra cotta for Portland buildings (glazed and unglazed) dating back to the 1880s. In 1925, Gladding, McBean & Co. acquired the Northern Clay Co. plant in Auburn, Washington, and, by 1926, had six plants: Auburn; Glendale, California; three plants near Los Angeles; and the original plant at Lincoln. In 1927, Gladding, McBean merged with the Denny Renton Clay & Coal Co. of Oregon and Washington.

According to a Clark descendant, N. Clark & Son originated when founder Nehemiah Clark's attempts at locating gold in the Sutter's Fort area turned up clay deposits instead.[8] The 1870 census listed four potters living in Clark's house, and his line was evidently limited to jugs. Around 1898, the firm was relocated to Alameda, California, and began producing architectural terra cotta.

The Washington Brick, Lime & Sewer Pipe Co., which dates back to the 1890s, ceased manufacturing in 1948 and N. Clark & Son in 1950[9,10]. Gladding, McBean & Co.'s Lincoln plant is the only producer of architectural terra cotta remaining from the glazed terra-cotta era. Although production methods have changed somewhat since the early 1900s (and even then the process varied from place to place), present production methods at the Lincoln plant can give a good indication of how terra cotta was produced prior to 1930.

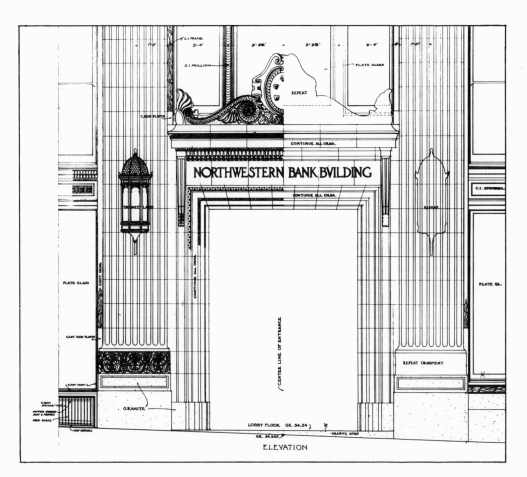

ELEVATION

Fig. I-24. Working drawing for main entrance to Northwestern Bank Building, 1913. This entrance was modernized in 1936 with a design in granite by Pietro Belluschi.

[7]*California Historical Society Currier,* Sept., 1981, as quoted in *Friends of Terra Cotta Newsletter,* Fall, 1981, p. 6.

[8]John Clark, Unrecorded interview by author, 1978.

[9]*Pacific Builder and Engineer,* "Development of Inland Empire Clay Industries," March 18, 1911.

[10]George D. Clark Jr., Letter to the author, 1979.

SHOP DRAWINGS

The first step in the translation of architects' drawings into terra-cotta ornament involves production of a set of shop drawings. These are done by draftsmen employed by the terra-cotta firms and are used both in the production of the terra cotta and by the contractor attaching it to the building structure. Shop drawings outline each individual piece of terra cotta, with details indicating generally how it is to be secured. (Actual sizes and shapes of anchors are determined by architects or engineers.) Each piece is labeled with one number for its configuration and, sometimes, a second unique number for its eventual location on the building. (Fig. I-24, 25, 26.) The shop drawings are used later as setting drawings when the terra cotta is installed.

MODELS

Although manufacturers had stock pieces that could be supplied on short notice, terra cotta for most, if not all, of Portland's downtown buildings was custom made. Custom work requires a complete set of plaster molds into which the clay is pressed. Because molds are cast around models, a complete set of models also has to be made. Model making was the responsibility of sculptors employed by the terra-cotta firms.

Fig. I-25. Gladding, McBean & Co. shop drawing for main entrance to Northwestern Bank Building. Notations beginning with "A" indicate configuration; other type of notation is unique for each location.

Fig. I-26. Gladding, McBean & Co. shop drawing, section through cartouche at main entrance to Northwestern Bank Building. Note holes where metal bars hook into pieces of terra cotta.

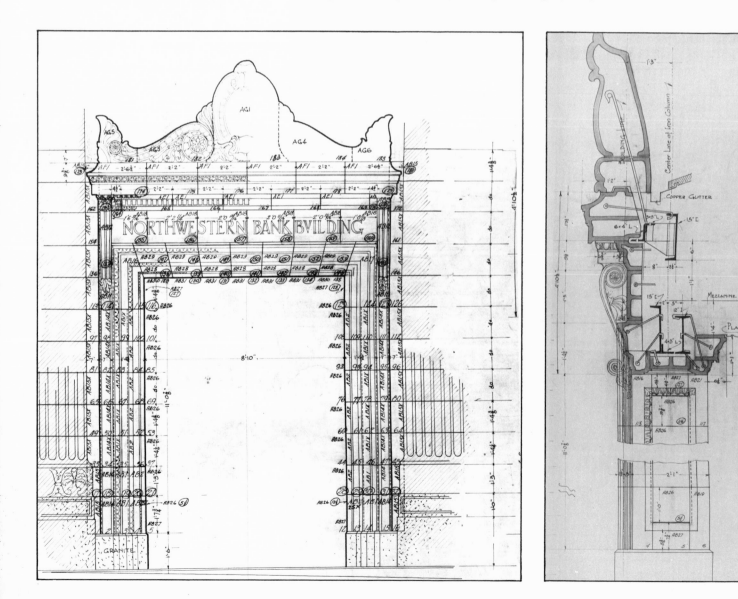

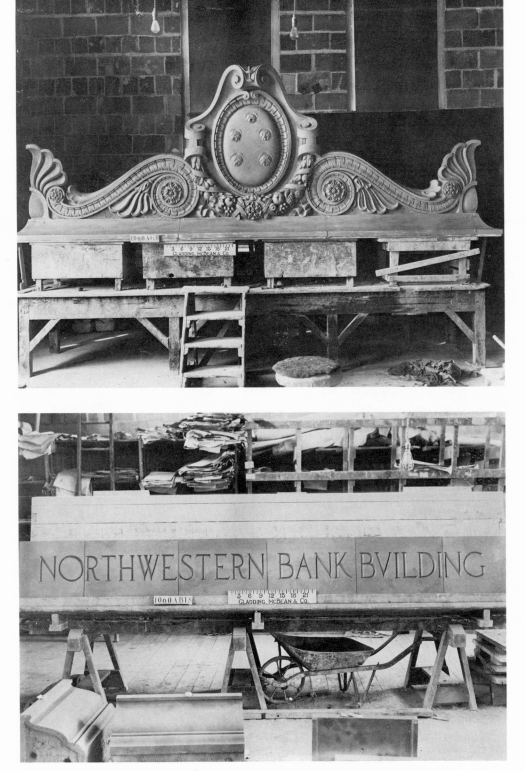

Fig. I-27. Plaster and clay model of cartouche, flanking scrolls and acroteria at main entrance to Northwestern Bank Building. A photograph like this was sent to the architect for his approval.

Fig. I-28. Model of name blocks with cornice pieces lying on floor in foreground.

Models are made out of a combination of plaster and modeling clay, plaster forming the main body and clay the details. (Fig. I-27, 28.) Even for large elements, such as column capitals and decorative panels requiring many separate molds, the model must be made of the whole element in order to get the overall effect. Since these models can be five-feet (or more) high, very large easels are provided to support them. By means of heavy chains, these easels can be lowered to a horizontal position on the floor or raised to a near-vertical

Fig. I-29. Model of cartouche for Journal Building on large easel. Easel could be lowered into horizontal position by allowing lower portion to move along track on wheels shown just below model.

Fig. I-30. Recent photograph showing easels in un-used model-maker's studio at Gladding, McBean & Co. plant in Lincoln, California.

position. (Fig. I-29, 30.)

Although the modeler works from shop drawings specifying the size and shape of each piece, the dimensions of the model have to be greater than those of the finished piece to allow for shrinkage during the drying-and-firing process. The amount of shrinkage varies with each clay mixture, requiring each terra-cotta plant to derive its own shrinkage ratio. Gladding, McBean & Co.'s ratio is approximately one in thirteen. This means that, for a piece with a final dimension of twelve inches, the model has to be 13 inches. Calculating these proportions is simplified for the modeler by an expanded ruler, called a "shrinkage ruler," with calibrations approximately one-twelfth farther apart than those on a normal ruler.

At the Gladding, McBean & Co. plant in Lincoln, California are innumerable photographs of completed models, taken to be sent to the architect for his approval. (Fig. I-31, 32, 33.) The modeler had his own darkroom adjacent to his studio where glass and celluloid negatives were developed, printed, and stored.

Producing models of architectural ornament required interpretation of the necessarily simplified details on the shop drawings. Modelers, therefore, had to master not only the mechanics of modeling, but also scale, proportion, and texture, and had to be familiar with sources of ornament. The scattered information available on modelers working in the Northwest indicates that they were born and educated in Europe. Victor G. Schneider, who worked with the Washington Brick, Lime & Sewer Pipe Co., was trained in Austria, came first to Chicago, and then went to California where he worked on the Panama Pacific Exposition Buildings (not of terra cotta, but requiring models for the cast-cement plaster). He died in 1930. Ernest Kadel, modeler at Gladding, McBean & Co., was born in Germany. He apprenticed at Gladding, McBean & Co. soon after he immigrated at about age 16 and worked there until he died in 1959 at age 75. (Fig. I-34, 35.)

Fig. I-31. Model of lion's head for cornice of 1912 Lipman, Wolfe & Co. building.

Fig. I-32. Model of capital for 1917 portion of United States National Bank.

MOLDS

To form a mold for a piece of terra cotta, liquid plaster is poured in sections over a completed model. If a mold is to be reused many times, it must be very sturdy and easy to take apart and reassemble. The number of parts for each mold depends on the complexity of the piece of terra cotta to be pressed. The simplest mold has five parts: a base and four sides. A piece of terra cotta with many complicated projections may require a mold with ten or more parts. Walls of a mold are about four-inches thick. Corresponding cone-shaped projections and holes on the edges where the walls meet and a removable encircling metal band tightened by wooden wedges hold the parts of the mold securely together.

Fig. I-33. Model of decorative panel for Meier & Frank Co. building.

Fig. I-34. Ernest Kadel, modeler at Gladding, McBean & Co., standing next to one of his last works. This photograph was tacked up on the wall of his office.

Fig. I-35. Ernest Kadel's office at the Gladding, McBean & Co. plant with photographs of models covering the wall above his desk.

CLAY.

The composition of clay used in the production of glazed terra cotta varied, depending on what the clay from a particular pit was like and on what was added to the raw clay. The present Gladding, McBean & Co. clay pit at Lincoln is not the same one used during the period 1905-30, and the clay is therefore different. Mining and mixing procedures also differ, chiefly in the use of large-scale machinery.

The present pit lies some three miles from the plant. Different types of clay suitable for different clay products lie at different elevations in the pit. The relatively fine-grade clay for architectural terra cotta comes from the top seven feet.

During late summer, a full year's supply of clay is hauled to the plant and stockpiled in a storage yard. Clay from the storage yard is transported as needed to the clay preparation shed where it is broken down and mixed with equal parts of finely-ground grog. (Grog is ground-up, previously-burnt clay, from brick, pottery, clay sewer pipe, terra cotta, etc.) Grog is added to the clay to control plasticity and firing behavior. It reduces shrinkage and tends to stabilize the clay mixture. Clay mixtures for architectural terra cotta contain more grog than either brick clay or ceramic-tile clay.

After being mixed with grog, the clay is wet down and run through a pug mill, which, by the action of large augers, thoroughly blends and breaks it down. The clay "body" is then covered and allowed to age 24 hours or more.

Up to this point, in the present process at Gladding, McBean and Co., the clay has been entirely processed by machines. It has been brought from the clay pit in enormous dump trucks, transported to the mixing shed by front-end loaders, and ground, screened and pugged by large pieces of mostly-automatic equipment. If the configuration of the final product is to include only simple projections of two-dimensional curves (such as one finds in ceramic veneer), the clay can be machine-extruded (squeezed out through a specially-shaped opening) and mechanically cut to the desired lengths. Ornament for early 20th-century buildings was, however, almost always based on three-dimensional curves, and these shapes could not be extruded. Except for a brief period of apparently unsuccessful experimentation with machine pressing, early 20th-century terra cotta was pressed into molds by hand.

PRESSING

Although it appears to be an easy process, pressing terra cotta requires a great deal of strength and skill. The presser first places the plaster mold open side up on the floor. He then takes one ball of clay (bat) at a time from the clay body. If the bat is for the face of the piece, he kneads it on a board until the lower surface is smooth and the grog particles covered. He then throws the bat into the mold, smooth side against the face of the mold, and socks it against the mold and against clay already pressed into the mold. In order that the surface ornamentation be clearly defined and there be no structural flaws, the clay must be tightly pressed against both the mold and adjoining clay. After the mold is lined with clay, approximately one-and-one-half-inches thick, webs are built up from side to side. (Fig. I-36.) Hand holes for lifting and holes for metal anchors are formed in the sides.

Clay is left in the mold for several hours. During this time, the plaster absorbs moisture from the clay, causing it to stiffen and shrink slightly. If left in the mold too long, there is a danger of protuberances, such as dentils, being sheared off as the clay shrinks. Clay pieces are then turned out onto wooden racks where the presser scrapes, brushes, or sponges the ornamental face to eliminate imperfections and obtain the desired finish. At this time, identification numbers are incised on the sides.

Terra-cotta pieces are left on the rack to continue drying for up to 24 hours. The rate of drying must be carefully controlled. If the exterior dries out too rapidly, the piece will warp or crack. Large, heavy pieces, therefore, require longer drying periods, and thicker sections of a piece are often covered with wet burlap to avoid too-rapid drying.

Fig. I-36. Harry Tracy at the Gladding, McBean & Co. plant pressing clay into a simple plaster mold.

Fig. I-37. Ed Crooks at the Gladding, McBean & Co. plant spraying glaze on a piece of terra cotta.

GLAZING

Because most architectural glazed terra cotta is fired only once (not once before glazing and again after the glaze is applied, as with some ceramic ware), the unfired pressed terra-cotta pieces are taken directly from the pressing area to the glazing room. There they are placed on a revolving stand and sprayed with a glaze as they rotate past the person wielding the spray gun. Although glazes can be applied with brushes, at the Gladding, McBean & Co. plant, they are sprayed on. (Fig. I-37.) This was also the usual method during the early 20th century.

For uniformity of color, glazes should be approximately 2/100-inch thick. To provide a smooth white base for the glaze, the piece may be sprayed first with an undercoat of fine clay suspended in water (slip). The spray gun nozzles can be adjusted to throw spots rather than a fine spray to give mottled and speckled effects. A glaze simulating granite (and marketed as "Granitex" by Gladding, McBean & Co.) was obtained in this fashion.

During the 1920s, development of glazes was subject to extensive scientific experimentation. Issues of the *American Ceramic Society Journal* contain innumerable papers by terra-cotta chemists conveying results of these experiments through complicated formulas. However, in spite of these efforts, glazing remained as much art as science. As with any natural product, the variables are infinite. Changes, not only in the glaze formula, but also in the clay composition and in firing temperatures, produce different colors. (Because Gladding, McBean & Co. is using a different clay pit now than when they produced terra cotta for Portland's buildings, the formulas in their job records are no longer applicable for replacement pieces.)

It is beyond the scope of this study to review techniques for obtaining all the possible terra-cotta glaze colors and textures. F. S. Laurence, author of the 1922 *Color in Architecture,* listed some of the colors available then: "...reds, ranging from a pale pink to deep madder; blues from a light sky blue to cerulean and deep indigo; greens from light emerald and malachite to grass greens and olive shades; yellows from a pale shade suggesting Naples to deep ochres; browns from café-au-lait to dark sunset; light and deep purples of both red and blue cast; mauve and, of course, black and white, the latter including several shades from pure white to deep cream or buff white. Also grays..."[11] Metals and alloys could also be applied to terra cotta: lead, zinc, tin, aluminum, nickel, copper, phosphor, bronze, silver, gold, and stainless steel.

A typical glaze composition might be feldspar 46%, clay 6.4%, flint 11%, white lead 21.3%, whiting 10.0%, and zinc oxide 5.3%. A variety of mineral additives gives the wide range of colors: iron oxide, cream; cobalt, blue; copper or chromium, green; and a chrome-tin lime combination, pink. Ingredients are carefully weighed and ground together with water for approximately two hours.

Not all colors are suitable for single firing. Bright red, deep yellows, gold, and silver usually require a second firing at a lower temperature.

Many of the ingredients giving color to terra-cotta glazes could theoretically be incorporated into the clay body, but at unreasonable expense. Applying color to the surface in the form of a glaze not only makes economical use of pigments, but also allows for a range of finishes. Variations in the proportion of bases, acids, and oxides determine whether the glaze will have a gloss, satin, or matte finish.

Glazing is one of the most ancient of arts. Mesopotamians utilized glazed ceramic decoration on their buildings. The Della Robbia family produced exquisite works of glazed terra cotta in Florence, Italy. And the term *faience,* which became synonymous with polychrome terra cotta, comes from the name of a town in France where the attaching of glazes to clay bodies was perfected. Large-scale application of glazes to architectural terra cotta became possible, however, only after 1885 with the introduction of barium carbonate, a substance which, by neutralizing them, prevents soluble sulphates in the clay from forming a coating on the surface of the terra cotta, thereby breaking the bond between the clay body and the glaze.

Full glazes for architectural terra cotta were not introduced commercially until about 1890. The earlier surface coatings were dull-textured slips, usually buff-brown or red in color. Because even the surface of unglazed terra cotta tends to have a slight sheen (from being finished after being turned out of the mold), it is often difficult to distinguish from terra cotta with a dull-textured slip. And, in many cases, matte glazes are hard to distinguish from slips. Thus, as with many classifications, the distinction between glazed and unglazed terra cotta, though useful, can be considered artificial.

Glazes on most of Portland's buildings are off-white or cream colored. The 1917-25 United States National Bank has a glaze with a speckled effect simulating granite. The 1920 Elks Temple, 1925 Bank of California, 1926 Pacific Building, and 1928 Public Service Building also have a stone-like finish. Glazes on the 1922 Fitzpatrick Building and 1922 Sovereign Hotel have a strong peachy cast. Terra-cotta glaze the green-color of weathered copper is combined with real copper on the 1913 Oregon Hotel's mansard roof. The only true polychrome terra cotta is found on the first and last of our group of buildings: the

[11]F. S. Laurence, "Color in Architecture, Part III," *The American Architect,* (Volume 122), p. 318.

1907 Wells Fargo Building and the 1930 Charles F. Berg. Accent colors on the Wells Fargo Building are strong and clear: red, blue, yellow, and green. Particularly delightful are the letters W-E-L-L-S F-A-R-G-O in blue above the ten upper windows. Berg's colors are typically Art Deco: black, gold, cream, and dark greenish-blue.

Fig. I-38. Pieces of glazed terra cotta being checked for proper fit.

FIRING

After having a glaze applied, pieces of terra cotta are loaded on open train-type cars for their trip through the pre-heater and tunnel kiln. The tunnel kiln, with its temperature varying along its length, subjects the terra cotta to a heating and cooling sequence similar to that of the beehive-shaped periodic kilns in which early terra cotta was fired. Periodic kilns, still in use for other clay firing, are first filled with the unfired clay pieces, gradually heated up, and then gradually cooled down.

Terra-cotta pieces are stacked on the tunnel kiln cars by a "setter" and his helper. Each piece is separated from the next by balls of unfired clay (bobbers).

Architectural terra cotta at the Gladding, McBean & Co. plant remains in the pre-heater for two days and for seven days in the tunnel kiln. The temperature in the kiln reaches a maximum of 2060°F. During firing, all perishable substances in the clay are consumed and the glazes fuse into a glassy finish (vitrify).

FITTING

After being fired, the glazed terra cotta is taken to a fitting shed where pieces are set up as they will be placed in the building and checked for size and fit. (Fig. I-38.) Some are rejected entirely and others trimmed to size with a special power saw. They are then packed with straw in wooden crates and shipped to the building site.

INSTALLATION

Construction of a glazed terra-cotta façade follows erection of the building's structural frame. Scaffolding for masons is suspended from the floors above. (Fig. I-39.)

Shop-drawing prints indicate for the masons where each piece should be placed and how it should be attached. Terra cotta is tied to the structure with metal anchors that hook into holes formed by the presser in the sides of the terra cotta. At lintels, projecting belt cornices, and roof cornices, these connections can become quite complicated, necessitating numerous detail drawings. Roof balustrades are held together with rods through the center of each balustrade. (Fig. I-40.)

It is the supporting iron work that has caused most deterioration of architectural terra cotta. Until the late 1920s, anchors (of wrought iron) were apparently, not galvanized — though a 1911 specification stipulated that anchors be dipped in "best red lead and linseed oil at least one week before being used"[12] and a 1923 specification called for a coating of "asphaltum, applied hot."[13] If, through poor design, construction, or maintenance, water is allowed to reach the iron, it rusts and, as it rusts, expands and literally explodes the terra cotta. Any section of terra-cotta wall with a large horizontal area is particularly vulnerable to this water penetration and rusting. The Northwestern Bank Building, for example, lost its roof balustrade to water-induced deterioration.

Although a specification published in a 1929 issue of *The American Architect* recommended "bronze, heavy copper wire or non corroding metal" for anchorage of exposed features such as balustrades,[14] there is no indication that Portland buildings used anything other than iron.

Cornices and window sills on some early glazed terra-cotta buildings had raised or lapped joints to reduce water penetration. These special joints also prevented rain from scouring out the mortar. The projections were, however, found to be susceptible to

[12]Reid Brothers, "Specifications of Building To Be Erected for the Journal…," 1911, Microfiche Collection, City of Portland, Bureau of Buildings.

[13]*The American Architect,* "Setting Terra Cotta," May 9, 1923, p. 425.

[14]*The American Architect,* "New York Building Congress Standard Specification for Setting of Terra Cotta," June 20, 1929, p. 837.

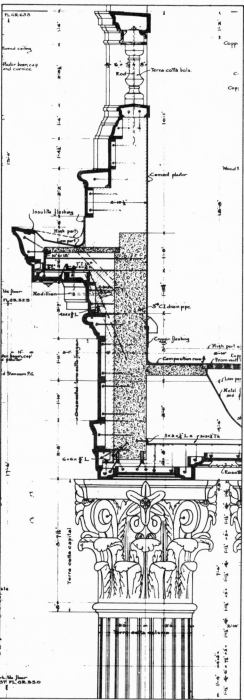

Fig. I-39. Glazed terra-cotta facing going up on steel frame of 1909 portion of the Meier & Frank Co. building.

Fig. I-40. Section through roof balustrade and cornice of United States National Bank. Supporting metalwork at cornices could become extremely complicated.

breakage and their use was gradually discontinued.

Vertical joints were also sometimes lapped, but merely as a means of concealing them. Rustication also tended to conceal joints, along with the inevitable slight irregularities in size, shape, and color. In fact, it could be said that some sort of surface decoration was a necessity for glazed terra cotta, which, no matter how carefully produced, would never have machine-like uniformity.

Most glazed terra-cotta walls are backed up with brick, mortar, or concrete. During the 1920s, the question of whether the cavities in the pieces of terra cotta should be entirely filled was quite a subject of dispute. Some experts claimed filling the cavities prevented water from entering. Others claimed that water was bound to enter somehow and that it was preferable to leave the cavity open and to provide weep holes for a quick exit. Because of its propensity for absorbing moisture, concrete backfilling was often blamed for the cracking of terra-cotta blocks. Whether filled or unfilled, however, tight joints and adequate flashing were essential.

MORTAR AND POINTING.

Terra-cotta units were saturated with water before being set. The approximately 1/4-inch joints were raked out to a depth of 1/2 inch and pointed. A specification published in a 1923 issue of *The American Architect*[15] called for mortar composed of one volume of Portland cement to three volumes of sand with lime "not to exceed 1/5 of a sack of lime to a sack of cement" added. Specifications for Portland buildings ranged from four parts of lime for each part of Portland cement to one part of lime for every four parts of Portland cement. The ratio of lime and Portland cement combined to sand was usually around one to two. Pointing mortar was generally of a different mix than setting mortar, with special sands or mortar stains producing colors compatible with glazes.

CLEANING.

Although glazed terra cotta was sometimes cleaned with a weak (3%) solution of muriatic acid (hydrochloric acid) and a coarse fiber brush, the preferred cleaning substance was a mild abrasive soap or washing powder. Muriatic acid removed dirt more effectively than soap, but etched the terra cotta glaze. When a muriatic acid solution had to be used, the terra cotta was sponged clean with clear water. One specification required that areas surrounding a portion to be cleaned with muriatic acid be thoroughly wet down to prevent absorption of the acid. This was a protection for mortar joints as well as for terra cotta.

Lumps of mortar were soaked with water and removed with a wooden stick.

CONTINUITY.

Surprisingly, most of the skills involved in producing and installing glazed terra cotta have been sustained through the past fifty anti-ornament years. Any significant resurgence of architectural design incorporating glazed terra-cotta ornament will, however, reveal one missing role — that of the modeler. With no continuing common language of ornament, there can be no artisans prepared to give sculptural form to an architect's drawings.

---

[15]*The American Architect,* May 9, 1923, p. 425.

COMPLEMENTARY FEATURES AND MATERIALS

Glazed terra cotta was just one of many materials used with remarkable consistency during the period 1905 to 1930. Brick did not, of course, fall into oblivion with the rise in popularity of terra cotta, but remained in favor as a companion facing material. Granite plinths provided an extra sense of solidity at the bases of terra-cotta and brick buildings, while cornices of sheet metal projected conspicuously at the roof line. A wrought-iron fire escape ran up the full height of each building. Upper windows usually had wood sash; street-level windows were framed either in wood, extruded metal, or cast iron. Cast bronze was found both inside and out — for doors, grilles, lighting fixtures, and hardware. Public spaces were decorated with marble and ornate cast plaster. Floors were of marble, terrazzo, ceramic tile, or smooth-finished concrete, depending on the importance of the space. And, finally, a standard palette tied the elements together in a harmonious whole.

NATURAL STONES.

Granite, limestone, and marble were used at the lower-floor exteriors of glazed terra-cotta buildings. Marble was also used inside.

Plinths were almost always of a medium- or light-grey granite with a bush-hammered finish. The grey granite on the United States National Bank has a slightly pinkish cast, to blend with the warm tones of the terra cotta above. (Fig. I-41.)

Some glazed terra-cotta buildings now have highly-polished black granite below the storefront windows and, sometimes, highly-polished black or reddish-orange (Carnelian) at the main entrance. These granites are not original, but were added during the first wave of office building "modernization," during the 1930s. It was at this time that the Northwestern Bank Building and Pittock Block lost their glazed terra-cotta entrances. The entrance to the Northwestern Bank Building is now faced with black granite and the entrance to the Pittock Block with travertine and Verde Antique marble. At about the same time, the entire street-level façade of the Selling Building was faced with polished Carnelian granite.

On both the Wells Fargo and the Spalding Buildings, limestone was used instead of glazed terra cotta at the lower floors. Limestone on the Spalding Building was replaced when the base was faced with travertine slabs, but that on the Wells Fargo Building remains intact. The use of limestone rather than terra cotta was probably due to their being, primarily, brick buildings, with glazed terra cotta confined to a few decorative elements.

Originally, travertine was not used at all with glazed terra cotta. Travertine at the lower floors of the Wilcox Building replaced the original glazed terra cotta.

Marble appeared infrequently on exteriors, but often in building lobbies and other interior public spaces. The Bank of California has an Escalette marble plinth and frieze on

Fig. I-41. Entrance to 1925 portion of United States National Bank building showing glazed terra cotta, granite plinths, marble-chip mosaic floor, and bronze grilles, doors, and lantern.

the exterior, both original. The Bedell Building apparently originally had marble underneath its first-floor windows.

Interior marble colors were more varied than those of exterior stones. Verde Antique was often used as a base and border for tile floors. The lobby vestibule of the Wells Fargo Building is an excellent example of the use of vari-colored marble, as is the main banking space of the United States National Bank. Floors of the bank are a cream-colored marble from Italy and a reddish marble from Hungary. Tellers cages are framed with Hauteville, a pinkish, cream-colored marble. Marble finishes continue into the basement level, which is paneled in a grey Tennessee marble.

Marble was used as frequently for its utility as for its decorative value. Wainscoting in office corridors was often of White Italian, Alaska, or grey marmor Tennessee marble, as were toilet-room stalls. Many of these stalls are still in place, as are the many stairs with marble treads.

Two atypical installations of stone are of particular note: the strikingly-figured grey-and-white marble in the Multnomah County Courthouse and the onyx wainscotting in the Seward Hotel lobby vestibule.

BRICK.

The transition in brick color and texture, from a smooth-faced, pressed yellow brick, to variously-textured red or buff brick, to rough-textured red, buff, or grey, which occurred between 1905 and 1930, can provide a quick clue to a building's construction date. This transition was partly stylistic and partly due to changes in the manufacturing process. The popularity of yellow brick during the late 1890s and early 1900s was apparently a nationwide phenomenon, perhaps a natural intermediate step in the change from dark-red Richardsonian Romanesque buildings to the white and off-white buildings popularized by the Chicago World's Fair.

Rougher textures were easier to obtain with highly-mechanized brick-making procedures than they had been with hand-pressed brick. The extrusion and wire-cutting process requires a stiff clay, and bricks produced by this method are inherently rough-faced. This roughness was often emphasized by giving the faces a combed finish and calling it "Rug" or "Tapestry" brick. Rough-faced red brick contrasts effectively with cream-colored glazed terra cotta on the Morgan Building and Pacific Telephone and Telegraph Co. building. The First Christian Church and Odd Fellows Building each have grey rough-faced brick. The 1907 Failing Building is a good example of early pressed yellow brick. Bricks on the 1910 Selling Building are a "Speckled Buff," Norman-size brick.

Glazed brick appears only on the 1909 Henry Building where bright blue bricks are laid in diamond-shaped patterns on the all-white brick façade. A promotional brochure for the building referred to the bricks as "Tiffany" brick. The choice of glazed brick resulted from owner C. K. Henry's appreciation of enameled brick buildings and the ease with which they could be cleaned.[1]

In order to reduce transportation costs, most brick was supplied by local brick plants. One such manufacturer, the Willamina Clay Products Co. was in operation in Yamhill County from 1907 to the mid-1970s. The Denny-Renton Clay & Coal Co. of Seattle (formed in 1905 when the Denny Clay Co. combined with the Renton Clay Works and acquired in 1927 by Gladding, McBean & Co.) also supplied brick for many Portland buildings, as did Gladding, McBean & Co.

WROUGHT AND CAST IRON.

The metalworking arts, so evident on late 19th-century buildings, continued to play an important role in commercial construction well into the 20th century. Like so many other building crafts, metalworking was sustained by European traditions and training transported to the United States by the waves of immigrants arriving prior to World War I.

Foremost among the immigrant metalworkers in Portland was Johann Konrad Tuerck, born in Germany in 1863. Tuerck was trained in Bayreuth, Munich, and Nuremberg before coming to America in 1888. He went first to Cincinnati, arriving in Portland in 1890.[2] After working for 18 months at Portland Ornamental Iron Works, he established Portland Art Metal Works. He is credited with the wrought-iron work for all of the major banks, clubhouses, churches, and residences built during the 1890s, 1900s, and 1910s. The curvilinear window grilles on the 1910 Arlington Club are undoubtedly his work. (Fig. III-7.)

On most glazed terra-cotta buildings, wrought-iron work was limited to fire escapes and elevator grilles. The fire escapes, virtually all of which remain, vary in ornateness from the strictly utilitarian to some graceful simplifications of classical design motifs.

[1] *Oregonian*, June 19, 1908, as quoted in E. Kimbark MacColl, *The Shaping of a City: Business and Politics in Portland, Oregon 1885-1915*, Portland, 1976, p. 314.

[2] *Portrait and Bibliographical Record of Portland and Vicinity, Oregon*, Chicago, 1903.

Many of the fire escapes and elevator grilles, as well as much miscellaneous ironwork, were fabricated by Columbia Wire and Iron Works, still in operation in Portland. Some elevator grilles were made of bronze, and Columbia Wire and Iron Works produced these also. Because, during a fire, an open elevator shaft acts as a chimney, quickly carrying superheated air upward through a building (a phenomenon not comprehended immediately after their introduction), open shafts with elevator grilles were eventually replaced with enclosed shafts and solid elevator doors.

Cast iron was utilized extensively for both exteriors and interiors. Window and door frames at the lower floors of glazed terra-cotta buildings that had ground floors occupied by banks were invariably of cast iron, as were those on some buildings with ground floor retail. Good examples are the United States National Bank, Northwestern Bank Building, and Lipman, Wolfe & Co. (Fig. I-42.) Street-level pilasters of the Yeon Building were of cast iron rather than terra cotta. Some exterior lighting fixtures and entrance marquees were also of cast iron, as well as some exterior grilles.

Inside glazed terra-cotta buildings, there were, and still are, many cast-iron stairs (popular because they were non-combustible) and railings. Mezzanine railings were also often of cast iron. Some railings were ornate copies of examples from the Renaissance, but most were made up of simple rectangular bars. Newel posts, also of cast iron, were a bit more elaborate, with moldings at the top and a paneled effect at the sides.

By weight, by far the most significant use of cast iron was for radiators. Steam heat was

Fig. I-42. Working drawing for 1913 Northwestern Bank Building. Window frames and spandrels at lower floors are cast iron.

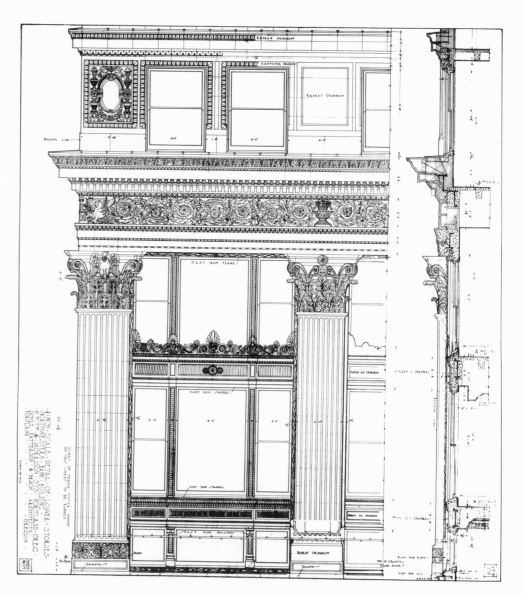

the rule, so each individual space had at least one of these hard-to-ignore features. Virtually all have been replaced.

SHEET METAL (COPPER AND GALVANIZED IRON).

Many of the exterior features of 1905-30 buildings, which appear to be of glazed terra cotta, are actually sheet metal painted to match the terra cotta. Roof cornices with wide overhangs were much more easily supported if fabricated of sheet metal rather than terra cotta; roof balustrades, because their exposure leads to freezing of entrapped water, were also likely candidates for fabrication in sheet metal.

Not all sheet metal masqueraded as terra cotta. The Oregon Hotel's copper roof was left unpainted and allowed to weather, as were the copper parts of entrance marquees and the Henry Building's copper-wrapped corner column.

While, up until the latter part of the 19th century, complicated sheet-metal decoration had been formed by pounding sheets of lead or zinc over wooden forms with wooden mallets, that on glazed terra-cotta buildings was machine pressed. In order to make the dies required for pressing, a model (similar to those made for terra cotta) had to be made out of plaster of Paris. A female die was cast by pouring molten zinc over the model. After coating it with graphite, the zinc die was used to cast a male die of lead. Then, both the zinc and the lead dies were cast into iron frames so they could be attached to a machine press.[3]

Depending on its complexity, a piece of sheet-metal decoration might be made up of many different parts requiring many different dies. The edges were lapped, notched at curved seams, and soldered together. The Morgan Building roof cornice and Pacific Telephone and Telegraph Co. roof balustrade are good examples of machine-pressed sheet-metal work. (Fig. I-43.)

Fig. I-43. Machine-pressed sheet metal cornice of the 1913 Morgan Building. Terra cotta ends at upper egg-and-dart course.

BRONZE WORK.

Providing lively accents at main entrances and lobbies was a variety of bronze features — lighting fixtures, name plaques, gates, doors, grilles, mail boxes, elevator pushbutton boxes, hand rails, and hardware. Decorative motifs in bronze work were the same as those in terra cotta, but at a smaller scale and with sharper definition.

Bronze can be rolled, extruded, forged, cast, and machined. The method by which it is formed is determined by the configuration of the finished product. A complex lighting fixture, for example, might have different parts produced by different methods.

Large, highly-sculptured pieces were fabricated by the Galvano method. This technique, like casting and so many other building processes of the time, required a model. The design was first modelled in clay; then, a plaster mold was poured around the clay model. Next, a plaster model was cast in the plaster mold and a glue (gelatin) mold made from the plaster model. The glue mold was lined with graphite and then electroplated with bronze, after which the glue mold was separated from the bronze electroplating. This method made possible more elaborate undercutting and finer detail than could be achieved by casting in a sand mold.

If left to weather naturally, bronze work will have streaks and blotches. For this reason, an artificial patina was developed chemically before pieces were installed. Features such as hardware and mailboxes, whose patina would likely be worn away in spots by constant handling, were generally polished.

Most, if not all, bronze work on glazed terra-cotta buildings in Portland was produced by Oregon Brass Works or its predecessor, Prior Bronze Works. Oregon Brass Works is still in operation and has in its files shop drawings of some early work.

Examples of bronze work of particular note are the entrance gates on the Wells Fargo Building, lobby doors and decoration on the Pacific Building, grilles on the Bank of California, and innumerable features of the United States National Bank.

[3]Lewis McArthur, Unrecorded interview by the author, 1982.

GLASS.

Windows for glazed terra-cotta buildings were of four basic types: one-over-one, double-hung; casement; fixed; and transom. As a rule, offices and hotel rooms had double-hung windows and ground-level retail space had fixed plate glass with transoms above. Steel casement windows were popular for office buildings in the late 1920s. "Chicago windows" (fixed glass flanked by double-hung windows) can be found on very few buildings. The number of office buildings with relatively widely-spaced, relatively small windows is especially surprising considering the scarcity of winter sunshine in Portland.

Plate glass was available in sizes up to 12 feet by 16 feet; fixed glass at ground level often approached these dimensions. The feeling of openness was increased by the use of lightweight metal frames. One framing system of copper, patented for the Kawneer Co. of Michigan in 1906, incorporated a flexible metal stop whose combination of firmness and resiliency prevented glass from cracking in high winds.

In the transom above the fixed plate glass, prismatic glass tiles ("prism glass") were often used instead of plate glass. These tiles were pressed glass, four- or five-inches square and set in zinc. On the inner face were tiny triangular ridges that deflected light up into the store interior. Small, operable sections were sometimes framed within the larger areas of prism glass.

Interior partitions on office floors incorporated large areas of glass — door lights, transoms, and relights. Most was obscure glass. Patterns were numerous and many are till available. Occupants' names and titles were painted directly on the glass.

Obscure glass in the Yeon Building was "glue chip" glass. This glass, which has the look of ice crystals forming on still water, is produced by applying a thin coating of glue to ordinary glass and then placing it in an oven where, as the glue dries, it contracts and chips off the surface of the glass. The process can be repeated, increasing the richness of the texture.

Colored glass occurred only occasionally in glazed terra-cotta buildings. Windows by the well-known local firm, Povey Brothers, are found throughout the First Christian Church. Originally there were Povey Brothers windows in the dining room of the Imperial Hotel. A leaded-glass skylight in the lobby of the Imperial Hotel may also have been by the Povey Brothers. A window of opalescent glass over the entrance to the Odd Fellows Building is similar to those in the First Christian Church and could also have been produced by the Povey Brothers.

Most notable of all remaining glasswork are the two leaded-glass panels flanking the entrance to the Seward Hotel, in which green-and-caramel-colored slag glass is arranged in geometric designs based on a setback motif. Also of interest are some slightly medieval-looking leaded-glass windows in deep rich tones in the board room of the United States National Bank.

A small leaded-glass window with a geometric design in the lobby of the Selling Building was a victim of its ground-floor renovation.

MOSAIC TILE AND TERRAZZO.

With the importance placed on achieving a "completely fireproof structure," it is not surprising that floors in glazed terra-cotta buildings were almost always of some incombustible material, rather than of wood.

Marble was reserved for floors of only the most important public spaces, primarily banking rooms and building lobbies. (Fig. I-44.) Lobby floors of the less-impressive buildings were finished with unglazed hexagonal ceramic tile ("hex tile"). These tiles, one-inch across, were available in white, black, bright blue, green, and earth colors. Darker tiles were arranged in various repeating figures on the white field. (Fig. I-45.) Rectangular tiles in the same colors were used for borders, usually in a meandering fret design. Cast-iron sills protected edges at entrance steps. Hex-tile floors were also favored for restrooms and office corridors. Many restroom floors remain.

Fig. I-44. Main banking space of United States National Bank with marble floor, columns, partitions, and desks. Coffered ceiling and column capitals are plaster. Lighting fixtures are bronze.

Fig. I-45. Hex-tile floor with border of square tiles in the Southern Pacific waiting room. Although not in a glazed terra-cotta building, this interior exhibits materials and features typical of the era, including decorative plasterwork, plain unornamented cabinetwork, and suspended incandescent lighting fixtures.

There were a few types of mosaic floors other than hex tile. Tiles in the Seward Hotel vestibule, of various sizes and shapes, are all in earth colors. Large bright-blue ceramic tiles are set in the terra-cotta ornament at the Seward parapet. The mosaic floor at the western entrance to the United States National Bank is made of marble chips.

Terrazzo floors occurred primarily in office corridors. The offices themselves usually had smooth-finished concrete floors with a 24-inch painted border. Each tenant supplied his own carpet.

Fig. I-46. Flexible rubber-mold in plaster "mother," made by Seattle modelmaker Matt Thewlis. Plaster piece cast in mold stands upside down in background.

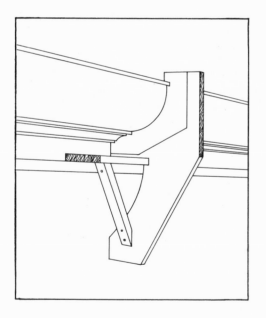

Fig. I-47. Mold for run-in-place ornamental plaster work: metal template mounted on wood frame. Frame rides along wood strip attached to wall.

⁴Christopher Weeks, "Preserving an Old World Heritage," *Historic Preservation*, November/December, 1981, p. 32.

ORNAMENTAL PLASTERWORK.

Plaster decoration was for the interiors of 1905-30 buildings what glazed terra cotta was for exteriors. The overall composition, style, and motifs were similar, if not identical.

Plasterwork ranged in complexity from the simple crown mold found in office and retail spaces to the elaborate coffered ceilings, pilasters, moldings, and bas-relief of major public spaces. Portland's best examples of highly-decorative plasterwork are in the main banking room of the United States National Bank and throughout the Elks Temple. Ornament in the Elks Temple has whimsical features including parrots, snakes, and female figures.

Plaster decoration is fabricated in two distinctly different ways: cast and run-in-place. Cast plaster, as the name implies, is cast in a mold. Run-in-place plasterwork includes only elements having no three-dimensional curves (such as simple moldings). Most installations involved both run-in-place and cast-plaster work. Some of the cast elements might have been stock designs selected from catalogues.

The production of cast-plaster work is similar to, but much simpler than, the production of terra cotta. For both, creation of a model is the first step. However, because plaster does not shrink as it sets, the model for cast plaster does not have to be made larger than the final piece, as it does for terra cotta.

Molds for cast plaster are made in two parts: a glue liner inside a plaster shell ("mother"). The flexibility of the glue mold, which can be removed from the mother, allows for deeper undercutting than would be possible with an all-plaster mold. The mother merely stabilizes the glue mold while the plaster is setting.

To fabricate a glue mold, a thin layer of water-based clay is first poured over the model. This is then covered with the plaster that forms the mother. The mother is taken away and the water-based clay removed. The mother is then replaced over the model, leaving a void where the water-based clay had been. Glue is poured into this void to form the glue mold.⁴ Molds to be reused many times are made of flexible rubber rather than glue. (Fig. I-46.)

For run-in-place work the "mold" is actually a metal template mounted on a wooden frame. (Fig. I-47.) This template, cut with the profile to be produced, is run along over many successive thin applications of plaster until the form is filled out. A vertical molding would likely be run on the floor and installed after it had set.

Plasterwork can be attached with wire or glue, or both, depending on size and weight. Wire and fiber are used to reinforce cast plaster. Ornamental plaster ceilings of the glazed terra-cotta era were hung in a manner similar to contemporary suspended ceilings. The vaulted plaster ceiling in the Elks Temple hangs several feet below the structural ceiling.

Modelers working in plaster were involved in many related operations. A 1908 advertisement for the Portland firm, Senn Nitschke & Company, read as follows: "Sculptors and Carvers. Manufacturers of Architectural Plaster Staff and Cement Ornaments; Makers of Composition for Wood, Artificial Marble and Granite;...Sculpturing Busts, Statues, Portraits and Monuments; Cement Vases; Lessons in Carving and Modeling."

The artificial marble and granite referred to in the advertisement was probably made of plaster. Numerous Portland buildings are decorated with plaster "marble." In some cases, it is impossible to tell real marble from false without touching it. (Real marble feels colder than plaster.) To simulate marble, colors were either mixed with the plaster ("scagliola") or applied to the surface. Scagliola involved casting marble colors and figures and giving the piece a high polish. The purely surface application tends to flake off when the plaster becomes wet or cracked.

The interior of the Bank of California is faced with travertine made of plaster, reportedly using a patented process. It has unfortunately been painted, but the pattern of small voids characteristic of travertine is still visible.

WOODWORK.

Although, because of its flammability, wood was not featured in glazed terra-cotta buildings, certain special spaces such as board rooms and hotel lobbies were sometimes paneled. Frames for office relights and doors, as well as the doors themselves, were made of wood; individual offices had wood bases, chair rails, and picture rails. Retail cases and shelving were also of wood. Until the mid-1920s, upper-story window sash and frames were wood.

While exterior wood was painted, interior woodwork was almost always stained very dark, varnished, and rubbed down to a flat finish. (Fig. I-48.) Philippine mahogany was preferred, but walnut was also used, most notably in the Oregon Hotel lobby, which is paneled in Circassian walnut. Lipman, Wolfe & Co. had fixtures of Circassian walnut on its third floor. The lines for wood moldings were extremely simple. The effect was of quality, not of elaborate show.

Fig. I-48. Office corridor of 1926 Pacific Building showing simple lines of dark-stained woodwork, obscure glass, terrazzo floor with marble borders and bases, and light neutral colors on plaster walls and ceiling.

PAINT COLORS.

The few exterior elements that required paint were not accented with colors contrasting to the building mass, but were, instead, keyed to the neutral glaze colors. Double-hung window sash and frames were apparently painted to exactly match the glaze. Steel sash of the late 1920s was painted a darker neutral. Cast-iron window and door frames were painted either dark green or bronze.

In order to maximize light levels, office interiors were painted light neutral tones. One specification called for walls of light tan and ceilings of light ivory. Pull-down shades at windows and relights were painted a light olive color.

Darker, richer colors could be found, however, in some public spaces — the main banking spaces of the United States National Bank and the Bank of California, as well as the lobbies of the Oregon Hotel and Public Service Building. Public spaces in the Elks Temple were also richly hued, with blacks and deep golds along with some surprisingly feminine pastels. Of these four buildings, only the United States National Bank main banking room and parts of the Elks Temple retain their original color schemes. The United States National Bank's coffered ceiling, with its gold leaf, golden yellows, dull red, and aquamarine, is a splendid example of classical coloration.

By the late 1920s, Art Deco color schemes had supplanted classical, as evidenced by the Charles F. Berg building with its black-and-gold exterior. The interior decoration of this building (none of which remains) must have been a prime example of the new palette. Colors mentioned in the detailed description published in the *Oregonian,* on the occasion of the building's grand opening, include bronze, silver-stipple lacquer, satin silver, black enamel, brown, jade green, light orchid, light violet, mauve, beige-grey, blue, and coral.

Stenciling was evidently practiced in Portland all through the glazed terra-cotta era and into the early 1940s. The ceiling in the Bank of California is elaborately stenciled, as was that in the Public Service Building lobby before it was remodeled. (Fig. I-49.)

LIGHTING.

Portland's glazed terra-cotta buildings are the only group of local commercial buildings for which lighting was originally almost exclusively incandescent. This is probably true also for glazed terra-cotta buildings in other American cities. Although the first successful carbon-filament lamp was made in 1879, it was not until the early 1900s that the vibration-proof tungsten filament was introduced. By the late 1920s, fluorescent lighting was beginning to replace incandescent.

As late as the 1910s, electricity was still not considered completely dependable, and many interior fixtures were a combination of gas and electricity, with from-one-to-six lamps for each on a single fixture.

Not long after the introduction of incandescent lighting, designers perceived the possibilities for indirect lighting. Light was reflected off the ceiling with the source either in a suspended opaque or translucent bowl or in a plaster cove. (The 1926 Pacific Building's lobby has cove lighting.) Simple glass globes mounted directly on the ceiling were, however, the more usual types of purely-electrical fixtures.

For public spaces, lighting fixtures were highly decorative, utilizing the same design motifs as the building's terra-cotta and cast-plaster decoration. Exterior lanterns were either iron or bronze. Interior ornamental fixtures were usually of bronze, although crystal was popular for clubs and hotels.

The person responsible for the design and manufacture of most custom fixtures from

Fig. I-49. Lobby of Public Service Building, 1928, with stenciled ceiling. None of this decoration remains.

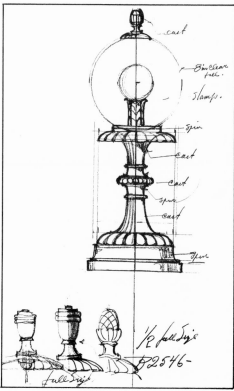

Fig. I-50. Interior of Baker-Harkness Company, mid-1920s. Men in background are operating drill presses; those at work tables are assembling lighting fixtures.

Fig. I-51. Recent sketch by Fred C. Baker of lighting fixture for a branch of the United States National Bank. Notations indicate how various components were to be fabricated: "cast," "stamp," and "spin."

1910 onward in Portland was Fred C. Baker, who died recently at the age of ninety-four. Baker was born in Bay City, Michigan in 1887 and came to Oregon in 1892 with his family. They settled on a ranch in Southern Oregon, but left for the East at the outbreak of the Spanish-American War, returning when it ended to settle in Portland.

Baker began his career as a draftsman. He was, for a time, apprenticed to architect Ellis F. Lawrence, who later became dean of the School of Architecture at the University of Oregon. In 1912, Baker opened his own shop where he began designing, assembling, and selling fixtures.[5] He would work for an architect as lighting-fixture designer, and the architect would then recommend that Baker be given the lighting-fixture contract. Some of the fixtures that he designed were fabricated by others. He also supplied stock fixtures. A building "lighted" by Baker could, therefore, have part stock and part custom-designed fixtures and, probably, also some fixtures assembled partly from stock and partly from custom-made components. (Fig. I-50, 51.) Prior Bronze Works of Portland produced many bronze castings for Baker, and he often collaborated with model makers Nitschke and Andrae. Baker also mentioned in an interview that a firm called the McBeth Evans Glass Company could make glass leaves for him from his models. Ordinary globes were purchased from Eastern manufacturers.[6]

The most elegant Baker fixtures remaining in Portland's glazed terra-cotta buildings are those in the United States National Bank. Featuring classical design motifs, they are direct fixtures of bronze with exposed bulbs. Baker's most unusual designs were found in the Elks Temple, where he fashioned pairs of parrots to perch on the fixtures in the billiard room. Although, so far as is known, these particular fixtures are no longer extant, his watercolor design-sketch shows them in detail.

The introduction of fluorescent lighting took its toll on Baker's business, as it did on others producing custom fixtures. He did, however, collaborate with Portland's architects on the "modernization" of many glazed terra-cotta building lobbies, often replacing his own classical designs with stripped-down modern fixtures.

The decorative possibilities of exterior electric lighting were celebrated at Portland's 1905 Lewis and Clark Exposition (as they had been in a somewhat more tentative fashion

[5]Charles Deemer, "The Draftsman as Artist," *Oregonian Northwest Magazine,* November 19, 1978, p. 14.

[6]Fred C. Baker, Recorded interview by Janet Charlton, George McMath, and Anne Murphy, 1978. Notes in author's collection.

Fig. I-52. Glazed terra-cotta cornice for 1911 Yeon Building with holes for electric light-bulb sockets.

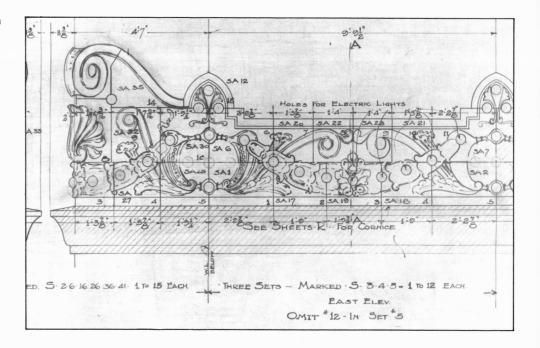

Fig. I-53. Section through Yeon Building cornice showing placement of light-bulb socket.

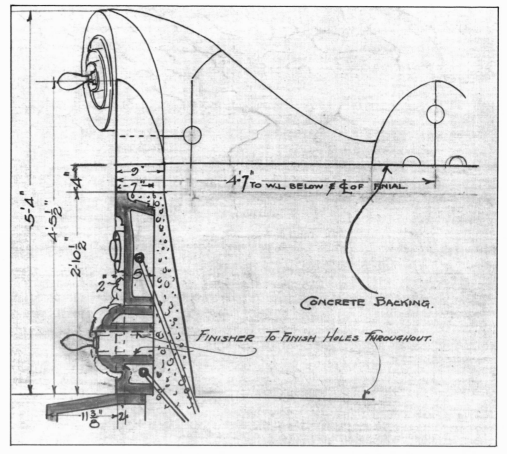

at the 1893 Columbian Exposition in Chicago) by outlining buildings with rows of light bulbs. This theme was subsequently adopted for many of Portland's downtown buildings built between 1905 and about 1922. The 1912 Journal Building is the only one with its lighting system in working order, though sockets remain in others. The 1911 Yeon Building's decoratively-lit, glazed terra-cotta cornice was removed entirely, but shop drawings show in detail how provisions for light bulb sockets were made when the terra cotta was pressed. (Fig. I-52, 53.)

Other decorative exterior lighting was provided by street-light standards, usually with a globe on each of three or four arms and a single globe on top. Standards of this type were placed all around the edge of the Olds, Wortman & King roof. All of the four-and five-globe street lights have been replaced by circa-1925 fixtures of a larger scale.

In 1914, intersections along Third were decorated with crossed, diagonal metal arches outlined with light bulbs. They were financed by the utility whose streetcars ran along Third as a means of promoting ridership.

Exterior decorative lighting also occurred on signs and on building marquees.

SIGNS, AWNINGS, MARQUEES, AND FLAGPOLES

Contrasting with the dignity and restraint of the glazed terra-cotta ornament was a variety of exterior appendages of a more sprightly nature. While entrance marquees, building-name signs, and flagpoles were likely parts of the original architectural design, awnings and individual business signs were selected by tenants and often differed widely in appearance.

Entrance marquees were typically the most elaborate features on the exteriors of glazed terra-cotta buildings. Made of sheet metal with glass panels and supported by chains, they often had cast-metal decorative motifs combined with the sheet metal. Some were made of copper, some of bronze, and some of galvanized iron. Many were outlined with light bulbs. (Fig. I-54.)

Corner buildings often had two marquees, one at each façade. Two glazed terra-cotta buildings, the Woodlark Building and the Failing Building, had marquees running the full length of both façades.

Extremely vulnerable to the elements, most entrance marquees have long since disappeared. Those on the Meier & Frank Co. building are still in place, though with bronze plates substituted for the original glass. The Seward Hotel's marquee recently emerged when the metal covering, which had encased it for years, was damaged and removed. Those on the Olds, Wortman & King building, though still intact, are not prime examples. Fortunately, the single example of a glazed terra-cotta-faced marquee, on the Odd Fellows Building, remains and is in good condition.

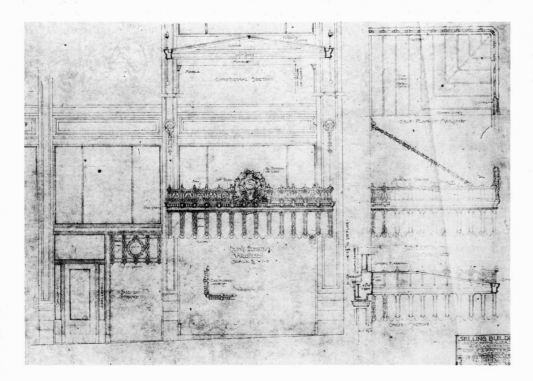

Fig. I-54. Entrance marquee for Selling Building, 1910, by Doyle & Patterson. Decorative motifs were of cast iron, side panels of plain glass, and upper panels of wire glass. Light bulbs screwed into the ends of the decorative cast-iron muntins.

Nearly every glazed terra-cotta building had a large flagpole on its roof. Some had two or more. Poles (of clear straight-grained fir) were often topped with large balls. Specifications for the Selling Building called for a spun-copper ball gilded with gold leaf. Although most buildings flew the American flag, there were exceptions; a perspective drawing for the Woodlark Building shows a large "Woodlark" banner. (Fig. III-15.)

Almost all buildings were designed with provisions for retractable awnings at ground-floor retail space. Some buildings also had awnings at office windows above. Storefront awnings were usually hung from the transom bar, thereby allowing sunlight through the transom lights and into the back of the store space. Awnings were of striped canvas with scalloped skirts.

Most building names were pressed into the terra-cotta frieze placed over the main entrance. Letters were large, but discreet, usually in one of the classic type-styles. The building name might also appear on a roof sign, an enormous construction with large individual letters supported on open trusswork. Letters would be outlined with individual light bulbs or, later, with neon. The Meier & Frank Co. building and the Sovereign Hotel both had signs of this type. (Fig. III-3, 30.) The most striking roof sign, a square structure atop the tile roof of the Public Service Building, did not display the building name, but rather "POWER," "GAS," "HEAT," and "LIGHT" on its respective four sides. (Fig. III-39.) In its place now is a pseudo-mansard metal roof.

Ground-floor tenants installed both projecting and frieze signs. Projecting signs were of sheet metal, sometimes with back-lit letters. Light bulbs often outlined signs and individual letters. As with roof signs, neon tubes eventually replaced bulbs. Metal frieze signs were either similar to projecting signs or had raised gold letters on a solid-colored panel. The Kress sign, with its traditional red background, ran continuously along both building façades. (Fig. III-38.)

Both street-level and upper-level tenants had signs painted on window glass. Those on upper windows were generally simple letters in gold leaf. Signs on street-level glass might be more assertive.

Billboard-type signs often appeared on brick party walls, either applied on panels or painted directly on the brick. In some cases, the name of the building was displayed in this fashion.

A 1926 photograph of the lower floors of the 1910 Selling Building shows a sampling of the features and materials found on glazed terra-cotta buildings: brick facing at upper stories, double-hung office windows, plate-glass shop fronts, leaded prism glass in transom lights, iron fire escapes and entrance marquees, awnings, and a full array of signs. It also indicates how glazed terra cotta can provide a unifying framework for the many *ad hoc* features appropriate to a lively and evolving downtown.

Fig. I-55. Photograph taken in 1926 of the 1910 Selling Building. Signs have raised gold letters, neon letters, or letters filled with incandescent bulbs. Names of upper-level tenants are lettered on window glass in gold leaf. Prism glass in transom is of larger-than-usual size. (Two-story glazed terra-cotta building to the right, designed by Houghtaling and Dougan, no longer exists.)

PART II

PRESERVATION

DISTRICT PRESERVATION

Survival of any group of downtown historic buildings depends on a combination of private and public activities. From 1930 to 1972 private actions predominated in shaping Portland's downtown development and, even though they were in general detrimental to the downtown area, their effects on the glazed terra-cotta buildings were, on the whole, benign. Following 1972 and the adoption of Portland's Downtown Plan, public actions took the lead in determining the course of development. Although to date the Downtown Plan has encouraged preservation of the terra-cotta buildings, its eventual full implementation could be harmful to them. The following review of past and likely future developments in the downtown area provides the basis for a look at the future of the district and at possible ways to protect it. The primary focus is on preservation of the glazed terra-cotta buildings along Washington and Morrison streets *as a group*. Preservation of individual glazed terra-cotta buildings, including those scattered around the district, is covered in Chapter II-B.

DOWNTOWN DEVELOPMENT, 1930-70s

From 1930 to the early 1970s Portland's downtown area experienced traumas typical of other American cities. Its streetcar system gave way to buses and automobiles. Streets were made one way. Many older buildings in the waterfront area were demolished for surface parking lots, and multi-level parking structures were built in the periphery of the retail core. Construction of a freeway loop around downtown began in 1959 and was completed in 1973. Downtown stores suffered from the competition of the new outlying shopping centers.

A spurt of office building construction commenced in 1963 and culminated in 1972 with the 42-story First National Bank tower (subsequently renamed First Interstate Center). With the exception of the Bank of California building, located on the north edge of the 1905-30 commercial district, these new office buildings were all south of Taylor Street, well out of the old streetcar center. The 1963 Hilton Hotel, the first major hotel built in Portland after the late 1920s, was located among these new office buildings. Although this new construction greatly enlarged the downtown commercial core, the retail center stayed put between Washington and Morrison, tied there by the major department store buildings.

Beyond the group of new office buildings, on the far south edge of the downtown area, an old predominantly Italian-and-Jewish neighborhood was cleared for an urban renewal project that included apartment towers as well as office buildings. A second urban renewal project made way for the newly-emerging Portland State University at the southern end of the South Park Blocks.

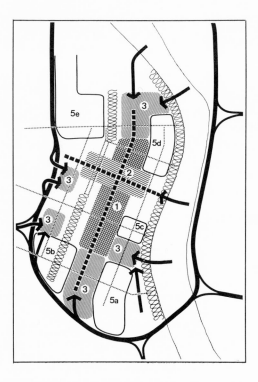

Fig. II-1. Concept plan included in 1972 *Planning Guidelines/Portland Downtown Plan.* (1) high-density offices related to north-south transit, (2) retail core related to north-south and east-west transit, (3) medium-density office, (5a) Portland Center, (5b) Portland State University, (5c) Government Center, (5d) Skidmore Fountain/Old Town District, and (5e) industrial. Housing areas, inadvertently omitted from this plan, were added soon afterward. Area 2, the retail core, coincides closely with the greatest concentration of glazed terra-cotta buildings.

[1]*Planning Guidelines/Portland Downtown Plan as adopted by City Council, December, 1972.*

DOWNTOWN PLAN (1972)

As the scale and pace of building in the downtown area increased, private citizens and local officials became concerned as to what kind of environment was being created. In 1970 a citizens' advisory committee was formed to produce goals for future development. Working with the City's planning staff and planning consultants, the committee produced a report, *Planning Guidelines, Portland Downtown Plan,* which was adopted by City Council in 1972. The advisory committee's vision of downtown is best expressed by the following goal statement from the 1972 report:

"Create in downtown an urban setting with a definite sense of place and identity by developing strong boundaries, emphatic focal points, unique physical designs for identifiable areas and by enhancing special views such as the waterfront and historic or architecturally significant buildings."[1]

The essential elements of the schematic plan concept (Fig. II-1) were straightforward: north-south transit corridor centered on a high-density office spine; retail core centered on east-west transit; remainder of land inside freeway loop in medium and lower density office, residential, and industrial use; waterfront esplanade; and strong pedestrianways linking development concentrations and special districts.

The office spine was to run from Market Street to Burnside Street between Fourth Avenue and Broadway, implying that Fifth and Sixth Avenues were to be the north-south transit routes. (If located to the east, this office spine would have collided with the Plaza Blocks and, if located to the west, with the Park Blocks, so its alignment was probably never in question.) East-west shuttle transit was roughly located on Alder and Morrison.

Downtown transit was to perform two roles: transport people to downtown and provide for circulation within the downtown area, including service from peripheral parking facilities. How downtown transit routes were to connect with the regional system was never specified, nor was the particular mix of modes (bus and rail).

TRANSIT MALL AND LIGHT RAIL LINES

A transit mall that consolidated most downtown bus routes on Fifth and Sixth from Burnside to Columbia Street was completed in 1978. With widened, brick-paved sidewalks, elegant metal-framed bus shelters, and other custom-designed street furniture, it created a strong visual north-south axis through downtown. Even before the transit mall was completed, planning commenced for an eastside light rail line to enter downtown on the Steel Bridge at Glisan Street, north of Burnside. After lengthy public debate, the route for this line was chosen: south on First Avenue to an east-west loop on Morrison and Yamhill Street. (Fig. II-2.) The reasons for not running it along the transit mall were two: the mall had not been constructed with the even slope required for the 180-foot-long light rail vehicles (mall streets flattened out at intersections) and major property owners in the Skidmore/Old Town and Yamhill Historic Districts were eager to have the line pass through the districts. The choice of Yamhill rather than Alder or Washington as the other half of the couplet (with Morrison) was due to the necessity of maintaining Washington and Alder for automobile traffic. (When the present Morrison Bridge was constructed in 1958, it was located midway between Alder and Washington, establishing these streets as a heavily-used automobile couplet.)

Plans are currently underway for a westside light rail line to be constructed by 1995. Although it was generally agreed, at the time First was chosen for the line serving the eastside, that, when the westside line was added, all light rail would be shifted to the mall (leaving only shuttle service on First, Morrison, and Yamhill), planners now say that both the First/Morrison/Yamhill route and the mall will be needed to accommodate the expected volume. Half the light rail cars will pass along the transit mall and west on Columbia and the other half along First and the Yamhill/Morrison couplet. Portland's 1905-30, streetcar commercial core will thus be served by regional bus and light rail lines

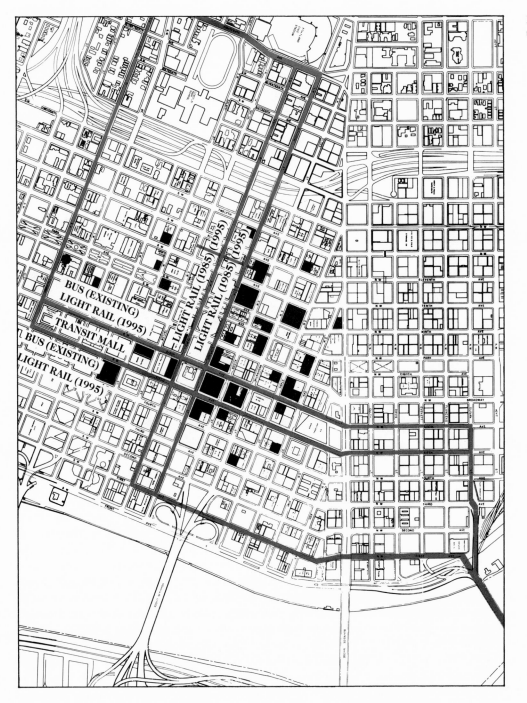

Fig. II-2. Downtown mass transit, existing and future.

intersecting one-and-a-half blocks south and one-half block west of its historical center of activity along Fifth between Alder and Washington. (Fig. I-6.) Assuming that ease of access continues, as it has historically, to result in demand for rental office and retail space, Portland's glazed terra-cotta district will in the 1980s and 1990s be subjected to considerable development pressure.

HEIGHT AND BULK REGULATIONS

Height and bulk regulations in the downtown area were established to reinforce the Downtown Plan concept. Maximum allowable total floor area for new construction varies from four square feet per square foot of building site area (4:1 floor/area ratio) to 15 square

Fig. II-3. Height and bulk limitations. Ratios indicate maximum allowable building floor area in relation to site area. Maximum allowable building height in shaded area is 460 feet. Maximum heights in other areas are lower, the lowest being 60 feet in one historic district. Maximum allowable heights for glazed terra-cotta building sites outside shaded area are indicated.

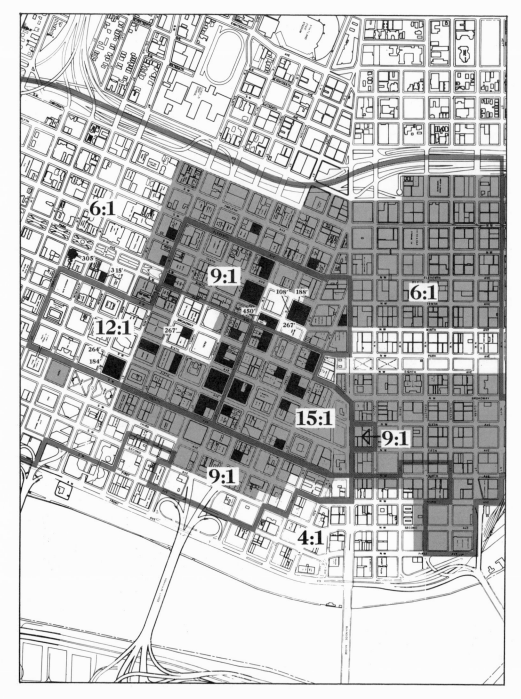

feet per square foot of building site area (15:1 floor/area ratio). Highest allowable ratios are along the high-density office spine with the northern portion set at 15:1 and the southern portion at 12:1 in recognition of the rise in terrain from north to south. These ratios compare to a maximum of about 12:1 for glazed terra-cotta buildings.

Maximum allowable building heights step down east and west from the high-density office spine and from north to south, again reflecting the change in terrain. (Fig. II-3.) The maximum allowable height around most glazed terra-cotta buildings is 460 feet. Exceptions are sites to the south and west of parks and along the South Park Blocks. By comparison, the tallest glazed terra-cotta building is 207-feet, six-inches.

In areas with a 6:1 floor area ratio (and probably also in 9:1 areas), the 460-foot building height limitation is superfluous. With Portland's 200-foot-by-200-foot blocks and with no provision to transfer allowable floor area from one block to another, it would be most unlikely for a building to have the small area per floor necessary to reach 460 feet. (In a 6:1 area, average floor areas would have to be approximately 6,400 square feet, compared to 16,000 to 20,000 square feet typical for present-day Portland office buildings.) Therefore, it is only in the 12:1 and 15:1 areas that very tall new buildings are likely to be constructed. Unfortunately, 23 of the 40 buildings in this study are located in these areas.

No new buildings approaching the allowable 460-foot height limit have been constructed in the glazed terra-cotta, streetcar-era district. The one office tower with a full-block site is only 15-stories tall. However, with the light rail system nearing reality and office sites in other areas of downtown becoming scarce, it would be naive to assume there will not eventually be pressure in the glazed terra-cotta district for construction of some large office buildings.

EXISTING DOWNTOWN DISTRICTS

Since the Downtown Plan was adopted in 1972, several districts have been delineated: Retail, Government, Housing, Industrial, North of Burnside, Chinatown, Yamhill Historic District, and Skidmore/Old Town Historic District. "Unique sign districts" are superimposed on three of these districts. (Fig. II-4.) Though the north-south office spine has never been outlined as a special office district, high-density office development has, in fact, occurred as intended along the transit mall.

Original functions of the glazed terra-cotta buildings coincide closely with designated functions of the districts in which they are located. Exceptions include two office buildings (Mayer Building and Portland Telegram Building) in the Housing District and an apartment house just outside the Housing District.

Twenty-two of the glazed terra-cotta buildings included in this study are located in the Retail District. Two regulations specifically promote sidewalk-oriented retail uses in this district: the "building line" requirement and retail use requirement. The building line requirement, which extends beyond the retail district past several peripheral glazed terra-cotta buildings (Fig. II-5.), stipulates that at least 75 percent of street frontage must extend to the property line and that these portions of the building must be at least one-story high. The retail use requirement states that new or substantially remodeled buildings in the district must devote at least 50 percent of their sidewalk frontage to retail use. (Retail includes restaurants, but not banks.) A third regulation, which applies to most of the entire downtown area, also encourages sidewalk-oriented activities: for all new or substantially remodeled buildings having non-residential ground floor uses, 50 percent of the width of all first-floor walls must be devoted to entrances or to windows with views into retail, office, or public spaces.

The Housing District, in which two office buildings, a church, and one former lodge (now converted to housing) are located, is not an exclusively residential zone. Also considered appropriate are "...institutional uses, together with appropriate office and retail activities that serve the area residents, as well as complement adjacent retail and office uses."[2]

On the whole, present districts recognize and augment the historical roles of the glazed terra-cotta buildings. The most important exception is the banking center, still in its historical location between Washington and Oak Street. This district is not recognized at all and, in fact, the southern portion is included in the Retail District.

DESIGN REVIEW

Construction within the entire downtown area is subject to design review by either the Portland Design Commission or the Portland Historical Landmarks Commission. A set of design guidelines applicable to all of downtown (excepting designated landmarks and the two historic districts) was adopted by City Council in 1980. Supplementary standards for the South Park Blocks were included in the 1980 design guidelines, with the comment that special guidelines for other districts might be developed in the future.[3]

[2]Portland Bureau of Planning, *Downtown Plan Handbook, Portland, Oregon, June 1981*, p. 125.

[3]Michael Harrison, *Downtown Design Standards*, July 1980, p. 60.

Fig. II-4. Downtown districts. Some districts relate to uses and others to visual qualities.

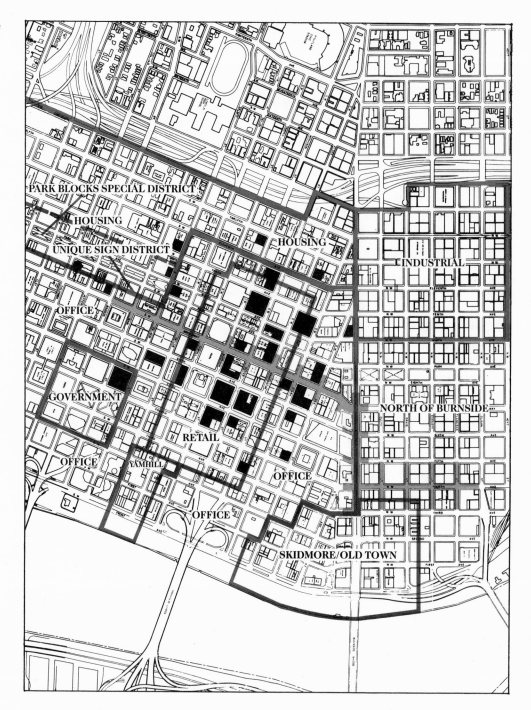

Although the 1980 guidelines were written for all of downtown, they reflect the special character of the glazed terra-cotta district. Three guidelines in particular speak to the glazed terra-cotta district: (1) maintain the street wall, (2) differentiate between the pedestrian-oriented uses at the sidewalk level and the office levels above, and (3) provide physical and visual contact between commercial space and the adjacent sidewalk.

Other guidelines serve to reinforce the identities of all districts, for example: maintain compatibility with design features of surrounding buildings that give continuity to the area.

Only one guideline seems inappropriate to the glazed terra-cotta district: reinforce the north-south orientation, and maintain active, pedestrian-oriented uses on the north-south avenues, on east-west streets designated as pedestrian or transit streets.[4] Although buildings in the Skidmore/Old Town and Yamhill Historic Districts consistently front on

[4]Portland Bureau of Planning, *Downtown Plan Handbook, Portland, Oregon, June 1981,* pp. 140-41.

Fig. II-5. Building line requirement. On streets indicated, at least 75 percent of the street facade (for a minimum of one story) must be built at the property line.

north-south streets, buildings in the terra-cotta district front equally on north-south and east-west streets.

POST-1972 DOWNTOWN DEVELOPMENT

Since 1972, most construction in the downtown area has taken place south of the 1905-30 streetcar-era commercial core and in the form of large office towers. One 42-story office building was constructed to the north, on Burnside. Extensive renovation and infill development have taken place in the historic districts. A major hotel was built in 1980 on the south waterfront.

Probably the most significant addition to the old streetcar-era commercial core was the

1978 full-block, three-story Nordstrom store building between Morrison and Yamhill and Broadway and Park. Nordstrom's faces the old federal (Pioneer) courthouse across Pioneer Courthouse Square, which was completed in 1984 on the site of the old Portland Hotel. Pioneer Courthouse Square is the second park block added to the streetcar-era commercial core since 1972. In 1973, buildings between Park and Ninth Avenues and Washington and Stark Street were razed to make way for O'Bryant Park, built atop one level of parking.

Two large city-owned parking structures have been built since 1972. One is west of Nordstrom's, adjacent to the 1910 Olds, Wortman & King department store building. The second parking structure is east of the 1905-30 commercial core, one block from the Morrison Bridge ramps. It will partly serve a major multi-block development, the Morrison Street Project, to be built under the auspices of the Portland Development Commission. This project, whose official role is to provide the "critical mass" of retail activity necessary for downtown to compete with large suburban shopping centers, will be located at the far southeast corner of the 1905-30 streetcar-era commercial center.

CHANGES TO GLAZED TERRA-COTTA BUILDINGS

To the author's knowledge, only four downtown glazed terra-cotta buildings (or their facades) were demolished between 1930 and 1972. During this span of 42 years, the rest remained essentially intact and in use as they were originally.

Three downtown glazed terra-cotta buildings have been demolished since 1972. The Orpheum Theater, a fine example with lions' heads, Ionic capitals, and a decorative cornice, was sacrificed for the new Nordstrom building in 1978. A relatively nondescript building with a minimum of ornament gave way to O'Bryant Park. The red brick and off-white glazed terra-cotta YMCA building was replaced by an office tower.

Of all the downtown glazed terra-cotta structures, the all-retail buildings have undergone the most significant changes since 1972. One of the three department store buildings, the five-story Olds, Wortman & King building, underwent a major (and very successful) conversion to three floors of shops and restaurants with two floors of offices above in 1976. Of the three small retail structures, the Graves Music Company building is vacant, the H. Liebes & Co. building is nearly vacant, and the Charles F. Berg building has been converted to ground-floor retail and upper-level office uses. The conclusion seems inescapable that upper-level retail activity has become difficult to sustain.

The Morrison Street Project will undoubtedly draw more shoppers downtown, but how many will filter out into existing retail establishments is not easy to predict. Certainly the project's location at the southeast corner of the 1905-30 commercial core will limit its benefit to glazed terra-cotta buildings along sections of Washington and Alder lying west of Broadway. Washington has already lost its standing as the northern half of the downtown retail couplet. Many of the men's specialty stores, historically located along Washington, are now found in the concentration of office towers south of Taylor.

Only one glazed terra-cotta building, the Odd Fellows Building, has been converted from non-residential to housing. Both the Sovereign Hotel and the Roosevelt Hotel have undergone renovations for apartment use. The Roosevelt rehabilitation was federally subsidized, as was the Odd Fellows.

Office building construction in downtown Portland from 1981 to 1983 added 2.4 million square feet of floor space. This has had a detrimental effect on glazed terra-cotta office buildings, which in late 1983 had vacancy rates averaging 20 percent.[5]

FUTURE OF DISTRICT

If present land use controls and design guidelines remain in effect and the light rail lines are built as planned, the concentration of glazed terra-cotta buildings in Portland's 1905-30 commercial core will gradually be obscured by new construction. Some glazed terra-

[5]Robert D. Scanlan, Coldwell Banker, Letter to author, September 23, 1983.

cotta buildings will be demolished for new office towers permitted by present zoning. Others will lose their character through remodeling.

On the other hand, if a decision is made to recognize the district as a special area that merits protection and enhancement, it could become an unusual and delightful commercial area.

The special character of a fully-realized terra-cotta district would be apparent both from within and without. The atmosphere inside the district would be established by a range of specific traits: light-colored, richly-decorated façades rising directly up from street building lines and divided into base, attic, shaft, and capital; glass-filled retail bases with retractable awnings at transom bars; awnings at some upper windows as well; metal-and-glass entrance marquees; a variety of signs — large silhouetted letters on roof-tops, gold-leaf letters on window glass, red panel signs with raised gold letters, and many types of projecting signs; flagpoles and, most importantly, outline lighting on buildings, marquees, and signs and around display windows.

The district would be distinguished from without, not, as commercial cores traditionally have been, by building heights greater than anywhere else in the metropolis, but by a dip in the skyline. This dip would be most striking from Portland's West Hills, where from some locations it would frame the view of Mt. Hood. Office towers north and south of the district would be tall, slender, and relatively widely-spaced. In contrast, buildings in the district would be lower and more densely packed. Outline lighting on buildings, signs, and other features would be visible from afar, clearly marking the area as a festive place to be.

Up to the 1940s, Portland's Front and First Avenues were an almost continuous streetscape of cast-iron façades. In a very short period of time, as building after building was replaced by surface parking, these streetscapes were decimated. In their own way, the streetscapes in the terra-cotta district are as fine as were those on Front and First. Today, unlike the 1940s and 1950s, there are tools available to protect such areas. They need only be applied.

ELIGIBILITY OF GLAZED TERRA-COTTA DISTRICT

Before evaluating possible tools for preservation and enhancement of the 1905-30 glazed terra-cotta, streetcar-era commercial core, its qualifications as an historic district should be examined.

Districts based on historical congruity (rather than on function or terrain, for example) must include an unusual concentration of buildings constructed during a particular span of time, termed the "period of significance." For the glazed terra-cotta, streetcar-era district, the period of significance is 1905 to 1930. Buildings constructed during that time, whether faced with glazed terra cotta or not, are considered of primary importance. Buildings of landmark quality, but not of the period, are also of primary importance, but do not play a role in determining boundaries.

A map showing the various types of primary buildings indicates where the district's official boundaries might be drawn. (Fig. II-6.) For the area shown within the boundaries, the percentage of buildable land occupied by each type of primary structure is as follows:

Glazed Terra-Cotta Buildings 49.4%
Non-Glazed Terra-Cotta Buildings — Designated Landmarks and/or Listed
on National Register 9.7%
Non-Glazed Terra-Cotta Buildings — Eligible for Landmark Designation and/or
Listing on National Register 1.9%
Non-Glazed Terra-Cotta Buildings — Not Eligible for Designation or Listing,
but Built Between 1905 and 1930 . . . . 16.0%

Total Percentage of Buildable Land Occupied by Primary Structures 77.0%

This is an unusually high percentage of primary structures. (By comparison, the percentages of primary structures in Portland's Skidmore/Old Town and Yamhill Historic Districts are 30% and 50% respectively.) If it were deemed desirable to enlarge the

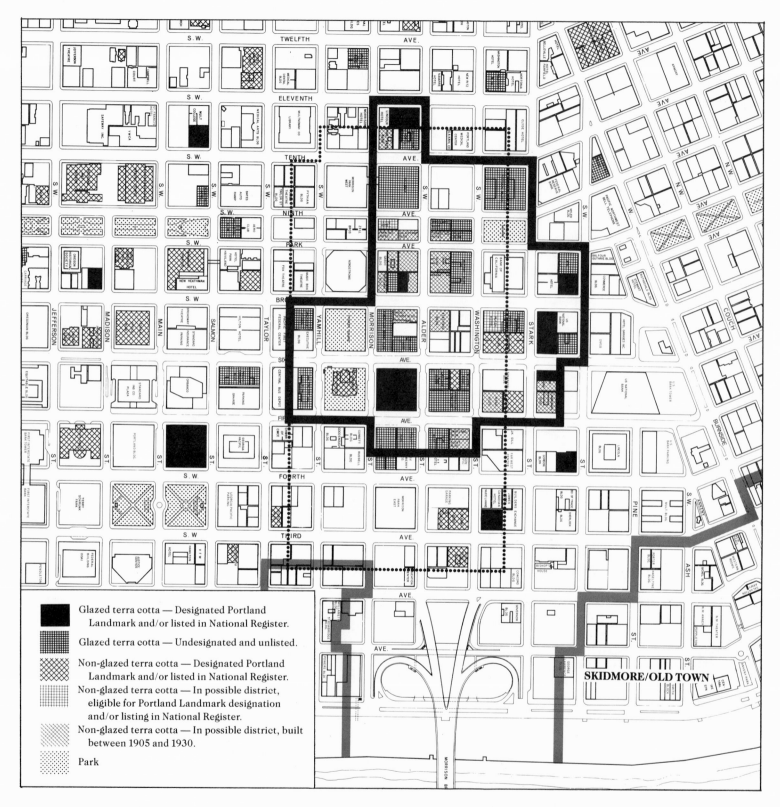

Glazed terra cotta — Designated Portland
Landmark and/or listed in National Register.

Glazed terra cotta — Undesignated and unlisted.

Non-glazed terra cotta — Designated Portland
Landmark and/or listed in National Register.

Non-glazed terra cotta — In possible district,
eligible for Portland Landmark designation
and/or listing in National Register.

Non-glazed terra cotta — In possible district, built
between 1905 and 1930.

Park

Fig. II-6. Possible glazed terra-cotta, streetcar-era district.

boundaries in order to encompass additional terra-cotta buildings, up to ten blocks around the periphery could be added to the glazed terra-cotta district, as shown, and still maintain a 50% percentage of primary structures. In evaluating these percentages, it should also be noted that 25 years is a relatively short period of significance for an historic district. Nationally, the usual period of significance for a commercial-center district is approximately 75 years. It is clear then that the suggested streetcar-era, glazed terra-cotta district satisfies, over and above, the requirements for designation.

LISTING DISTRICT IN NATIONAL REGISTER

Listing of the glazed terra-cotta district in the National Register of Historic Places would make available to owners of primary buildings, as well as other buildings that contribute to the historic significance of the district, federal grants for rehabilitation, federal income tax credits for rehabilitation, and special state property tax status (15-year property tax assessment freeze). Many district buildings that would never qualify individually for listing in the National Register would, because of their importance in maintaining the district's sense of time and place, be determined eligible for these tax benefits. (It should be noted that granting special property tax status to large numbers of buildings in the downtown area could result in an increase in property taxes for other property owners.)

Rehabilitation plans for any buildings taking advantage of federal grants and investment tax credits must be approved by the State Historic Preservation Office. Those utilizing investment tax credits must also receive approval from the National Park Service. Although no design review is required for properties with special state property tax status, this status can be lost because of incompatible alterations. Owners are, therefore, encouraged by State Historic Preservation Office staff to submit rehabilitation plans to them for approval before proceeding with reconstruction.

Other than for buildings taking advantage of federal financial aid, there is no requirement for design review of alterations in National Register districts. Neither is there any design review of new construction, nor provision for delaying demolition. National Register listing offers, therefore, very little ongoing protection to districts.

National Register districts do, however, enjoy a certain amount of protection from detrimental federal activities. Federal agencies are required to consider the effects on district properties of any federally-sponsored project. If effects are adverse, alternatives and mitigations must be considered. This review is also required for districts determined eligible for listing in the National Register.

LOCAL HISTORIC DISTRICT DESIGNATION

Under the Portland Historical Landmarks Commission ordinances, there are two forms of district designation: historic district and conservation district. Differences between the two types of districts are based on the way they are regulated rather than on their degree of historicity or integrity. For both, there is design review of new construction (exteriors) and the possibility of a 300-day demolition delay imposed by the Commission and City Council on primary structures. Only in historic districts must alterations to existing structures undergo design review.

Portland's two historic districts are commercial in nature and its two conservation districts, primarily residential. Although the district ordinances do not distinguish between residential and commercial districts, it is generally accepted in Portland that design review of alterations is desirable in commercial districts but not in residential districts. Following this precedent then, if given local designation, the glazed terra-cotta district would be an historic rather than a conservation district.

Designation of a glazed terra-cotta, streetcar-era historic district would have both advantages and disadvantages. Advantages to the general public would be protection and enhancement of a prime urban resource. Advantages to building owners would be the intangible benefits of location in a strongly-identified and well-publicized district, as well as eligibility for low-interest loans from the Portland Development Commission's Urban Conservation Fund. (It should be noted, however, that this is not a large fund and is presently available only to buildings in the Waterfront Urban Renewal Area.)

Disadvantages to building owners and managers would be possible delays in issuance of demolition permits and, possibly, a more restrictive design review process.

Upon designation, design review would shift from the Design Commission to the Landmarks Commission. A set of detailed design guidelines would be developed especially for the district. These guidelines could emphasize clearly and strongly the image of the district and point designers more directly toward a particular ambiance. The advantage of consistent application of tailor-made guidelines can be seen in the Skidmore/Old Town and Yamhill Historic Districts, which, since they were designated, have developed a more distinctive and appealing character. Design guidelines written specifically for the glazed terra-cotta, streetcar-era district could insure realization of its potential as well.

SPECIAL DESIGN REVIEW DISTRICT

The district would not have to be officially designated as an historic district to have its own set of design guidelines. This could be accomplished by establishing a special design review district under the purview of the Design Commission.

The glazed terra-cotta district incorporates about one-half of the Retail District. (Fig II-6.) Having a special set of design standards for a portion of the Retail District could be confusing. The situation in the downtown, vis-à-vis districts, is already confusing, however, in that some districts are design districts (Skidmore/Old Town, Yamhill, Park Blocks, and Unique Sign Districts) and others are functional districts (Retail, Government, Housing, and Industrial). Because the boundaries of functional districts are more appropriately shifted over time than those for districts that are based on clusters of particular historic building forms, it would probably make sense to have two separate sets of districts, design and functional, which overlap only as appropriate. This is already the case with the Park Blocks and Housing Districts.

The northern two blocks of the glazed terra-cotta district from Washington to Oak are functionally a banking district and should be recognized as such. There is no reason, however, why the same design guidelines could not apply to this area as to the rest of the glazed terra-cotta district.

CHANGES TO HEIGHT AND BULK REGULATIONS

The most direct way to prevent construction of overpoweringly large buildings in the glazed terra-cotta district is to reduce the allowable floor/area ratio to 12:1 throughout the district and the maximum allowable building height to approximately 250 feet. The allowable building size would then correspond reasonably well with the size of the glazed terra-cotta office buildings, effectively reducing the pressure to replace them with larger structures.

For the several really-low glazed terra-cotta buildings, some form of development rights transfer mechanism should be considered. The principal difficulty in developing such a mechanism is that allowable densities have been set so high in most of the downtown area that there is no pressing need to purchase development rights. One area in downtown to which development rights might be appropriately transferred lies along Tenth Avenue on the northwestern, western, and southwestern edges of the Retail District. This area, which has an allowable floor/area ratio of 9:1, has a few developable sites and is scheduled to be served after 1995 by light rail.

PUBLIC PERCEPTIONS

As a group, Portland's downtown glazed terra-cotta buildings have received little public attention. This is undoubtedly partly because they are not the oldest group of commercial buildings downtown, nor have they ever become derelict or fallen into disuse. They have, rather, since the 1910s been synonymous with "downtown" in the minds of most Portlanders. That a thriving commercial core could be "historic" is for most western Americans inconceivable. It has been left for visitors from the East Coast or Europe to remark on the wonderful "historic" buildings in Portland's downtown core. The first step in district preservation must, then, necessarily be an expanded awareness on the part of Portland's residents.

BUILDING REHABILITATION

Preservation of individual glazed terra-cotta buildings, whether located within the proposed district (Fig. II-6.) or on the periphery, will depend on their successful accommodation to changing needs. Adapting to new or modified uses calls for an understanding, not only of market demands and building code restrictions, but also of the innate qualities of the buildings themselves and of some of the special preservation tools available to historic buildings.

REHABILITATION OBJECTIVES

When 19th-century buildings in Portland are renovated, those portions visible to the public are generally restored to their near-original condition. Early 20th-century buildings, regardless of the number and extent of incompatible alterations made over the years, are, however, usually simply refurbished. If Portland's downtown glazed terra-cotta buildings are to achieve their full aesthetic and functional potential, their particular characteristics must be understood and exploited.

The primary attribute of any glazed terra-cotta building is its façade — richly ornamented and divided into human-scaled elements. Each façade is different, so that each building has its own special identity. Interior spaces in glazed terra-cotta buildings are commodious and yet contained. They lend themselves to the creation of distinctive and personal environments, but are, at the same time, relatively efficient. The special features (such as lighting fixtures) and materials (such as bronze and marble) on glazed terra-cotta buildings are the handsomest on any buildings in Portland. They impart a feeling of dignity and elegance unusual for commercial structures. Finally, because their underlying aesthetics are not based on a clean, spare look (as in modern architecture), glazed terra-cotta buildings can gracefully accommodate the great variety of temporary appendages (signs, awnings, flags, etc.) intrinsic to an active commercial area.

In order to capitalize on these assets, rehabilitation plans for a glazed terra-cotta building should take the original design as a starting point. The appropriateness of any non-historical features and materials should be judged within the context of the original design. Treatment of façades above the first floor should *always* be an accurate restoration. For buildings, such as banks, with no storefronts, the ground-floor façade should also be restored. Storefronts and public spaces allow for somewhat more latitude in design. For rental spaces the design treatment need not be historical at all.

There are several glazed terra-cotta buildings for which the nature of present adjacent development makes a combination of new construction and rehabilitation a distinct possibility. Such projects would offer interesting design possibilities, particularly in the treatment of spaces between buildings. New courtyards could provide pleasant views for interior space in both old and new buildings. A good example of such a project, in St.

Louis, incorporated the 1891 Wainwright Building.[1] Architect Walker C. Johnson, of Holabird & Root, and a team that included a developer and a planner, produced schematic designs for similar developments in Chicago.[2]

STOREFRONT REHABILITATION

Most glazed terra-cotta buildings were designed with the expectation that storefronts would be modified to accommodate various ground-floor tenants. During the glazed terra-cotta era, however, materials and detailing conformed to the rather narrow range in general use. (See Chapter I-D.) Design integrity was further maintained by the containment of modifications within each structural bay. During the 1930s, 1940s, and 1950s, whole ground-floor façades were stripped and faced with materials appropriate for modern buildings. It is, unfortunately, these portions of the glazed terra-cotta buildings that are most evident to the pedestrian. Neither the glazed terra-cotta buildings, nor the streetcar-era district, can achieve any real distinction until these ground-floor façades are rehabilitated in a manner compatible with the original design.

Office buildings in need of ground-floor remodeling are the Failing Building, Henry Building, H. Liebes & Co., Northwestern National Bank Building, Pittock Block, Platt Building, Selling Building, Woodlark Building, and Yeon Building. One hotel, the Imperial, has also been disasterously remodeled at its street level (with a facing of *fieldstone* at one portion!). Although these ground-level façades do not necessarily need to be returned exactly to their original condition, the overall original composition should be restored. For office buildings, this would mean plate-glass windows and transoms filling each bay, with recessed entrances located as needed. Retractable fabric awnings should be attached to the transom bars and entrance marquees, either duplicating the original designs, or with harmonious contemporary detailing replaced.

REHABILITATION OF PUBLIC SPACES

Most public spaces in Portland's glazed terra-cotta buildings have been "modernized." Although many of these renovations were designed by highly-regarded architects, they are often aesthetically incompatible with the buildings' overall design.

Office building lobbies, because they are relatively small, could, without incurring too great an expense, be either restored or remodeled to an approximation of their original design. This would undoubtedly increase the buildings' appeal to office tenants, many of whom are attracted to the glazed terra-cotta buildings because of their distinctive architecture.

One hotel, the Imperial, could also benefit from a sensitive remodeling of its public spaces, which in their present state are totally out of character with the building. Restoration of the original leaded-glass lobby skylight would re-create a lighting effect similar to that in Huber's, Portland's only remaining glazed terra-cotta-era restaurant.

Plans and photographs showing the original interiors are available for most terra-cotta buildings, as an aid for either restoration or compatible remodeling.

REHABILITATION OF RETAIL SPACE

Of the three basic types of retail space originally in glazed terra-cotta buildings — ground floor and mezzanine in office buildings, small two- and three-story store buildings, and department stores — only the office building ground floors are functioning as they did originally. Upper-level retail space in the small store buildings is either virtually vacant or being converted to office space. The three upper levels of one department store have been converted to office use and Meier & Frank has considered renting its upper floors for office use.

The difficulty in maintaining upper-level retail use is probably due to changes in the nature of the downtown shopper. When the glazed terra-cotta buildings were con-

[1] Carleton Knight III, "Wainwright rededicated as state office complex," *Preservation News* (Aug. 1981) pp. 1, 18.

[2] Carleton Knight III, "Our Kind of Town; Saving buildings in Chicago's North Loop," *Preservation News* (March, 1981), pp. 1, 11.

structed, most women were working solely as housewives. Few had cars, so shopping for other than day-to-day needs involved a trip downtown by streetcar. In most cases, this was at least a half-day excursion, with lunch at one of the department store restaurants. These restaurants were usually located on one of the upper floors, so it was natural to stop off at intermediate levels to shop. Today, the typical downtown shopper is an office worker out on a lunch hour. Many people working downtown live in suburbs with two-to-three-level shopping centers, so horizontal shopping is what they have come to expect. With neither the time nor the inclination to ride up several floors on an escalator or elevator, they do most of their shopping at sidewalk-oriented retail establishments.

Retailers also prefer fewer, larger floors, rather than multi-level stores, because of the flexibility and, as a result, the economy they allow for in staffing. This puts less than full-block buildings (such as Lipman, Wolfe & Co.) at a real disadvantage.

Although these constraints can be counteracted to some extent by staging special evening and weekend events and by creating special multi-level "festival" spaces (as in the remodeled Olds, Wortman & King building and the proposed Morrison Street Project), it is unlikely that the trend away from upper-level retail space will be reversed in the near future. We can probably expect to see much remaining upper-level retail space converted to office use.

Ground-level retail space in glazed terra-cotta buildings was typically 18-feet or more in height at the front with a mezzanine across the back. Where this spatial configuration remains intact, it should certainly be retained. Where obliterated, it should, if possible, be re-created. The loss in floor area would be more than compensated for by the increased attractiveness of the space.

Rehabilitation Of Office Space

At the time glazed terra-cotta buildings were constructed, very few offices were more than several hundred square feet in area and office floors were more or less permanently partitioned into enclosed rooms (sometimes connected as suites), on either side of central corridors. In contrast, the typical new office building has an open, 35-to-40-foot-deep, doughnut-shaped floor area around an elevator core, with one or more entire floors typically given over to a single business.

There are still, however, a sizable number of tenants requiring small offices, and glazed terra-cotta buildings have come to fill this niche in the market. A large proportion of office space in glazed terra-cotta buildings has outside windows and this spatial configuration makes them attractive to firms with a high ratio of professional to clerical staff.

Some large organizations, requiring more square feet of space than is typically available on one floor in a glazed terra-cotta building, find that the lower rents more than compensate for space restrictions. (In late 1983, rental rates for office space in glazed terra-cotta office buildings averaged around $10 per square foot, while rates for recently-constructed office towers ranged from about $16 to $24 per square foot.) Strategic location of the required exit corridors can create a relatively-large open area suitable for open-plan offices. It is also possible to fill in light wells at the lower levels and to connect floors with private stairs.

By the 1970s, physicians' offices, which originally filled much space in glazed terra-cotta buildings, had relocated en masse to new office buildings adjacent to hospitals. Now, with the patient-doctor ratio increasing and doctors being forced to consider the patients' convenience as well as their own, the downtown location is beginning to regain appeal. However, in the interim, plumbing for individual offices has been removed from most buildings, making them unsuited for doctors' use.

Historical Buildings And The Building Code

Renovation of glazed terra-cotta-era buildings can be complicated by the local building code, which, like codes in other cities, was written for new construction. Fortunately, however, Portland's Building Code Board of Appeals is a reasonable body and has often approved realistic alternative solutions.

The code specifically states that historical buildings "shall not be required to comply with the requirements of this code for those items approved to be exempted by the Historical Building Review Committee [Building Code Board of Appeals plus a representative from the Landmarks Commission] and judged to be in the public interest to the preservation of such buildings." An historical building is defined as "any building or structure designated under a local government landmark or historic district ordinance or buildings or structures listed in the State of Oregon Inventory of Historic Sites and Buildings, and properties approved for nomination to the National Register of Historic Places by the State of Oregon Advisory Committee on Historic Preservation."[3]

Structural Requirements Of The Building Code

Prior to 1979, Portland's building code required that any building whose alterations within a 12-month period exceeded 50% of its value must conform to the requirements of the code. The present code simply states that all new work shall comply with the code. Now, therefore, a building's structure is reviewed only when structural changes are being made, or when the occupancy is changed (in which case all aspects are reviewed). Although most glazed terra-cotta buildings have either steel or reinforced concrete frame structures, they generally do not meet present requirements for seismic loading. In carrying out structural review, officials strive for the maximum increase in earthquake resistance feasible within each rehabilitation project.

Exiting Requirements Of The Building Code

Most glazed terra-cotta buildings have only one enclosed stair, with an exterior fire escape serving as the second emergency exit. If a building being renovated is sprinklered, the Appeal Board will not require construction of a second exit stair. However, when there is a length of corridor greater than 20 feet with only one possible direction of travel to the stair or fire escape, the corridor system must be revised to create a loop. The fire escape can be accessed through an office.

The popularity of open-plan offices has complicated review by the Bureau of Buildings for compliance with code exiting requirements. Theoretically, any partition over five feet, nine inches in height, regardless of its length or continuity, establishes a corridor; and, if this corridor serves 30 persons or more (3000 square feet or more of office space), the partition must be of one-hour, fire-resistive construction. But, because strict application of this principle to the open-plan office would be absurd, layouts in both new and old buildings that are totally sprinklered and have smoke detectors in the plenums can receive special dispensation as "discontinuous corridor systems."

Office partitions as originally constructed in glazed terra-cotta buildings, with relights comprising up to 25 percent of the enclosed wall area, can also be considered discontinuous corridor systems by the Appeal Board, making possible their retention in renovated space. The transoms commonly found over corridor doors must always, however, be closed off.

Atrium Requirements Of The Building Code

Multi-story interior spaces with mezzanine-type open floors, popular during the glazed terra-cotta era, have, as "atriums," regained favor both for new construction and for rehabilitation of historic buildings. In glazed terra-cotta buildings, atriums can be created by removing portions of one or more floors, by introducing new floors over portions of a previously high-ceilinged space, or by enclosing a light court. (Fig. II-7.)

---

[3]State of Oregon, 1983 Edition, Structural Specialty Code and Fire and Life Safety Regulations, Based on the 1982 Edition of the Uniform Building Code.

Fig. II-7. Re-created atrium in Olds, Wortman & King building, completely remodeled in 1976 for three floors of retail with offices above and renamed "Galleria."

Portland's code requirements for atriums were revised in 1983. The minimum width for atriums three-or-four-stories-high is now 20 feet. For atriums five to seven stories in height, the minimum width is 30 feet. For atriums eight or more stories high, the minimum width is 40 feet. For office and retail space, the number of stories opening into the atrium is limited to three, and then only with an 18-inch draft stop and sprinklers on six-foot centers all around. Open exit balconies are permitted, however, as long as the travel distance from the tenant door to an enclosed exitway does not exceed 100 feet.

With the exception of the Pittock Block, light courts in Portland's glazed terra-cotta buildings are less than 20-feet wide. Special authorization would, therefore, be required in order to convert the light courts to atriums. Permission is usually given in such cases, however, with the stipulations that a maximum of two floors be left completely open and that windows at other floors have fixed, fire-resistive glazing.

In new atriums created by removing portions of existing floors in retail or office buildings, only three floors can be completely open. Additional floors have to have wired, tempered, or laminated glass, either at the the atrium wall or at the partitions between the office or retail space and exit balconies opening onto the atrium.

LANDMARK DESIGNATION

In spite of the prestige associated with landmark status, only six of the 40 glazed terra-cotta buildings in this study are designated landmarks: Bank of California, Elks Temple, Multnomah County Courthouse, Oregon Hotel, Sovereign Hotel, and United States National Bank. There are 18 to 20 others that would qualify.

Designation as a landmark shifts review of alterations from the Design Commission to the Landmarks Commission. It also makes it possible for the Landmarks Commission and City Council to delay for up to 300 days the issuance of a demolition permit. In addition to public recognition, benefits of designation would include eligibility for low-interest Urban Conservation Loans for rehabilitation. (It should be noted, however, that this is not a large fund and is presently available only to buildings in the Waterfront Urban Renewal Area.)

LISTING IN NATIONAL REGISTER

Nine glazed terra-cotta buildings in downtown Portland are listed in the National Register of Historic Places: Bank of California, Charles F. Berg, Elks Temple, Henry Building, Meier & Frank Co., Multnomah County Courthouse, Odd Fellows Building, Sovereign Hotel, and Spalding Building. At least 15 others would qualify for individual listing. Probably all 40 of the buildings in this study could be listed as part of a thematic group. (According to National Register rules and regulations, a thematic group is one that includes "...a finite group of resources related to one another in a clearly distinguishable way."[4]) Within a glazed terra-cotta, streetcar-era district listed in the National Register, any glazed terra-cotta building would be considered a primary structure with the same benefits as a structure listed individually. (See Chapter II-A.)

Financial benefits associated with listing in the National Register can be considerable. Owners are eligible for a special property tax assessment that freezes the assessed value for 15 years. Properties with the special assessment must be opened for public viewing one day a year. Maintenance and any alterations must be satisfactory to the State Historic Preservation Officer.

Owners of properties listed in the National Register are also eligible for a 25 percent federal investment tax credits for rehabilitation expenses. To qualify, the rehabilitation cost must be equal to the depreciated value of the property (not including land) or $5,000, whichever is greater. Based on present market values in Portland and typical rehabilitation costs, it appears that glazed terra-cotta buildings in need of substantial rehabilitation would easily meet this requirement. Plans must be approved by the State Historic Preservation Officer and by the National Park Service. Rehabilitation carried out in phases over a period of up to 60 months is eligible for investment tax credits, provided that plans for all work are approved at the outset.

National Register properties are also eligible for federal preservation development grants. These so-called "bricks and mortar" grants are only available when Congress allots funds, which in the recent past has happened infrequently. During 1983, only projects *not* using investment tax credits were considered for development grants and it is expected that this restriction will continue.

FAÇADE EASEMENTS

Buildings listed in the National Register, or located in an historic district and certified as being of historic significance to the district, are candidates for façade easements. A façade easement can be donated by the owner of a building to any organization qualified to accept it. This could be a local or state government, or a preservation organization, such as the Historic Preservation League of Oregon.

A legal document in deed form is drawn up; it outlines responsibilities and rights of both parties. For glazed terra-cotta buildings, the primary responsibility of the party

[4]Federal Register, Vol. 46, No. 220, Monday, November 16, 1981, Rules and Regulations, 56189.

donating the façade easement would be preservation of the terra cotta. Any alterations to the façade would require approval of the easement holder. The building owner might be required to make certain improvements to the building.

In that a façade easement limits future use of the property, it decreases its market value. This decrease in value can be taken as a charitable deduction for income and estate tax purposes. When restrictions have already been placed on the structure by landmark or historic district designation, the decrease in market value resulting from donation of a façade easement is not as great as for a building with no special prior restrictions. There is always some difference, however, in that easements apply in perpetuity and local ordinances can be revoked at any time. Prior listing in the National Register does not decrease the valuation of the easement because no restrictions (design review or demolition delays) are involved.

Development rights for additional stories, which local codes would allow to be constructed above a National Register building, can also be donated to an organization that can hold and sell them later on. In order to be valued at any substantial amount, a façade easement would probably include such development rights.

Property owners are generally asked to make a donation to the organization accepting the easement to cover administrative costs. The Historic Preservation League of Oregon currently asks for five percent of the value of the easement.

INDIVIDUALITY

It should be obvious from the preceding discussion that there will be no standard approach to rehabilitation of the glazed terra-cotta buildings. The type of work performed and the way it is financed will depend on the condition of the building, its possible uses, and its ownership. With the wide range of assistance available, there should, however, be a way to maintain and enhance each of the 40 buildings in this study.

PRESERVATION OF GLAZED TERRA COTTA

During the past few years, knowledge of the types of deterioration and preservation techniques peculiar to terra cotta has increased tremendously. Because much of the data is highly technical and constantly being revised, any terra-cotta restoration project should include a person who specializes in its preservation. The following overview is intended merely to acquaint non-experts with the fundamental principles involved.

DETERIORATION OF GLAZED TERRA COTTA

Failures in glazed terra-cotta facings are of several types: cracking, spalling, separation of block face from the webs, and rusting of the metalwork that secures the glazed terra cotta to the structure.

Cracking can take several forms. Crazing, a web of tiny cracks occurring over the whole glaze, is a natural result of the firing process and is of no significance. Other types of cracks, hairline cracks confined to single blocks and larger cracks running through several adjacent blocks, are potentially serious. (Fig. II-8.)

The term "spalling" refers to both the blistering up of the glaze and the loosening of pockets of glaze along with portions of clay behind the glaze. The former is called "glaze spalling" and the latter, "material spalling." Both of these conditions require attention. (Fig. II-9.)

Separation of the block face from the webs can be potentially life threatening, in that loose portions can break completely away from the façade and fall to the ground, possibly striking a passerby.

Rusting of the metal anchors that hold the blocks to the structure can cause serious damage. As an iron or steel anchor rusts, it expands and can literally explode a terra-cotta block. Rusting is difficult to detect in its early stages and, even when detected early, is hard to correct. Usually a rusted anchor cannot be replaced without removing and, in the process, running the risk of destroying the glazed terra-cotta block attached to it.

The supporting structural framework for projecting terra-cotta features (such as cornices) may also be almost completely rusted away without any outward signs. Fortunately, it is often easier to gain access to the interior of projecting terra-cotta elements, for both inspection and repair, than it is to terra cotta that is completely built into a wall.

CAUSES OF DETERIORATION

The four types of failure in glazed terra cotta — cracking, spalling, separation of block face, and rusting of metalwork — result from the action of one or a combination of five

Fig. II-8. Cracked terra-cotta blocks at Elks Temple balcony, probably caused by rusting of metal anchors. Close examination of glazed terra-cotta roof cornices on other Portland buildings would undoubtedly reveal similar conditions.

major external forces: water, temperature extremes, wind, air pollution, and gravity. Terra cotta that has inherent faults resulting from improper production methods, was incorrectly installed, or has received inadequate maintenance is especially susceptible to these forces.

Water, alone or in conjunction with wind and temperature extremes, is the prime enemy of glazed terra cotta. On first consideration, it appears that the glaze on terra cotta, by providing an impenetrable finish, would prevent any water-related problems. Unfortunately, the situation is not that simple. Glazes are subject to cracking. Mortar joints, even if scrupulously maintained (which they seldom are), admit water. Horizontal mortar joints (for window sills, cornices, and parapets) are especially susceptible to water penetration. All vertical mortar joints, but especially those at parapets, are subject to wind-driven rain. Roofing materials and flashings, unless frequently and properly repaired, permit water entry. Water also enters through holes and slots made for signs, awnings, etc., and around windows and doors, if the joints aren't properly sealed.

It is clear from the technical literature of the glazed terra-cotta era that penetration of a certain amount of water was accepted and that the primary strategy for dealing with errant water was to provide weep holes for a speedy exit. It was also assumed that mortar joints would allow for passage of a significant amount of water out of the wall. In most cases, voids were left in the wall so that any trapped water would have room to expand during freezing without creating extreme stresses.

Excessive water trapped behind the glaze on a terra-cotta block can cause spalling (both glaze and material spalling). Once begun, the spalling process escalates, with spalled pockets allowing in more water, which in turn causes more spalling. This process is intensified during periods of freezing and thawing. Freezing of trapped water can also cause major cracking and the separation of the face of the block from the webs. And water is, of course, what causes anchors and other iron and steel supports to rust.

An overall absorption of water by a wall will cause corresponding expansion of brick and terra cotta, setting up a uniform low level of stress over the face of the wall. This stress by itself would not be serious, but, when combined with thermal and wind stresses, it can become significant enough to cause cracking. Cracks resulting from such a combination of stresses are generally vertical and run over substantial distances, whereas cracks resulting from rusting anchors are generally localized.[1]

Although terra cotta has a relatively low coefficient of thermal expansion, and its mass moderates temperature fluctuations, when subjected to high temperatures it can expand enough to create stresses. When the glaze and body of the block have different coefficients of expansion, heat can cause crazing and spalling.

Temperature-induced stresses can occur over the whole face of the wall, as well as in isolated locations. Stresses are likely to be the greatest in freestanding elements, such as columns and balusters, where the mass of terra cotta is not great. Metal rods placed inside balusters can expand at a greater rate than terra cotta and cause major cracks. (Fig. II-10.) (Metal railings attached to terra cotta can cause similar problems.)

Deflection due to wind loads would probably not be great enough in Portland's typically twelve-story buildings to cause significant stresses in glazed terra-cotta cladding. Wind does, however, increase water penetration.

Air pollution in Portland is, fortunately, not serious enough to cause deterioration of terra cotta.

Unequal settling of some older buildings may have caused stresses on parts of the façade. Reinforced concrete structural frames shrink over time, and this may have induced compressive stresses in the exterior walls. The latter phenomenon is significant only in tall buildings. Both can cause cracking of terra cotta.

Faults due to improper production methods are generally visible within a few years. Crazing, the most common and harmless defect, occurs when, after firing, the glaze shrinks more than the body. Dunting, very fine hair-like cracks that extend into the body, is caused by the inability of the body to withstand cooling after being removed from the kiln. A crack of this type would have the same degenerative effects as cracks that develop following installation.

Incomplete bonding of the glaze to the body can result from improper production methods. The widespread spalling of the glaze on the Graves Music Company building suggests it was never properly bonded.

Faulty installation can include too few anchors, inadequate protection of anchors and

Fig. II-9. Extensive spalling on the Graves Music Company building (right) is probably due to faulty production. Although it appears that the S.H. Kress & Co. building (left) has been infected by the Graves Music Company building, its spalling is undoubtedly being caused by water entering at the party wall.

Fig. II-10. Cracked balusters at roof of Portland Telegram Building. Because rods have not rusted, stresses must have been caused by thermal expansion of rods, or possibly by freezing of entrapped water.

[1]Theodore H.M. Prudon, "Architectural Terra Cotta: Analyzing the Deterioration Problems & Restoration Approaches," *Technology & Conservation*, III, no. 3 (Fall, 1978), 36.

other support members, too coarse sand in mortar, poor workmanship in filling and striking mortar joints, too rich a mortar in back-up masonry, omitted or clogged weep holes, and inadequate flashing. Too coarse sand in mortar causes point-loading, which can cause cracking. Too rich mortar absorbs too much water. Some technicians would add solid masonry or solid concrete back-up for terra cotta to the above list of faulty installation procedures, claiming that no wall could be completely watertight and that the back-up material would inevitably become saturated with moisture.

Most glazed terra-cotta buildings were constructed without any consideration of stresses caused by thermal expansion, moisture-induced expansion, wind, or settling of the structural frame. Only late in the 1920s were expansion joints introduced to accommodate these stresses. The author is not aware of any such expansion joints on Portland's glazed terra-cotta buildings.

INSPECTION

Determination of the extent and causes of terra-cotta deterioration is a complicated process involving techniques ranging from primitive to technologically advanced.

Of great help in any inspection are sets of working drawings and shop drawings. These drawings can serve not only as the basis for the set of restoration drawings, but also, by showing the locations of anchors and other hidden construction, as indicators of the locations where invisible deterioration is occurring and its causes. (If drawings of the building under study are not available, drawings of similar buildings constructed at about the same time will suggest likely construction details.) Building maintenance records also aid in assessing the condition of the terra cotta.

Advanced deterioration can be located visually, using binoculars or a camera with a powerful telephoto lens, for up to four or five stories. Above this height, scaffolding or some other means of elevation is required.

While spalling and cracking can be determined from a visual inspection, there are often no visible signs of separation of the face of the block from the web. Separation of the block face can usually be detected by tapping the block with a wooden mallet. Undamaged blocks give a pronounced ring and deteriorated units produce a hollow sound. Not surprisingly, detecting the difference requires experience. This method of inspection entails the expense of erecting scaffolding. If, however, patterns of deterioration become evident, it may be possible to estimate fairly accurately the extent of restoration required without testing the whole façade.

Rusting of anchors and other supports may not be evident until the deterioration is in an advanced state. Metal detectors can indicate missing or badly-deteriorated anchors. If the terra cotta was not completely backed up with masonry, a borescope (with a built-in light source) can be inserted in holes as small as one-half-inch in diameter to check conditions inside the wall.[2] It is sometimes possible to remove the flat pieces of terra cotta covering cornices to inspect the supporting framework and anchors.

Patterns of stress in a terra-cotta façade will indicate whether deterioration is resulting from excess water, temperature extremes, gravity loading, or a combination of these. To measure stress, strain gauges are attached to the surface of the terra-cotta block and a reading taken. The block, with the gauge attached, is then cut loose from the wall and a second reading taken. The difference indicates the stress relief. By taking spot tests over the whole façade, stress patterns can be mapped. A marked increase in vertical stresses from the upper portion to the lower portion of the façade indicates either gravity stresses resulting from inadequate support of the facing at intermediate stories or stresses resulting from shrinkage of the structural frame. Heat- and water-induced stresses (both horizontal and vertical) will be more uniformly distributed, with heat stresses varying with temperature and exposure. Portland's glazed terra-cotta buildings are probably not tall enough for gravity stresses to be a major factor in deterioration and, without large gravity stresses, the facings can probably withstand water and thermal stresses. However, only individual building analyses can confirm this.

[2]Sven E. Thomasen, Wiss, Janney, Elstner and Associates, Inc., "Inspecting, Testing and Analyzing Terra Cotta," (Unpublished Typescript), no date, p. 3.

In some cases, it might be helpful to know to what extent terra-cotta blocks have lost their original properties — compressive strength, glaze adhesion, absorption rate, thermal coefficient of expansion, etc. These can be determined through laboratory tests. Water absorption can also be measured on blocks still in place.[3]

While inspecting for deterioration, weep holes should be checked to see if they are clogged, and mortar joints, caulking, flashing, etc. should be examined for water tightness.

CLEANING

Manufacturers of glazed terra cotta often claimed that it cleaned itself. With the abundant rainfall and clean air in Portland, this assertion is generally valid. North façades, window surrounds, and other sheltered areas not subject to winter rains do, however, have a tendency to become soiled. In any case, the owner of a building undergoing rehabilitation, usually wants the façade cleaned as part of his effort to create a new image for the building. The danger is that this bit of optional maintenance, if not done properly, will permanently damage the terra cotta.

Terra cotta should *never* be cleaned by sandblasting, steam cleaning, or high-pressure water cleaning. All abrasive cleaners and most chemical solutions should also be avoided.

Cleaning experts often recommend cleaning with water and an alkaline detergent. The wall surface is first wet down and then scrubbed with the detergent and a natural bristle brush. It is then thoroughly rinsed with water at four gallons per minute and at a maximum pressure of 500 pounds per square inch. Even this method can be damaging, however. Any cleaning agent has the potential for reacting with an unknown substance in the terra cotta. Alkaline substances can cause efflorescence. Water can dissolve soluble salts in the terra cotta, transport them to the underside of the glaze through evaporation, and thereby cause spalling.

Some experts recommend cleaning with water alone, simply allowing a sprinkler hose to run for 24 to 100 hours.[4] Even with this method, there is a danger of efflorescence.

In cities, such as New York and Chicago, where dirt is more of a problem than in Portland, terra cotta has been cleaned using proprietary products. To clean the Alwyn Court Apartments in New York, the terra cotta was first hosed down with hot water and then fiber-brushed with a diluted alkaline pre-wash. After five minutes, the pre-wash was rinsed off with hot water under moderate pressure. The surfaces were then scrubbed with natural bristle brushes. A diluted acidic afterwash was then brushed on by hand to neutralize the pre-wash. The terra cotta was rinsed again with hot water under pressure.[5] When using this method, all window glass, metal, and painted surfaces must be masked. As with all "wet" methods, joints must be watertight; therefore, any tuckpointing must be completed before cleaning.

Anyone contemplating the cleaning of a terra-cotta building is advised not to select a particular method without first testing each technique under consideration on a small area of the building. (On polychrome terra-cotta buildings, each technique should be tested on each color.) Every terra-cotta façade has its own peculiar characteristics, and what works for one may not be appropriate for another. The method selected should be the gentlest possible. And if, even after a method has been selected and cleaning is underway, any damage is observed, cleaning should cease and a gentler method should be tried.

Experts do not agree on the advisability or methods of removing paint from terra cotta. Some recommend either heat guns (for *glazed* terra cotta *only*) or chemical strippers.[6] The type of stripper used depends on the type of paint to be removed. Any method of paint removal should be tested on a small area, keeping in mind that any chemical that removes paint is likely to damage the terra-cotta glaze.

Although experts do not agree on the best method for removing paint from terra cotta, or even whether it should be removed at all, there is consensus that glazed terra cotta should never be painted, except in small isolated spots. Paint forms a vapor barrier, trapping moisture inside the block and eventually causing the terra cotta to deteriorate.

[3]J.G. Stockbridge, "Evaluation of Terra Cotta on In-Service Structures," *Special Technical Publication* 691, p. 223.

[4]Nancy D. Berryman and Susan M. Tindall, *Terra Cotta: Preservation and Maintenance of an Historic Building Material* (manuscript), 1984, p. 15.

[5]Dr. James Marston Fitch, "Renovation of Alwyn Court, New York City: Restoring the Façades & Improving Public Spaces," *Technology & Conservation* (Summer, 1980), p. 24.

[6]Berryman, Tindall, p. 17.

REPAIR OF GLAZED TERRA COTTA

Crazing or other hairline cracks not extending into the terra-cotta body do not require repair. Spalled areas, however, must receive attention. Blocks with deep cracks or blocks whose faces have broken away must be either reattached or replaced. Blocks with badly-rusted anchors or other supports must also either be reattached or replaced.

Glaze spalling is simple to repair. Loose material is cleaned away with small hand tools and the spalled area then painted with an acrylic-based paint.[7]

Patching material-spalling presents some of the same problems as filling dental cavities: all deteriorated material must be cleaned out, the filling material must be compatible with the material being filled, and the filling must be keyed in so that it doesn't pop out. Because of the difficulties in obtaining filling materials with coefficients of thermal and hydroscopic expansion similar to those for terra cotta and of achieving a good bond, it is sometimes preferable to replace deeply-spalled terra-cotta blocks rather than patching them. However, in situations where this is not possible, the spalled areas can simply be cleaned and painted or they can be cleaned out, filled with patching mortar, and painted. For patches, a bonding agent should be used. Patches can be locked in by dovetailing and with rustproof pins (preferably, stainless steel).[8]

Major cracks can be filled with epoxy. To secure cracked blocks and block faces, holes can be drilled and filled with either epoxy or a stainless-steel tube grouted with epoxy. If cracks in terra cotta have been caused by unrelieved stress (thermal, gravity, or moisture induced), stress must be relieved by new, strategically-placed expansion joints. Replacing badly-rusted anchors usually can be accomplished only by removing the terra cotta, thereby running the risk of destroying it. For this reason it is usually preferable to devise a system of pinning or bolting the terra cotta to the building structure or masonry back-up without having to remove the terra cotta.

Deteriorated terra cotta that is in danger of falling can be temporarily secured with metal straps, wire mesh, or nylon netting.

WATER PROTECTION

At the same time terra-cotta blocks are repaired, measures should be taken to prevent future water damage. Unsound mortar joints should be tuckpointed, cracks around windows and doors (as well as miscellaneous holes) caulked, deteriorated flashings replaced, and the roof made watertight. Interior roof drains should also be checked for leaks.

Tuckpointing should be done with mortar rather than with waterproof compounds, which impede the outward passage of moisture in a wall. Mortar should have a compressive strength *less* than that of the glazed terra cotta. This will ensure that any stresses that develop in the wall due to settlement or expansion will be accommodated by the mortar rather than by the terra cotta. Hard or coarsely-screened sand may cause point loading and should not be used.

Old mortar should be removed to a minimum depth of one inch or until solid mortar is encountered, leaving square corners at the back of the joint. New mortar should completely fill the joint. Where weep holes are found to be insufficient, new ones should be created.

The appearance of new mortar should match unweathered existing mortar, even if this means that repointed areas are visually obtrusive at first. The unweathered appearance of existing mortar can be determined from samples taken from the interiors of existing joints. Because they may be harmful to adjacent terra cotta, stain mixtures applied to new mortar to produce immediate color matches are not recommended.

Ideally any new mortar should have exactly the same composition as the original mortar. Specifications for original mortar are still available for many glazed terra-cotta buildings. (See Chapter I-C.) There is, however, no guarantee that the specifications were followed and often the specifications did not stipulate exactly what kinds of sand and pigment were used. Mortar tests, though imprecise, can be used to identify the original in-

[7]de Teel Patterson Tiller, "The Preservation of Historic Glazed Architectural Terra-Cotta," *Preservation Brief*, No. 7, Heritage Conservation and Recreation Service (1979), p. 7.

[8]James L. Lucas, "Causes and Cures for Deteriorating Masonry," *The Construction Specifier* (March, 1983), p. 70.

gredients (with the exception of pigmentation, which must be determined by trial and error).

Care should be taken to match existing joint profiles. It is surprising how much difference a small change in joint tooling can make in the appearance of a wall.

Waterproof sealants may be used for horizontal joints, such as those on parapets and cornices, that were originally filled with pitch. Either polysulfide or polyurethane sealants would be suitable. Joints around windows and doors and on window sills may also be caulked. Lead weather-caps can be placed over joints in parapet copings and, in some cases, the top of the parapet can be completely capped with sheet metal.

Wholesale waterproofing of glazed terra-cotta façades is *not* recommended. A waterproof coating seals joints, creating a vapor barrier and trapping moisture inside the wall. Although some vapor barriers are said to breathe, they have to be renewed periodically and, with each subsequent coat, the breathing qualities are progressively lost.

Replacement Of Glazed Terra Cotta

In many cases, glazed terra-cotta blocks are too deteriorated to be successfully repaired and must be replaced. Replacement of a terra-cotta block is almost always necessary when its anchors have to be replaced.

Because adjacent units are likely to be damaged in the process of removing terra cotta, it is a good idea to remove all units to be replaced before ordering new units.

The ideal replacement for terra cotta is, of course, new terra cotta. However, because of the cost and long lead time required to produce terra cotta, in-kind replacement is not always economically feasible. Likely substitute materials are pre-cast concrete, fiberglass, and stone. Other possibilities might be stucco, porcelain-enameled panels, prefinished galvanized metal, and aluminum.

In considering the use of substitute materials, it should be remembered that the behavior of these materials when exposed to heat and moisture differs from terra cotta and brick. Although recognized experts in the field of terra-cotta restoration sometimes recommend pre-cast concrete as a replacement for deteriorated terra-cotta units located here and there in a façade, it is the author's opinion that substitute materials should not be intermingled with terra cotta in a patchwork fashion. Substitute materials are only appropriate for discrete elements, such as cornices, capitals, panels under windows, etc.

In-Kind Replacements

The fabrication of glazed terra-cotta replacements must follow the same procedure outlined in Chapter I-C. The only step that might not be necessary would be the production of shop drawings in cases where they are still in existence. To the author's knowledge, the only shop drawings remaining for Portland buildings are those at Gladding, McBean & Co.

With some ingenuity, it might be possible to utilize machine-extruded ashlar, window sills, and parapet copings, considerably reducing production costs and time. This option would depend on the configuration of existing terra cotta and the extent of the required replacement.

To forestall future deterioration, new metal anchors for replacement terra cotta should be of a non-rusting metal (preferably stainless steel). Holes are bored in the back-up masonry, and the anchor and new unit are both bedded in mortar.

Precast Concrete Replacements

Precast concrete, which as "cast stone" during the 1920s and early 1930s gradually supplanted glazed terra cotta for exterior ornament, still maintains an economic advantage. Because its shrinkage is negligible, molds can be developed from existing ornament, obviating the need for an expanded model. It can be cast hollow, and designed to accommodate metal anchors.

In order to minimize bulk and weight, reinforcement is sometimes of glass fibers. However, because concrete's alkalinity "eats up" fiberglass, alkaline-resistant glass fibers must be used.

Concrete can be tinted to match existing terra-cotta glazes. The surface is lightly sanded or etched to bring out the color. A clear masonry coating is applied to reduce moisture absorption and to give a glaze-like sheen.[9] Polychrome effects can be achieved by pouring different colors at different depths.[10] The surface can also be speckled with latex or acrylic paint to achieve a granite-like finish.[11]

The primary disadvantages to precast concrete are that, unless it is treated with an acrylic sealer, it changes color when wet (no longer matching the terra-cotta glazes) and that its finishes are not as permanent as terra-cotta glazes. Other disadvantages are the difference in coefficients of thermal expansion of concrete and terra cotta and the tendency of glass fibers to absorb water and expand, thereby causing the concrete to deteriorate.

To the author's knowledge, precast concrete has never been used as a replacement for terra cotta in a restoration in the Portland area.

FIBERGLASS REPLACEMENTS

Portland, unlike some cities, has no regulations prohibiting the use of fiberglass as a building material, so it can be used to replace damaged and missing glazed terra-cotta blocks. (Fiberglass is a plastic resin, typically polyester, reinforced with glass fibers.)

Shrinkage for fiberglass is, like that for precast concrete, negligible and so, like precast concrete, it does not require an expanded model.

Fiberglass pieces are much lighter than either terra cotta or precast concrete. This reduced weight is an advantage, particularly when deep overhangs are involved. Fiberglass pieces can be much longer than terra-cotta blocks, with joints simulated at the intervals at which they would occur in terra cotta. Because the coefficient of thermal expansion for fiberglass is much greater than for the structural materials to which it will be attached, joints and attachments must be carefully designed to accommodate movement.

Plastic resins deteriorate when exposed to ultraviolet rays. For this reason, pieces should have a protective gel coat, an unreinforced layer of resin (high in pigment content) that is better able to withstand exposure to sunlight. The gel coat also provides a protective coating for the glass fibers, which, because of their "wicking quality" (tending to absorb moisture), should not be exposed to water. Any surfaces of the finished fiberglass unit that are cut or drilled during construction should be coated with a protective resin.

Gel coats will also deteriorate over a period of ten years, so should, in turn, be coated with urethane paint (or other appropriate coating). Paints can be mixed to simulate existing glazes and, in case the paint ever is chipped or worn away, gel coats should be colored to match the paint. Modern-day paints have a relatively long life, but are not, of course, as durable as terra-cotta glazes. There also may be a problem with color fastness with any other than earth tones.

Fiberglass is essentially a laminated product and is not well suited to production of ornament with small protuberances in which it would be difficult to achieve good distribution of glass fibers. Resin not well reinforced with glass fibers has a tendency to crack, exposing the interior of the piece and the glass fibers to moisture. Ornament with small protuberances would be more appropriately made of cast aluminum or precast concrete.

Fiberglass is best suited for discrete pieces of ornament with relatively large three-dimensional curves. Building elements, such as cornices, with two-dimensional curves are better fabricated of sheet metal.

According to a past owner of the Lipman, Wolfe & Co. building, a few of its cornice lions' heads were replaced some years ago with fiberglass replicas.[12] Differences between the original and replacements are not detectable from street level.

When glazed terra cotta from the ground floor of the demolished Congress Hotel was

[9] deTeel Patterson Tiller, p. 8.

[10] Theodore H.M. Prudon, Presentation at Friends of Terra Cotta Seminar: "The Deterioration and Preservation of Architectural Terra Cotta," New York City, Fall, 1982.

[11] Mary J. Matthews, "Kansas City Experiments with Terra Cotta Replacement," *Friends of Terra Cotta Newsletter*, Fall, 1983, p. 4.

[12] Bill Roberts, Unrecorded interview by the author, Winter, 1980.

reinstalled on the 1981 gazebo of the Orbanco Building (on the site of the Congress), fiber-glass (made with urethane rather than polyester) was used to fabricate several missing units. The original terra cotta had a pinkish granite finish and this was duplicated with paint on the replacements. Streaks were even added to correspond to dirt on the original pieces.

STONE REPLACEMENTS

Ironically, cut stone, the material for which glazed terra cotta was originally considered a less expensive substitute, is in some cases less expensive than glazed terra cotta for replacement units. This would be true only for pieces on which there is no decoration.

Matching the color would be most likely possible when the terra cotta being replaced had originally been colored to simulate a particular stone. Even in such cases, the match might only be temporary; stone, like precast concrete, changes color when wet and weathering might eventually alter its color altogether.

STUCCO REPLACEMENTS

Stucco was used to simulate terra cotta on the ground floor of Portland's Journal Building. In place since 1975, the stucco is still in good condition. The appearance is so similar to the adjacent glazed terra cotta that only a person with prior knowledge would detect the difference. Its satisfactory use in this case is probably due to the fact that a large contiguous area, rather than small isolated areas, were faced with the stucco. Stucco tends to pull away from terra cotta and to crack, so that without continuous repair it would not be weather-tight. The success of the Journal Building stucco replacement is due also to the glazed terra-cotta finish (an off-white, matte glaze) having been exceedingly easy to match.

METAL REPLACEMENTS

Metal replacements could conceivably be of iron, steel, or aluminum, and be cast or formed. Because metal has a much greater coefficient of thermal expansion than terra cotta, it would only be appropriate for discrete elements such as cornices or small pieces of applied ornament. As with precast concrete, fiberglass, and stucco, there are inherent problems in achieving a shiny, durable finish. The finish on porcelain enamel panels is shiny and durable, but only if not chipped or drilled during installation (which is very unlikely). Prefinished galvanized metal panels are probably more practical.

When the S.H. Kress & Co. building was renovated in 1975, porcelain enamel panels were installed above the ground-floor storefronts where the Kress sign had been located. Their color and sheen are similar to those of the terra-cotta glaze. Perhaps with greater care the match could have been perfect. There are no signs of chipped enamel or rusting to date.

Dentils on the glazed terra-cotta cornice of the Multnomah County Courthouse were replaced with sheet-metal replicas, probably in the 1950s. They were then painted.[13]

Aluminum panels were used on the upper stories of the Woolworth Building restoration in New York City, with different colors applied to suggest articulation.[14]

Although cast aluminum has been suggested previously as a replacement material for terra cotta,[15] to the author's knowledge, it has never been used.

ONGOING MAINTENANCE

Once repaired, the glazed terra-cotta façade should be inspected every five years for any subsequent deterioration. With an organized and technically appropriate maintenance

[13]Carl Moseley, Facilities & Property management Division, Multnomah County, Unrecorded interview by the author, March, 1984.

[14]Prudon Presentation.

[15]James Marshall Hamrick, Jr., "A Survey of the Use of Architectural Terra Cotta in American Commercial Architecture: 1870-1930," (Masters Thesis), University of Oregon, December, 1979.

program, it could last indefinitely.

Maintenance is also very important for the longevity of any materials substituted for terra cotta. Because their finishes are not as durable as the glaze on terra cotta, particular attention should be paid to repainting.

PRESERVATION OF COMPLEMENTARY FEATURES AND MATERIALS

Many of the original features and materials on Portland's terra-cotta buildings are missing. Although some have been lost through deterioration, most were simply removed, usually in the course of "modernization." Restoration of a glazed terra-cotta building requires, therefore, an understanding of a wide variety of crafts. It also inevitably leads to difficult choices, when budgets do not allow for historically-accurate reproductions and alternate features and materials must be substituted for the original.

NATURAL STONE

Most of the original stone on Portland's terra-cotta buildings is still in place. The one notable exception is the Spalding Building, from which the original limestone at the first floor was removed and replaced with travertine panels. Reconstruction of the limestone base, even in a simplified approximation of the original form, would add immeasurably to the appearance of this building.

Limestone at the first floor of the Wells Fargo Building is intact and, except for some staining, nearly new in appearance. Limestone on the Multnomah County Courthouse is also intact.

The marble at the base of the Bank of California is badly deteriorated. Cracks and holes have, however, been filled so that they do not detract from the overall appearance of the building. The marble frieze has been plastered over and painted. Marble is susceptible to water damage and, therefore, not a good choice for an exterior material in a climate as wet as Portland's.

Granite plinths, which are found on almost all of Portland's terra-cotta buildings, are in excellent condition.

Cleaning of stone in Portland is rarely necessary and, like the cleaning of terra cotta, is likely to cause damage and create more stains than it removes. The reaction of calcareous rocks, such as limestone, with acids precludes cleaning with any acidic compound. Damage can occur even from slightly acidic tap water. Alkaline cleaning substances can cause efflorescence on older limestone and marble,[1] as can water soaking. Water may also oxidize minerals in the stones, leaving yellow-brown stains.

If, for some reason, limestone *must* be cleaned, there are three possible methods: (1) water soaking, (2) detergent wash and plain water rinse, and (3) alkaline wash followed by acidic rinse.

The latter method requires protection of all metal, glass, wood, and vegetation. This is usually accomplished with a special masking substance supplied by the manufacturer of the cleaning compounds. The wall is first pre-wet. The alkaline wash remains on the wall for 20 minutes to one hour. The stone is then rinsed with clear water at 400 to 500 pounds

[1]Norman R. Weiss, "Exterior Cleaning of Historic Masonry Buildings, Draft," United States Dept. of the Interior, Heritage Conservation and Recreation Service, 1976, p. 10.

per square inch and at a minimum of four gallons per minute. The acidic neutralizing rinse is applied immediately following this rinse. The wall is then rinsed again and tested with litmus paper to make certain that the alkaline wash has been neutralized. Stubborn stains can be scrubbed away with natural bristle brushes and wooden scrapers. Wire brushes cause iron staining, and synthetic brushes wear out too fast.

Detergents used on stone should have a neutral pH (i.e., be neither alkaline nor acidic) and be very mild. They also require pre-wetting and thorough rinsing.

Water soaking has been used successfully on some exceptionally dirty stone buildings in New York City. Curtains of water were allowed to run down the stone façade for 24 to 72 hours. The water softens the outer surface of the stone, thereby loosening the bond between it and the layer of dirt. To avoid contaminants that might react with the stone, only purified water and plastic pipes are used.[2]

Though granite is much more impermeable than limestone, it is also subject to iron staining. The author could find no agreement among experts on the cleaning of granite.

Sandblasting and high-pressure water cleaning should never be used on any stone. All cleaning should be done by professionals. Cleaning methods should be tested on small areas and allowed to weather, ideally for one year.

Discoloration and disintegration of stone are often caused by excessive dampness, resulting from faulty rain protection at roofs, parapets, cornices, and window sills, as well as from deteriorated mortar joints. These water-protection features should, therefore, be scrupulously maintained.

Stone, like terra cotta, needs to "breathe." For this reason, voids behind stone veneer (such as the marble frieze and base on the Bank of California building) should be left open and vented. Waterproof coatings should *never be* applied and tuckpointing should be done with mortar, not sealants. Mortar for tuck-pointing stone should match the original in visual and physical properties. (See Chapter II-C.)

BRICK

Except for a few small areas on the Henry Building and Seward Hotel, all brick in Portland's glazed terra-cotta buildings is in place. The worst fate met by any brick to date was the recent painting of both the Northwestern National Bank Building and the Selling Building. It is the author's fervent hope that the painting of the brick on these two buildings is not the beginning of an epidemic.

Painting brick on glazed terra-cotta buildings is aesthetically wrong and potentially damaging to the brick itself. Buff-colored brick was chosen for the main body of the typical office building to contrast with the off-white glazed terra-cotta at the base and top floors, thereby emphasizing the classical three-part composition. Painting the brickwork to match the terra cotta effectively destroys the basic façade design. It also obliterates the texture of the brick wall, giving the building a flat, cardboard look, and adds a new maintenance cost for the life of the building.

Although one coat of paint may not cause damage to the bricks themselves, subsequent layers of paint will create a vapor barrier, which, by trapping moisture in the wall, will cause subfluorescence (depositing of soluble salts beneath the surface of the brick) and eventual spalling. Even if the paint is one that allows for moisture transpiration, this quality will be lost through application of many coats. It is difficult, if not impossible, to remove paint from a brick wall without damaging the brick itself. Paint could probably be safely removed from brick with a heat gun, but this method would be extremely slow and expensive.

If Portland is to preserve the visual and structural integrity of its downtown brick-faced buildings, it should adopt an ordinance prohibiting painting without permission from either the Design or Landmarks Commission. It should at the same time initiate an educational campaign to acquaint the public with the importance of not painting any but very soft (usually pre-1900) brick.

Though a brick wall is more of a dust-catcher than a wall faced with glazed terra cotta, in Portland's clean environment most brick buildings have remained fresh and clean-

[2]Paul Hemp, "Cleaning Those Grime-Encrusted Façades," *New York Times*, Jan. 22, 1984.

looking. Cleaning should then, in general, not be required and should, in fact, be avoided. The cleaning of brickwork is fraught with many of the same dangers as the cleaning of terra cotta and stone. The hard outer skin characteristic of brick can be eroded, increasing water penetration and future soiling. Mortar can be eroded. Chemicals, and even plain water, can cause efflorescence and subfluorescence, leading eventually to spalling.[3]

If brickwork *must* be cleaned, the gentlest method possible should be used. Low-pressure washes and steam cleaning are generally preferred.[4] When a chemical assist is needed, it should be acid rather than alkaline (unless the brick is glazed, in which case it should be cleaned like glazed terra cotta). Proprietary cleaning products are available. The wall should be pre-wet. The cleaning solution can be sprayed or brushed on. It should be left on for two to three minutes and then rinsed with clear water at 400 to 500 pounds per square inch and a minimum of four gallons per minute. Stubborn dirt can be scrubbed off with a natural bristle brush.

As with terra cotta and stone, brick cleaning should be carried out by professionals. Methods should be tested on small areas and allowed to weather, ideally for a full year. Under no circumstances should brick be sandblasted.

Tuckpointing of brick walls should be carried out in a similar manner to that of terra cotta. (See Chapter II-C.) Except for joints around window and door frames, sealants should not be used. At these locations, a polysulfide or polyurethane sealant would be appropriate.

As for glazed terra-cotta wall facings, waterproof coatings for brick are *not* recommended. Brick walls also need to "breathe."

WROUGHT AND CAST IRON

Original exterior ironwork missing from glazed terra-cotta buildings includes window and door frames, pilasters, grilles, and marquees. Replicas of cast iron could be fabricated of cast aluminum, fiberglass or, of course, cast iron. Wrought-iron elements are generally lighter and more delicate in profile than cast iron and so would probably not be reproduced in a substitute material.

In most cases, there are no remaining features from which molds for replacement pieces could be derived. Original construction drawings with large-scale details are, however, available for most buildings.

Developing molds from existing architectural elements would be complicated because both cast iron and aluminum shrink as they cool from a liquid to a solid state and, thus, molds must be made larger to compensate. The shrinkage of fiberglass is, however, negligible. For small decorative elements, shrinkage would not be a consideration.

When installed in a building, aluminum must be isolated from cast iron in order to avoid galvanic corrosion.

Fiberglass replacements for cast iron are subject to all the production and installation-related considerations that apply to its use as a substitute material for glazed terra cotta. (See Chapter II-C.) Matching a painted finish on cast iron would, however, be much easier than matching a terra-cotta glaze.

Much remaining iron on Portland's glazed terra-cotta buildings is heavily encrusted with paint, which will have to be removed at some future repainting. Paint can be cleaned from iron by a variety of methods: hand scraping, wire brushing, sandblasting, flame cleaning, and with chemicals. Hand scraping and wire brushing are the more common methods for small elements. Rotary wire-brush attachments to drills can be used. Sandblasting pressures should be kept to 80 to 100 pounds per square inch.[5] (Because of the elaborate means of protection necessary for adjacent building parts and passersby, it is unlikely that sandblasting would be the method chosen for downtown terra-cotta buildings.)

In that new paint adheres better to paint than to bare iron, only loose paint should be removed. To avoid rusting, completely-cleaned iron should be repainted the same day with a rust inhibitor.

[3]Robert C. Mack, "The Cleaning and Waterproof Coating of Masonry Buildings," *Preservation Brief*, No. 1, National Park Service (no date), p. 3.

[4]Anne E. Grimmer, "Dangers of Abrasive Cleaning to Historic Buildings," *Preservation Brief*, No. 6, Heritage Conservation and Recreation Service (1979), p. 6.

[5]Margot Gayle, David W. Look, John G. Waite, *Metals in America's Historic Buildings*, p. 136.

SHEET METAL

With the exception of signs, marquees, and miscellaneous storefront elements, most sheet metal on Portland's glazed terra-cotta buildings is intact. Only the Mayer Building has lost an entire cornice.

Reproducing ornate sheet-metal cornices like the one originally on the Mayer Building would not be feasible at the present time. Even if a plaster of Paris model could be produced at a reasonable price, no sheet-metal workers would know how to fabricate the dies.[6] (See Chapter I-D.) Replacements could, however, be made of fiberglass, fabricated in essentially the same manner as terra-cotta replacements. (See Chapter II-C.) Cornices with simple straight lines like the one on the Olds, Wortman & King building, could be replicated in sheet metal.

Most sheet metal on glazed terra-cotta buildings was galvanized iron, painted to match the terra cotta. Both galvanizing and painting protect the iron from rusting. There are, nevertheless, rust stains apparent on several cornices, indicating that the iron has lost both protective coatings. Rusting is a condition that demands immediate attention. Rust, unlike many oxidized surfaces, does not form a protective coating. It is porous, permitting penetration of oxidizing elements. It also acts as a reservoir for water, accelerating corrosion.[7]

Rust and loose paint should be cleaned from galvanized iron using the gentlest means possible. The high pressures inherent in sandblasting will deform sheet metal and, with any abrasive cleaning, there is the danger of removing the remaining galvanized coating.[8] Cleaning can be done using chemical or thermal methods.[9] Following cleaning, the galvanized iron should be primed with a rust inhibitor, and painted with a compatible top coat.

Sheet metal on glazed terra-cotta buildings was sometimes copper, the most prominent remaining example being portions of the Oregon Hotel roof. If properly installed and not subjected to corrosive chemicals, copper surfaces should be maintenance free. Over a period of eight-to-ten years of exposure to the elements, copper develops its own protective patina. This patina, which is brown at first and finally stabilizes as green, is formed when the surface copper combines with hydrogen sulfide and oxygen or sulfur dioxide to form a copper carbonate or copper sulfate coating.[10] Except for the possible resoldering of joints, which requires a clean metal surface, there is no reason for this patina to ever be removed.

Structural failures do sometimes occur in copper when adequate provisions for thermal expansion and contraction have not been made, causing bulging and cracking. All soldered joints eventually crack, as a result of expansion and contraction of the copper.

Copper can be corroded by contact with asphaltic roofing compounds and acidic water.[11]

BRONZE WORK

Most of the original bronze features on Portland's downtown terra-cotta buildings were removed when the entrances and elevator lobbies were remodeled. A few items were stored in the building basements; most were evidently hauled away by contractors.

Original working drawings, which show bronze grilles, lanterns, hardware, etc., are available for most buildings; and these drawings are detailed enough to make new patterns and castings. Present-day casting procedures are the same as they were during the glazed terra-cotta era and are the same for bronze as for cast iron and aluminum. Reproduction in bronze is, however, more expensive than in cast iron or aluminum because the material itself is more costly. Replicating small items, such as door hardware, for which pieces are available to use as patterns, could, however, be done at reasonable prices. Because there are no alternative materials with the surface richness of bronze, using substitute materials for replicas is not a possibility.

There has been some confusion among building owners in Portland regarding appropriate finishes for bronze work. Several pieces have been cleaned inappropriately and left a shiny gold color. Most bronze work on Portland's terra-cotta buildings was intended to

[6]McArthur, Lewis, Unrecorded interview by the author, 1983.

[7]Gayle, Look, Waite, p. 131.

[8]Grimmer, p. 5.

[9]Gayle, Look, Waite, p. 99.

[10]Ibid., p. 118.

[11]Ibid., p. 119.

have a green or brown patina. Exceptions were pieces, such as door hardware, that were subject to constant handling, which would wear away the patina. The natural patina for bronze is green; brown patinas are artificially induced. With artificial patinas, gold highlights are generally left to accentuate the decoration. A lacquer is applied to prevent further oxidation. Patinas that develop naturally tend to be uneven and splotchy, especially in the early stages, and finally become very dark.

Cleaning should not be necessary for the bronze on Portland's glazed terra-cotta buildings. If, for some reason, cleaning *is* necessary, a slurry mixture of 5% oxalic acid and water with finely-ground India pumice is recommended. Bronze should never be sandblasted. Re-patinizing is accomplished by swabbing the surface with highly-diluted yellow sodium or ammonium polysulfide ("liver of sulfur"). Both cleaning and re-patinizing should be done by professionals.[12]

GLASS

Upper-level windows on Portland's glazed terra-cotta buildings are almost all intact and, apparently, in good condition. However, very few original storefront windows remain.

With the exception of the prism-glass transoms, storefronts can easily be reconstructed in modern-day systems that approximate the original configurations. To the author's knowledge, the prism glass that frequently filled transoms is no longer available, except very rarely as salvaged material. Its reinstallation, though unlikely, would be an interesting and attractive part of a restoration project.

Upper-level window sash in several pre-1900 Portland buildings has been replaced and tinted glass used instead of the original clear glass. The dark color gives the buildings a bombed-out look, distorting the original solid-void relationship. For some restorations of pre-1900 buildings, highly-reflective glass has been used. Any waviness is especially noticeable in this type of glass, and its mirror-like quality gives the buildings a surreal look. It is the author's opinion that energy savings incurred with dark or reflective glass do not outweigh the aesthetic losses and that only clear glass should be used for glazed terra-cotta buildings.

With present-day office systems and building code requirements, it is unlikely that office partitions like the originals will be reconstructed. For those remaining in place, however, it should be possible to obtain appropriate obscure glass. Glass craftsmen can even custom make the "glue-chip" glass originally used in a few glazed terra-cotta buildings. (See Chapter I-D.)

MOSAIC TILE AND TERRAZZO

Because most floors in glazed terra-cotta buildings now have wall-to-wall carpeting, it is unknown how many of the original terrazzo and mosaic tile floors remain. It is certain, however, that many hexagonal tile floors survive in building entrances and in toilet rooms of 1905-30 buildings throughout downtown. Most are in good condition.

Unglazed hexagonal tiles are once again in production. White tiles are readily available, and other colors (brown, gold, black, blue, and green) can be ordered. Coordinating one-inch-square tiles, such as were used for borders, are also available. Border designs and field figures must, however, be arranged by the tile setter for each specific installation.

Terrazzo is probably the most durable flooring material available and, though expensive, is still preferred for heavily-used public spaces. The only form of deterioration to which terrazzo is generally susceptible is cracking, which is caused by building settlement. The terrazzo remaining in view in Portland's glazed terra-cotta buildings is in excellent condition.

ORNAMENTAL PLASTERWORK

Re-creation of ornamental plasterwork could greatly enhance the main entrances and

[12]Ibid., p. 127.

elevator lobbies of Portland's glazed terra-cotta buildings, many of which are bleak-looking at present. In some cases, portions of the original ornament remain behind wood paneling or above suspended ceilings; they could be used to develop molds for new work. Where no original plaster ornament remains, original working drawings could be used to fabricate patterns and molds.

Ornamental plasterwork is produced in essentially the same way today as it was from 1905 to 1930. There are still craftsmen versed in even very special techniques, such as "squeeze-bag" work, in which liquid plaster is applied like cake-icing decoration to create *bas relief* ornament.[13]

The recently-developed method of using glass reinforcing fibers for ornamental plasterwork may be relevant to certain special restoration installations. Substituting glass fibers for the traditional natural fibers makes possible a much stronger and thinner-walled piece.[14] Because glass fibers are subject to deterioration by alkaline substances, non-alkaline plasters must be used.

WOODWORK

Wood paneling remains in the Oregon Hotel and Elks Temple. That in the lodgeroom of the Odd Fellows Building was lost when it underwent conversion to apartment use. No retail spaces retain their original casework and, given the self-service nature of most present-day retailing, their restoration is unlikely. Though most original office partitions have been removed, there are a number of office floors with original wood doors and trim. Most of the wood has, however, been painted.

PAINT COLORS

Most upper-level office window frames and sash retain their original neutral colors, light for wood sash and darker for metal windows. Colors at ground-floor storefronts have, as one would expect, been frequently changed. Ground-level, cast-iron window frames on both the United States National Bank building and the Wells Fargo Building still have their historical dark-bronze color. Cast-iron window frames on the Northwestern National Bank Building, which were a bright, weathered-bronze green, were recently painted a dull medium brown.

Although glazed terra-cotta building façades can accept a certain degree of variation in paint colors for window frames and sash, too light, too dark, or too intense colors throw a façade composition out of balance, greatly diminishing its aesthetic qualities. If striking color is to be added, it should be on appendages, such as awnings, signs, and flags.

Very few interior color schemes remain. In that most interior paint colors were cream colored, even in public spaces, they could easily be restored. Anyone contemplating decorative color schemes should study the ceilings of the United States National Bank and Bank of California.

LIGHTING

The extensive loss of interior and exterior decorative lighting has been extremely detrimental to the character of individual buildings and to the streetcar-era district in which they are located. Nothing could more effectively identify the district than re-creations of the lighting that originally outlined buildings, signs, and marquees. Replacement of the numerous nondescript modern fixtures with decorative incandescent fixtures would enliven many interior public spaces.

Locations and types of exterior lighting for most buildings could be determined from original working drawings. For some reason, which the author has been unable to determine, few photographs were taken at night showing original exterior lighting. Light standards and lighted signs are, however, visible in daytime photographs.

[13]United States Gypsum Company, "Plasterers Add 100 Years to Landmark's Life," *form & function*, Issue 1 (1983), p. 14.

[14]United States Gypsum Company, "Classic elegance at a bargain price; Glass-reinforced gypsum recreates the authentic look of traditional plaster craft," *form & function*, Issue 1 (1984), p. 10.

Drawings for lighting fixtures designed by Fred C. Baker were, after his death, given to the Oregon Historical Society. There are an enormous number of drawings depicting fixtures from about 1910 to 1982.[15] These drawings are a great resource for remodeling and restoration work. Even when the original drawings for a particular building are not included, there are designs of fixtures for other similar buildings that indicate the general size and type of fixtures used. If fixtures of a contemporary design are to be installed, designers could still benefit from understanding the original design effect.

For important considerations in reproducing (or reactivating) lighting systems, the reader is referred to sections on the materials into which they were incorporated: glazed terra cotta, cast iron, sheet metal, and bronze work.

SIGNS, AWNINGS, MARQUEES, AND FLAGPOLES

One of the primary goals of any glazed terra-cotta building renovation should be creation of a festive look. This could be achieved through the use of signs, awnings, marquees, and flagpoles, as well as with decorative lighting.

Portland's present-day sign code does not allow any sign above the second floor. This means that not only roof signs, but also roof-top flagpoles, and even the historic gold-lettered window signs above the second floor, are illegal. Some provision should be made in the code so that these historic features can be retained, and reinstituted, on glazed terra-cotta-era buildings.

The size and number of lower-level signs found on glazed terra-cotta buildings would in many cases exceed what is permissable under the present-day code. Code standards should also be revised so that signs of an historical nature could exceed these limitations. Examples of signs for which special allowances should be made are the "dime-store" type sign with raised gold letters on a red background and sheet-metal signs with outline lighting. (It should be stipulated, however, that signs must not obscure architectural details.) The only type of historical sign that the author would like prohibited outright is the billboard or large party-wall sign.

The non-retractable awnings in general use today are not as complementary to glazed terra-cotta buildings as the original retractable type. Because the non-retractable awnings have closed sides and are hung above the transom, they obscure many architectural features and overpower adjacent entrance marquees. If, for some reason, retractable awnings cannot be used, continuous metal-and-glass marquees along all street façades should be considered.

Most missing marquees could be reconstructed using original working drawings. To reduce costs, decorative elements could be fabricated of aluminum or fiberglass and the whole assembly painted the color of weathered copper or bronze. Contemporary metal and plexiglass marquees might also be considered (Fig. II-11.) Whether reproductions or contemporary adaptations, marquees should certainly incorporate decorative lighting.

Fig. II-11. Contemporary entrance marquee in same spirit as those original to Portland's glazed terra-cotta buildings. Light bulbs outline both marquee and display windows.

PART III

SURVIVING BUILDINGS

CHRONOLOGICAL INVENTORY

Names of buildings are original names. Present-day names are given in the alphabetical list that follows the Inventory. Dates are for the year built. Unless otherwise indicated, designers were located in Portland.

The Wells Fargo Building was Portland's first skyscraper. It was built for joint occupancy by Wells, Fargo & Co. Express, the Southern Pacific Railroad Company, and the Oregon Railway and Navigation Company. According to a 1908 newspaper article, it was through the influence of Colonel Dudley Evans, then president of Wells Fargo, that "... the Wells Fargo skyscraper was erected" in Portland. Evans had at one time been the company's Portland agent and was "...'in consequence, well posted on [the city's] present and prospective needs."

The Wells Fargo façade is unlike others in Portland. The great variety of materials, colors, and compositional elements gives the building some of the richness and complexity of Victorian architecture.

Polychrome glazed terra cotta occurs at the third story and at the top two stories. Terra-cotta motifs include a bright blue wave-scroll belt course above the third story, green keystones and wreaths above the tenth story, and the letters WELLS FARGO above the top-story windows. The roof balustrade is also of terra cotta.

Above a gray granite plinth, the lower two floors are sheathed in limestone, with cast-iron window and door frames set into the two-story arches. Buff-colored brick on the main body of the building is laid in decorative diamond and cross patterns. Window surrounds at the upper two stories are of red brick. The roof cornice is copper. The cast-bronze entrance gates were said by lighting fixture designer, Fred C. Baker, to have been produced by Prior Bronze Works.

The vestibule and elevator lobby are in near-original condition, with vari-colored marble paneling and ornamental plasterwork. The original cast-iron stair is visible through a door at the rear of the lobby. Other portions of the interior were altered in 1923, following designs by A.E. Doyle. Subsequent remodeling was designed by Annand & Kennedy and by Skidmore, Owings & Merrill.

The first (1853) Wells, Fargo & Co. office in Portland was on Front Avenue near Morrison. Around the turn of the century, the company's express and banking operations were separated, and the banking operation was subsequently acquired by the United States National Bank. The Wells Fargo Building was, however, before its purchase by the United States National Bank, owned by Andrew Porter. It is still sometimes referred to as the Porter Building.

FIG. III-1.
WELLS FARGO BUILDING
Southwest corner of Sixth and Oak
1907
Designed by Benjamin Wistar Morris (New York City)
Built for Wells, Fargo & Co.
Terra cotta by Gladding, McBean & Co.

SOURCES
Baker, Fred C. Recorded interview by Janet Charlton, George McMath, and Anne Murphy, 1978. Notes in author's collection.
MacColl, E. Kimbark. *The Growth of a City; Power and Politics in Portland, Oregon*, 1915 to 1950. Portland, 1979.
Oregonian, June 7, 1905, p. 14; September 20, 1905, p. 14; January 1, 1908; September 8, 1974.
Scrapbook #60, p. 162, and #67, p. 125. Collection, Oregon Historical Society.
Vaughan, Thomas and Virginia Guest Ferriday. *Space, Style and Structure; Building in Northwest America*. Portland, 1974.

FIG. III-2.

FAILING BUILDING

Southeast corner of Fifth and Alder
1907-Lower six floors
1913-Upper six floors
Designed by Whidden & Lewis
Built for Henry E. Failing Estate
Terra cotta by Gladding, McBean & Co.

Although constructed for the Failing family, this building was not called by that name until after 1928 when the 1901 Failing Building at Third and Washington was renamed the Postal Building. It apparently originally had no official name at all. From circa 1918, when the Portland Gas and Coke Company became the major tenant, until 1928, it was commonly referred to as the "Gasco Building."

Working drawings for the original 1907 structure show doors (nine lights over four panels) all along the Alder Street façade with multi-light transoms above, double-hung windows at the upper stories, rusticated brickwork, and a simple cornice with block modillions. Specifications included: sill courses of even-colored Tenino Stone; street walls faced with standard pressed face brick (of Gladding, McBean & Co's make) laid in colored mortar with ruled joints; floors of reinforced concrete; and poultry netting as reinforcing for column fireproofing. The brick is a rich ocher.

The 1910 rendering pictured is apparently an accurate portrayal of the 1913 alterations and addition. New brick was an exact match for the old. Glazed terra cotta at the upper two stories is cream colored. Decoration includes keystones with fishscale pattern and window surrounds with a laurel leaf design.

The main entrance was remodeled in 1937 by H. Abbott Lawrence, architect, with bronze door frames produced by Oregon Brass Works and a surround of Verde Antique marble. In 1951, the lower floors were remodeled by Glenn Stanton, architect, for J.J. Newberry. Though the base at both façades was faced with ceramic veneer, the 1937 entrance was left intact. The building elevator lobby is of recent vintage.

Gevurtz (a furniture store) was the original tenant. In 1914, the building housed part of the Meier & Frank Co. store while its 1898 building was being replaced by a new structure.

Henry E. Failing (1834-98) was born in New York City where he went to work at age twelve in a New York counting house. In 1851, at age 17, he came to Portland with his brother John and father Josiah. Within two years Josiah had established a business, J. Failing & Co., on Front Street and had been elected mayor. In 1858, Henry married Henry W. Corbett's sister, and five years later he and Corbett bought control of the First National Bank. In 1871, the brothers-in-law merged the two family merchandise houses into the Corbett-Failing Company, which became the largest hardware supply business in the Northwest. Henry Failing was a generous supporter of cultural and religious activities. He was widely read in literature, science, and the arts. He was twice elected mayor of Portland. At his death in 1898, his estate listed 38 lots of prime downtown property.

SOURCES

MacColl, E. Kimbark. *The Shaping of a City; Business and Politics in Portland, Oregon, 1885 to 1915.* Portland, 1976.

Oregon Brass Works (Shop drawings for Failing Building) H. Abbott Lawrence, Architect, December 9, 1937.

Oregonian, January 1, 1907, p. 2; January 27, 1907; March 31, 1907, p. 30; January 1, 1908, p. 4.

Roduner, Pat. Portland Historical Landmarks Commission Inventory Form, 1978.

Vaughan, Thomas and Virginia Guest Ferriday. *Space, Style and Structure; Building in Northwest America.* Portland, 1974.

Whidden & Lewis. "Building for H. Failing Et Al" (Working drawings), March, 1906. Microfiche Collection, City of Portland Bureau of Buildings.

Whidden & Lewis. "Alterations & Additions to Building for H.E. Failing Et Al" (Working drawings), July, 1911. Microfiche Collection, City of Portland Bureau of Buildings.

Wilding, (Delineator). (Watercolor rendering of Failing Building), 1913. Collection, Oregon Historical Society.

The 1915, east half of the present building replaced an 1898 structure designed for Meier & Frank Co. by Whidden & Lewis. The 1909 portion of the present building was to have been built to match the 1898 structure, but the design was changed at Sigmund Frank's request after he visited the glazed terra-cotta Carson, Pirie, Scott & Co. building in Chicago. Both the 1915 and 1932 portions repeated the 1909 design, with only one major change — two additional stories rising directly above the main cornice and topped by a balustrade.

The building is sheathed entirely in white glazed terra cotta. Salient decorative features are the roof balustrade, flagpole support, pilasters, ornamental panels, cornices, and belt course. Motifs include double-key Greek frets, rosettes, lamb's tongue, wave scroll, bead-and-reel, cable mold, and egg-and-dart. Plinths at the base of the terra-cotta pilasters are granite.

Upper windows are double-hung with wood frames and sash. Storefronts, most of which have been modified, have metal frames.

There are at present three sets of marquees, two on the north façade and one on the south façade. Those on the west end of the north façade are all that remain of a wrought-iron marquee that ran continuously along both façades of the 1909 portion.

Upon completion of the full block in 1932, there were six entrances: two each at the north and south façades and one each on the east and west façades. One of the north entrances was substituted for an entrance at the northwest corner. The east and west entrances were closed in 1976.

At the time of the 1915 construction, interiors of the 1909 portion were completely refurbished. The store then enjoyed the latest in mechanical equipment: a vacuum sweeping machine with 165 outlets, a complete automatic sprinkler system, a four-stage automatic centrifugal fire pump with 90 hose racks and 7600 feet of hose, 19 elevators, six spiral chutes, thousands of feet of mechanical belt conveyors, and the first escalators in Portland. A grocery, bakery, creamery, and delicatessen were located on the ninth floor. The tenth floor, where the restaurant was located, had a two-story space with mezzanine. Little, if anything, of the 1915 interior remains.

In 1932, the entire ground-floor was remodeled in the Art Deco style. A 1964 remodeling obliterated all but a few details: stainless steel railings and trim, floor directory, mail box, marble paneling, and travertine steps. The ground-floor interior was remodeled again in 1977 by Assad Design Inc. of Pittsburgh.

The basic structure is steel with masonry or concrete fireproofing.

The Thompson-Starret Company was contractor for the 1909 portion, Dinwiddie Construction Company for the 1915 portion, and Dinwiddie and Hoffman for the 1932 portion. J.D. Tresham did the 1909 ornamental plasterwork. Hanford & Sutthoff of Seattle supplied the 1909 Philippine hardwood (mahogany).

Meier & Frank Co. grew from a small store established by Aaron Meier at Front and Taylor Streets. Emil Frank, like Meier a native of Germany, joined the firm in 1870 and Emil's younger brother Sigmund in 1872. Meier took Emil in as a partner a year later, and the business became Meier & Frank Co. The store was moved one block west in 1885, where it remained (with two enlargements) until the 1898 move to the present location. In 1888, Emil Frank sold his interest in the store to Aaron Meier and to Sigmund, who three years previously had married Aaron's daughter, Fannie. When Aaron Meier died in 1889, Sigmund Frank became president; he managed the store for the next 21 years. The company remained in family hands until acquired by the May Company in 1965-67. Most widely known member of the Meier and Frank families was Aaron's son Julius, who became governor of Oregon in 1930.

SOURCES

Clark, John. Unrecorded interview by the author, 1978.

DeYoung, Moscowitz & Rosenberg, Architects, New York City; Herman Brookman, Associate Architect. "Alterations & Additions to Department Store for Meier & Frank Co." (Working drawings), January 15, 1930. Microfiche Collection, City of Portland Bureau of Buildings.

Doyle & Patterson. "Meier & Frank Co." (Ink-on-linen working drawings), 1908, 1914. Collection, Oregon Historical Society.

McMath, George. "National Register of Historic Places Inventory — Nomination Form, Meier & Frank Building," 1981.

Oregon Brass Works. "Bronze Marquies [sic] for Meier & Frank, DeYoung, Moscowitz & Rosenberg, Architects" (Shop drawings),August 11, 1931.

Oregonian, January 1, 1910, sec. 2, p. 2, sec. 3, p. 10; September 11, 1977, p. C7.

Photographs. Collection, Oregon Historical Society.

Portland Architectural Club Yearbook, 1909, 1910, 1913.

Fig. III-3.

MEIER & FRANK CO.

Entire block between Fifth and Sixth, Morrison and Alder
1909-Northwest portion
1915-East half
1932-Southwest portion

Designed by Doyle & Patterson (1909 & 1915) and DeYoung, Moscowitz & Rosenberg with Herman Brookman (1932)
Built for Meier & Frank Co.
Terra cotta by N. Clark & Son (1909), Gladding, McBean & Co. (1915, 1932)
Listed in National Register

FIG. III-4.
HENRY BUILDING
Southwest corner of Fourth and Oak
1909

Designed by Francis C. Berndt
Built for Charles K. Henry
Terra cotta by N. Clark & Son (New entrance, 1940s)
Listed in National Register

The exterior walls of the Henry Building are faced with a glazed "Tiffany" brick produced in Denver, Colorado. They are all white except for some blue diamond-shaped motifs in the spandrels. There are eight large glazed terra-cotta cartouches with lions' heads directly under the galvanized-iron roof cornice. The belt cornice above the first floor is also glazed terra cotta. The original glazed terra-cotta entrance, which incorporated decorative motifs similar to the cartouches, was replaced in the 1940s by the present Moderne glazed terra-cotta entrance.

Exterior walls at the first floor were originally almost entirely of glass, with masonry extending to the ground only at the party walls and at the main entrance. A recessed corner entrance with free-standing cast-iron column encased in copper served to further dematerialize the base. The base was remodeled in 1924. Subsequent alterations have included a fieldstone veneer wall, which is still in place.

The lobby originally included a decorative tile floor, wood-paneled walls, and bronze elevator doors. Only the original cast-iron stair with marble treads remains.

Hex tiles were used at the corner entrance and in many interior spaces, such as the office corridors and the "... beautiful and sanitary Henry Building Barber Shop," located in the basement and still intact, though not in use. Marble was used in the barber shop and in toilet rooms.

Office partitions were glass-filled, with transoms above the doors. Picture rails were provided throughout. The original lighting fixtures were reportedly left in place when suspended ceilings were installed. The original safe remains on the ground floor.

The 100-foot-by-100-foot plan is roughly doughnut-shaped, with three light courts, one in the center and one at each party wall.

Essentially of wood construction, the building has reinforced concrete "Kahn" window lintels.

E.B. White was the carpenter and general contractor. Hanford & Sutthoff of Seattle supplied Philippine hardwood (mahogany).

Charles K. Henry (1856-?) was born in Liverpool, England, when his Irish parents were immigrating to California. The senior Henry mined for a short time and then moved to San Francisco where he operated a hotel until his death. Henry graduated from St. Mary's College in San Francisco in 1874 and then learned the cabinetmaker's trade. In 1878, he moved to Walla Walla and went into the furniture business. He subsequently became involved in real estate and, in 1890, came to Portland to live. In 1903, he suffered heavy financial losses but paid off all his debts. In 1909, Henry formed a syndicate of Portland and Seattle men who purchased William Ladd's Hazelfern Farm. Henry was a member of the Arlington Club, Chamber of Commerce, and Commercial Club. E. Kimbark MacColl quotes an *Oregonian* article as saying that Henry, in comparing Portland's buildings with Denver's, liked Denver's enameled brick buildings because they were "easier to keep clean."

SOURCES
Berndt, Francis, Architect. "Office Building for Mr. C.K. Henry" (Working drawings), 1908. Microfiche Collection, City of Portland Bureau of Buildings.
N. Clark & Son Job List. Collection, Gladding, McBean & Co.
Gaston, Joseph. *Portland, Oregon; Its History and Builders*. Chicago, 1911.
The Henry Building, Portland-Oregon (Promotional pamphlet). No publishing date or place. Photocopy in author's collection.
MacColl, E. Kimbark. *The Shaping of a City; Business and Politics in Portland, Oregon, 1885 to 1915*. Portland, 1976, p. 314.
Photographs. Collection, Oregon Historical Society.
Portland Architectural Club Yearbook, 1909.
Randolph, Thomas, Michael J. Lilly, and Marianne Schimelfenig. "National Register of Historic Places Inventory — Nomination Form, C.K. Henry Building," 1982.

The father of Phil Metschan, Jr. was owner and manager of the original (1894) Imperial Hotel (now the Plaza), to which this structure was annexed.

The exterior wall is faced with buff-colored brick. Cream-colored glazed terra cotta at the upper story blends with the sheet-metal cornice and brackets. Quoining is also glazed terra cotta, as are the belt courses. Terra cotta at the first-floor disappeared in 1956 when fieldstone veneer, cement plaster with a dashed-pebble finish, and resawn redwood strips were applied, following a design by an architect in Hollywood, California.

Windows of the hotel dining room, originally located on the first floor corner, were made by the Povey Brothers of Portland. They were probably also responsible for the skylight, which was originally in the main lobby. Metal-and-glass canopies originally hung over entrances at both façades. The vestibule had a marble tile floor. No original ground floor features, either exterior or interior, remain.

On a 100-foot-by-100-foot site, the L-shaped plan encloses an interior light well into which approximately one-third of the rooms face. Up until a 1927 remodeling, all rooms shared connecting baths. According to Fred C. Baker, guest room fixtures were the "one and one" variety (one gas light and one electric light) manufactured in Chicago.

Structural design was by Northwest Bridge Works. The first-floor structure consists of an 8-inch-thick, flat concrete slab supported on round concrete columns with flared capitals, referred to in the drawings as the "Turner Mushroom System." Upper floors have the typical riveted-steel frame and ribbed reinforced-concrete floor system formed with integral terra-cotta tiles.

Theodore Burney Wilcox (1856-1918), for whom three glazed terra-cotta buildings in downtown Portland were built, was born in Agawam, Massachusetts. Shortly after 1877, while working in a bank in Westfield, Massachusetts, he so impressed visiting Asahel Bush of Portland that Bush offered him a job — which he promptly accepted — at the Ladd & Tilton Bank in Portland. W.S. Ladd made Wilcox his administrative assistant in the early 1880s and, later, general manager of the Albina Flour Mills. Wilcox became a major shareholder in the Ladd & Tilton Bank and used it as a tool to enhance his fortunes. At his death, his estate was estimated to be worth over $10 million.

Phil Metschan, Jr. was a native of Canyon City, Oregon; he later lived in Heppner, where his father was in the hotel business. In his twenties, Metschan bought and ran a small hotel in Heppner. He became a local power in the Republican Party, serving as Chairman of the Republican State Central Committee from 1924 to 1930. In 1930, he ran unsuccessfully for governor. He was a Port of Portland Commissioner for 16 years, the last ten as treasurer. Metschan bought out the Wilcox Investment Company's interest in the Imperial in 1926. Perhaps because of Metschan's roots in Eastern Oregon, the Imperial has been the traditional stopping place for cattlemen and houses the offices of the Oregon Cattlemen's Association.

SOURCES

Baker, Fred C. Recorded interview by Janet Charlton, George McMath, and Anne Murphy, 1978. Notes in author's collection.

MacColl, E. Kimbark. *The Shaping of a City; Business and Politics in Portland, Oregon, 1885 to 1915*. Portland, 1976.

MacColl, E. Kimbark. *The Growth of a City; Power and Politics in Portland, Oregon, 1915 to 1950*. Portland, 1979.

Oregonian, January 1, 1909, page 4; January 1, 1910, page 3.

Photographs. Collection, Oregon Historical Society.

Portland Architectural Club Yearbook, 1910.

The Pacific Coast Architect, vol. 3, no. 1 (April, 1912). (Ad for the Lithic Manufacturing Co. with photo of Imperial Hotel lobby.)

Povey Brothers Exhibit, Oregon Historical Society.

"Reminiscences of Fletcher Linn." Collection, Southern Oregon Historical Society.

Vaughan, Thomas and Virginia Guest Ferriday. *Space, Style and Structure; Building in Northwest America*. Portland, 1974.

Whidden & Lewis, Architects. "Hotel Building, S.E. corner of 7th & Stark Sts; Mr. T.B. Wilcox" (Working drawings), November, 1908. Microfiche Collection, City of Portland Bureau of Buildings.

FIG. III-5.

IMPERIAL HOTEL

Southeast corner of Broadway and Stark
1909

Designed by Whidden & Lewis
Built for Theodore B. Wilcox and Phil Metschan, Jr.

FIG. III-6.

SEWARD HOTEL

Southwest corner of Tenth and Alder
1909

Designed by William C. Knighton
Built for G. Rosenblatt

The glazed terra-cotta ornament on this building is exceptional, especially for its date. Decorative motifs are predominently geometric in form: squares, diamonds, and ball courses. A nearly-shield-shaped element, which is repeated in numerous locations, both inside and out, was Knighton's trademark, applied to both residential and commercial work. The terra cotta is glazed off-white; brick is gray.

The copper entrance marquee is original. Flanking the entrance are leaded-glass panels with green-and-caramel-colored slag glass. The entrance vestibule has onyx wainscoting and a mosaic tile floor.

The lobby was originally in the corner space. Except for a check-in area and a small reading room, the rest of the street floor was given over to retail. The first-floor corner windows have been altered, but much of the lobby cast-plaster decoration remains. Much of the original interior woodwork on the first floor and in the main stairway is also in place.

There are two light courts, one in the center and one along the south wall. Many rooms face into these light courts. Outside rooms have connecting baths; interior rooms share common baths. The common baths have hex-tile floors and marble toilet stalls.

Fire escape balcony railings have been replaced. Mosaic tile from the center of one large parapet cartouche is missing. The terra cotta itself is badly spalled and is in dire need of attention.

The basic structure is wood with 10x10- and 12x12-inch posts and 4x16- and 6x16-inch joists.

SOURCES
Knighton, W.C., Architect. "Business Building for Mr. G. Rosenblatt" (Working drawings). Microfiche Collection, City of Portland Bureau of Buildings.
Oregonian, January 1, 1910, p. 3, section 4, p. 14.
Photographs. Collection, Oregon Historical Society.

FIG. III-7.

ARLINGTON CLUB

North side of Salmon between Park and Ninth
1910

Designed by Whidden & Lewis
Built for Arlington Club
Terra cotta by Gladding, McBean & Co.

This is the second building designed by Whidden & Lewis for the Arlington Club; the first stood on the northwest corner of Park and Alder.

Exterior walls are of smooth-faced red brick laid in Flemish bond. The terra cotta has been painted off-white. Photographs taken prior to its painting show blotchy areas on the terra cotta so it is possible that the glaze was faulty or that it was a slip rather than a full glaze, though by 1910 this would have been unusual. Decorative terra cotta includes balusters at roof parapet, roof cornice with block modillions, window heads, brackets, belt course with fret motif, and Ionic columns flanking the entrance.

Windows are one-over-one, double-hung with wood frames and sash. Set in the smaller windows at the upper two stories are wrought-iron grilles, probably made by Johann K. Tuerck.

The Arlington Club was first organized as a "Social Club" on December 9, 1867 by 35 business and professional men. The purpose was "...to commit its members to finance a club where they could fraternize for mutual enjoyment and relaxation, and to provide a meeting place for discussing their own and Portland's destiny." In 1881, when the "Social Club" was given a formal structural organization and named "Arlington Club," it had a "carefully selected membership of about 100," and its members leased the old Ainsworth Mansion at Southwest Third at Pine Street for its headquarters. Some of the prominent founding members were Henry Failing, William S. Ladd, C.H. Lewis, Capt. J.C. Ainsworth, Simeon G. Reed, Donald Macleay, and J.A. Chapman.

SOURCES
Arlington Club. *Arlington Club and the Men Who Built It*. Portland, 1968.
Gladding, McBean & Co. Job List.
Oregonian, January 1, 1910, section 3, p. 8
Photographs. Collection, Oregon Historical Society.
Vaughan, Thomas and Virginia Guest Ferriday. *Space, Style and Structure; Building in Northwest America*. Portland, 1974.
Whidden & Lewis. "New Arlington Club" (Working drawings), April, May, 1909. Microfiche Collection, City of Portland Bureau of Buildings.

This quarter-block office building was the best of Portland's new commercial buildings according to Herbert D. Croly in an 1912 *Architectural Record* article. The plan is U-shaped with a light court facing north. Exterior walls are grey brick with deeply raked joints. The off-white, glazed terra-cotta ornament has been painted. The glazed terra-cotta roof cornice has been recently restored. Lower floors were originally finished with Indiana limestone. Limestone remains at the "attic" story, but has been painted. Window frames at the ground floor were of cast iron, and there was a metal-and-glass entrance marquee.

The Ladd & Tilton Bank, which originally occupied the main floor, had a separate entrance on Washington Street. There were two large cast-iron lamps at each side of the bank entrance. The bank interior had a marble floor, Kasota stone paneling, and ornamental plaster ceilings. Fixtures were of Breccia Pavonazza marble and bronze. Chandeliers were by the Frink Lighting Company.

The building lobby had a marble floor, marble wainscoting, and ornamental plasterwork.

Two stairwells with cast-iron railings, oak handrail, and marble treads are all that remain of the original bank and building lobby interiors.

The building has a structural steel frame. The original heating system was a forced-air system, utilizing "Harrison Heaters." Because it did not allow for individual room control, this system was replaced with steam radiators in 1917.

Col. Z.S. Spalding was head of the Spalding Company, a California corporation located in Los Angeles. The contractor was James Stewart & Co. of New York, St. Louis, and San Francisco.

The Spalding Building was the headquarters for the Oregon Bank from 1925 to 1980 and is still generally known as the Oregon Bank Building.

SOURCES

Croly, Herbert D. "Portland, Oregon, The Transformation of the City from an Architectural & Social Viewpoint," *Architectural Record*, XXI (June, 1912), 591-607.

Gilbert, Cass. "Office Building for Col. Z.S. Spalding (Working drawings), June 30, 1909. Microfiche Collection, City of Portland Bureau of Buildings.

Oregonian, Jan. 1, 1910, sec 2, p. 2.

Portland Architectural Club Yearbook, 1910.

Randolph, Thomas, Miller/Cook Architects. "National Register of Historic Places Inventory — Nomination Form, The Spalding Building," 1982.

Vaughan, Thomas and Virginia Guest Ferriday. *Space, Style and Structure; Building in Northwest America*. Portland, 1974.

FIG. III-8.

SPALDING BUILDING

Northwest corner of Third and Washington
1910

Designed by Cass Gilbert (New York City)
Built for Col. Z.S. Spalding
Terra cotta by Gladding, McBean & Co.
Listed in National Register

FIG. III-9.

SELLING BUILDING

Southwest corner of Sixth and Alder

1910

Designed by Doyle & Patterson

Built for Ben Selling, C.S. and R.S. Moore, and
Moses Blum

Terra cotta by Gladding, McBean & Co.

The first office building designed by A.E. Doyle, the Selling Building was originally flanked by two Richardsonian Romanesque buildings — the Marquam Building to the south and the Oregonian Building across the street to the north.

It is faced with speckled, buff, Norman-size brick (unfortunately, recently painted white). Glazed terra cotta includes a decorative roof cornice (with block modillions), Venetian windows and pilasters at the top two stories, belt cornices, and column and spandrel facings at the "attic" story. Some terra cotta at the lower floors was removed in 1931 when the retail base was redone in the Art Deco mode for a Lerner store and the columns faced with black glass. During a 1937 remodeling for the same tenant, designed by architect Harry A. Herzog, the retail base was faced with polished Carnelian granite, obliterating the original design. This granite facing, which is still in place, did not, however, cover the bay just east of the building entrance, which had been remodeled in 1934 for Wegert's Prescription Pharmacy. This storefront, also designed by Harry A. Herzog, was faced with travertine and had bronze letters, window frame, door frame and door, all produced by Oregon Brass Works. It is essentially intact.

The storefronts originally had prism-glass transoms with small, inset, awning-type windows. There were iron grilles below the plate glass store windows.

An unusually attractive cast-iron-and-glass marquee, with a large "S" on its face, sheltered the building entrance. By 1934, it had already been removed.

The building lobby was originally finished with marble wainscoting and ornamental plaster-work. It had a terrazzo floor. A cast-iron stair with marble treads led to the basement. Elevator doors were bronze, and bronze fixtures with red-and-white glass ball lights indicated the elevators' direction of travel. Building corridors also had marble wainscoting. In 1958, automatic elevators were installed, and the corridors and other public spaces renovated. The main entrance was again remodeled in 1966.

The structure is riveted steel with reinforced concrete floors.

James Stewart & Co. was general contractor for the original construction. Hanford & Sutthoff of Seattle supplied Philippine mahogany.

Ben Selling (1852-1931) was born in San Francisco and came to Portland with his parents at age ten. He worked in his father's general merchandise store on Front Street (and later First Street) and in 1880 went into business for himself. He launched a wholesale boot and shoe business and then opened a clothing store. Both thrived, and he died a millionaire. A staunch Republican, he was a member of the Public Docks Commission, charter member of the Port of Portland Commission, State Senator, director of the Portland Symphony Society, director of the National Jewish Consumptive Hospital, and president for more than 20 years of the Hebrew Benevolent Association. A great philanthropist, Selling raised money for Armenian relief work, established kitchens for the unemployed during the depressions of 1893 and 1907, supported the Waverly Baby Home and Jewish Neighborhood House, and established a scholarship loan fund at the University of Oregon Medical School. In 1928, the Portland Realty Board voted Selling Portland's leading citizen — the first time the honor was conferred by the board.

SOURCES

Doyle & Patterson, Architect. "Building for Ben Selling et Al" (Working drawings), 1910. Microfiche Collection, City of Portland Bureau of Buildings.

Gladding, McBean & Co. Job List.

Hendrickson, Ann Williams. Portland Historical Landmarks Commission Inventory Form, 1974.

MacColl, E. Kimbark. *The Growth of a City; Power and Politics in Portland, Oregon, 1915 to 1950*. Portland, 1979.

Oregon Brass Works. Job List and Photographs.

Oregon Journal, July 15, 1966, p. 5M.

Photographs. Collection, Oregon Historical Society.

Portland Architectural Club Yearbook, 1910, 1913.

Vaughan, Thomas and Virginia Guest Ferriday. *Space, Style, and Structure; Building in Northwest America*. Portland, 1974.

In 1916, Olds, Wortman & King was said to be the only retail store in the Northwest occupying an entire city block. The building's exterior is, with the exception of the galvanized iron cornice, finished entirely in white glazed terra cotta. Ornament is flat and sparse: dentils at the cornice, a hint of capitals at the columns, raised spandrel panels, and some rustication. There were originally five-ball light standards around the edge of the roof, and awnings were placed below the transoms above the large ground-floor windows. An original entrance marquee remains on the south façade.

The interior was also spare. The original first-floor maple flooring has been replaced by marble. Upper floors were originally fir.

The building's basic structure is steel frame (utilizing "I" beams) with ribbed concrete slabs. Bays are 21-feet square. A grand stairway to the second floor was located in the central light well. Smaller stairs on the east wall gave access to the upper floors. The light-well stair was later replaced by escalators and the light well itself enclosed. When the building was remodeled in 1976 for shops and offices (and renamed "Galleria"), the light court was re-opened and enlarged.

The Trustee Company, founded by A.L. Hawley of New York and Judge W.D. Wood of Seattle, dealt in real estate in Spokane, Los Angeles, and Seattle. In 1907, the company held options on ten other sites in the vicinity of the Olds, Wortman & King store, including the site of the Pittock Block. Later that year, the *Oregonian* reported that the Trustee Company had attempted to raise money from adjoining property owners for construction of the department store building. The author did not determine how construction was ultimately financed.

The Olds, Wortman & King department store originated as McLaren Bros. This firm was sold to John Wilson, who in 1878 sold it to employee William Parker Olds. Olds formed a partnership with his stepfather, Samuel Willard King, and the name was then changed to Olds & King. Charles Willard King, son of Samuel Willard King, began carrying parcels for the store in 1878. He was admitted to the firm in 1891. In 1890, John Wortman bought part interest in the firm. In 1901, his brother Hardy joined the business, and it was renamed Olds, Wortman & King. Olds, born in 1857 and a native of Washington County, Oregon, was president after 1897.

Successive locations of the store are illustrative of the move of Portland's commercial area from the river: 1852 at Front and Taylor; 1868 to Front and Morrison; 1870 to Third and Morrison; 1878 to Third between Morrison and Alder; 1887 to First and Taylor; 1891 to Fifth and Washington; and 1910 to the Tenth Avenue location. This final location had previously been the site of the home of Sylvester Pennoyer, lumberman, Portland mayor, and governor of Oregon.

SOURCES

Aldrich, C.R. "Department Store Building for Olds, Wortman & King, Constructed by The Trustee Company" (Working drawings), Dec. 24, 1908. Microfiche Collection, City of Portland Bureau of Buildings.

Doyle & Patterson. "Olds, Wortman & King Building" (Working drawings for fixtures), 1910. Collection, Oregon Historical Society.

Gaston, Joseph. *Portland, Oregon; Its History and Builders*. Chicago, 1911.

King's Hill Inventory. Collection, Goose Hollow Foothills League Association.

Lockley, Fred. *History of the Columbia River Valley*. Chicago, 1928.

MacColl, E. Kimbark. *The Shaping of a City; Business and Politics in Portland, Oregon, 1895 to 1915*. Portland, 1976.

McMath, George. Lecture on A.E. Doyle. A.I.A. Meeting: January 17, 1983.

Oregon Journal, April 26, 1877, p. 3.

Oregonian, Feb. 27, 1907, p. 14; April 14, 1907; June 23, 1907, p. 32; July 23, 1907, p. 10; Aug. 16, 1908, p. 10; Jan. 1, 1909, p. 12; June 13, 1909, p. 5; July 1, 1909, p. 12; Aug. 1, 1909; Jan. 1, 1910, sec. 1, p. 2, sec. 2, p. 2, sec. 4, p. 2; Jan. 1, 1916, p. 7.

Photographs. Collection, Oregon Historical Society.

Plamondon, Al J., compiler. "The Plamondon Scrapbooks," vol. V, Nov., 1955. Collection, Alfred Staehli.

Spencer, Arthur. Notes for the author, 1984.

FIG. III-10.

OLDS, WORTMAN & KING

Entire block between Ninth and Tenth, Morrison and Alder

1910

Designed by C.R. Aldrich; Doyle & Patterson, Associate Architects

Built for The Trustee Company to be occupied by Olds, Wortman & King

Terra cotta by Gladding, McBean & Co.

FIG. III-11.
GRAVES MUSIC COMPANY
West side of Fourth between Alder and Morrison
1910
Built for Milton J. Jones

Off-white glazed terra cotta faces the entire façade of this eighth-block building. Ornament in terra cotta includes diamond motifs in spandrel panels, pierced parapet flanked by cartouches, and cornice with scroll modillions and consoles. Paint was recently removed from the terra cotta, revealing generalized glaze spalling.

The storefront was altered as early as 1914 when cast-iron columns were substituted for reinforced concrete piers.

The building was occupied for a time by the Lucas Music Store and, most recently, by the Star Furniture Company.

SOURCES
Card Files, City of Portland Bureau of Buildings.
Portland City Directories.

FIG. III-12.
MULTNOMAH COUNTY COURTHOUSE
Entire block between Fourth and Fifth, Main and Salmon
1911-East half
1914-West half
Designed by Whidden & Lewis
Built for Multnomah County
Terra cotta by Gladding, McBean & Co.
Portland Landmark
Listed in National Register

This courthouse replaced the 1886 courthouse, which stood on the west half of the block and which remained in use until the east half of the present structure was ready for occupancy.

The exterior of the present courthouse is faced with Indiana limestone and has a grey granite plinth and off-white glazed terra-cotta entablature. A ten-foot-high glazed terra-cotta parapet wall has been removed, exposing the two-story penthouse (originally constructed for use as a jail). Decorative motifs in terra cotta include lions' heads, rondels, and meandering fret panels. Limestone columns have Ionic capitals. Major entrances are framed with carved granite. (The west entrance has been closed off.) Entrances are flanked by bronze lanterns (with inappropriate replacement parts). Decorative bronze screens on the north and south windows have been removed. All original wood windows have been replaced with anodized aluminum units.

Public interior spaces were finished with ornamental plasterwork and had marble floors, wainscoting, and stairs. Main stair railings were bronze and newel posts were Italian statuary white marble. Doors and trim were oak. Only the entrance lobbies, halls, stairs, and two courtrooms remain in their original condition.

The building has a central courtyard faced with white glazed terra-cotta tile. The structural frame is riveted steel with a ribbed reinforced concrete floor system. There was originally a forced air system combined with radiant heating.

General contractor was the Lewis H. Hicks Company. Schanen Blair Company provided marble and granite.

SOURCES
Moseley, Carl P. "National Register of Historic Places Inventory — Nomination Form, Multnomah County Courthouse," 1978.
Oregonian, Jan. 1, 1913, sec. 3, p. 3.
Portland Architectural Club Yearbook, 1913. (Photo of lobby.)
Whidden & Lewis. "Multnomah County Courthouse" (Ink-on-linen working drawings), 1909-1914. Collection, Oregon Historical Society.

With the exception of the retail base, the Yeon Building is faced entirely with off-white glazed terra cotta. Terra-cotta elements include rustication at the "attic" story and at the third-story windows, cartouches above the third-story windows, and an Ionic colonnade at the "cap." The decorative glazed terra-cotta roof cornice, originally lighted with bulbs screwed into sockets in the terra cotta, was removed in the 1930s after a lion's head fell from the Lipman, Wolfe & Co. building cornice and all downtown building cornices found unsafe by City building inspectors had to be either repaired or removed.

As originally built, the retail base had cast-iron pilasters with plate glass below the transom bar and prism glass above. Small awning-type operable windows were set in the fields of prism glass. The cast-iron pilasters were painted a dark color; as a result, the base tended to dissolve, leaving the masonry mass floating above.

The main building entrance on Fifth is framed in glazed terra cotta. The building name appears in terra cotta over the doorway and was originally also set in the mosaic tile vestibule floor. Before the entrance was remodeled in 1930 (following a design by DeYoung, Moscowitz, and Rosenberg), the entrance had cast-metal lighting fixtures, cast-metal door and window frames, and a revolving door. An early photograph shows the lobby with marble-faced walls and columns, mosaic tile (hexagonal?) floor, globe lights, and cast-metal grilles.

A metal-and-glass marquee hung at the Alder Street entrance. Early photographs show randomly-placed striped awnings at office windows.

The plan is U-shaped with light court facing east.

John B. Yeon (1865-1928) was born in Canada, one of eight children. His parents, who spoke only French, operated a 70-acre farm near Plantagenet, Ontario. At age 17, Yeon went to Ohio where he worked as a lumberjack. In 1885, he arrived in Portland with assets of $2.50. After working as a lumberjack and running a lumber camp in Oregon and Washington, he went into the lumber business himself with $1200 capital. In 1906, he sold his by then prosperous logging business and extensive timber interests and moved to Portland to invest in real estate. Yeon was active in the "Good Roads" movement. In 1913, he accepted the position of Multnomah County Roadmaster at $1 a year, and, under his management, the county assumed the "Good Roads" leadership of the Northwest.

SOURCES

Carey, Charles Henry. *History of Oregon*. Chicago, 1922.

DeYoung, Moscowitz and Rosenberg. "Yeon Building, Alterations to Vestibule and Elevator Lobby" (Working drawings). Microfiche Collection, City of Portland Bureau of Buildings.

Gladding, McBean & Co. Yeon Building Shop Drawings.

Hendrickson, Ann Williams. Portland Historical Landmarks Commission Inventory Form, 1979.

Oregonian, Sept. 29, 1905, p. 16; Jan. 1, 1912, sec. 2, p. 2.

Photographs. Collection, Oregon Historical Society.

Portland Architectural Club Yearbook, 1910.

Reid Brothers. Yeon Building (Ink-on-linen working drawings). Collection, Melvin Mark Properties.

Vaughan, Thomas and Virginia Guest Ferriday. *Space, Style and Structure; Building in Northwest America*. Portland, 1974.

Yeon Building (Watercolor rendering). Collection, Melvin Mark Properties.

FIG. III-13.

YEON BUILDING
Northeast corner of Fifth and Alder
1911
Designed by Reid Brothers (San Francisco)
Built for John Yeon
Terra cotta by Gladding, McBean & Co.

FIG. III-14.

WILCOX BUILDING

Southeast corner of Sixth and Washington
1911
Designed by Whidden & Lewis
Built for Theodore B. Wilcox
Terra cotta by Washington Brick, Lime &
Sewer Pipe Co.

The design for this steel-frame office building was repeated in simplified form for the Stevens Building, also designed by Whidden & Lewis for Theodore B. Wilcox.

The main body of the building is sheathed with smooth-faced, buff-colored brick. Off-white terra cotta was used at the lower and upper floors and for window sills. Terra-cotta elements at the cornice include antefixae, lions' heads, block modillions, and egg-and-dart. There are fleur-de-lis along the frieze, scrolls and faces on the spandrel panels, and *putti* and fruit-filled urns on the vertical panels. Except for a wave-scroll belt course above the second story, all the original terra cotta at the lower floors has been replaced with travertine (probably in 1947).

The storefronts originally had terra-cotta-faced columns, mullioned transoms, and awnings hung at the transom bar. The second floor had smaller windows with rusticated terra cotta and a band of fleur-de-lis.

There were originally two copper-and-glass marquees — a semi-circular one on Washington and a rectangular one on Sixth.

Architects Whidden & Lewis moved their offices into the Wilcox Building upon its completion.

The building lobby, elevators, and corridors underwent extensive remodeling in 1956.

For information on Theodore B. Wilcox, see data on the Imperial Hotel. (Fig. III-5.)

SOURCES

Oregonian, Jan. 1, 1912, sec. 2, p. 2.

The Pacific Coast Architect, vol. 2, no. 4 (Jan., 1912).

Photographs. Collection, Oregon Historical Society.

Portland Architectural Club Yearbook, 1913.

Roduner, Pat. Portland Historical Landmarks Commission Inventory Form, 1979.

Vaughan, Thomas and Virginia Guest Ferriday. *Space, Style and Structure; Building in Northwest America*. Portland, 1974.

Whidden & Lewis. "Office Building at S.E. corner of Sixth & Washington for Mr. T.B. Wilcox" (Working drawings), Oct., 1910. Microfiche Collection, City of Portland Bureau of Buildings.

This nine-story, 50-foot-by-100-foot building was originally entirely occupied by the Woodard, Clarke & Co. retail drugstore.

The basic structure is steel frame with ribbed concrete slabs. There is no light court, and elevators are arranged along the east party wall.

Except for the base, the exterior is sheathed in smooth-faced, buff-colored brick. The cornice is galvanized iron. There are glazed terra-cotta arches above the top windows. The present glazed terra-cotta entrance dates from 1924.

The ground-floor exterior has been entirely altered, and no photographs or plans have been located to indicate whether or not it was faced with terra cotta. An architect's rendering shows plate glass with prism-glass transom lights and a metal marquee supported by chains attached to rosettes (still in place) running the full length of both façades. A photograph of the original store entrance shows a ceramic tile floor with meandering fret border.

The ground-floor interior was originally two-stories high with a mezzanine on all four sides and a grand stairway opposite the entrance. Mezzanine and stair railings were cast iron, and the stair had marble treads. The floor was finished with white tile laid with contrasting figures. Cabinetwork was mahogany. Large globe lamps hung on chains along the center of this space. The mezzanine has been filled in to create a full second floor.

Charles Henry Woodard (1832-1909), a native of western New York, came to Portland in 1865 and went to work for the retail drug house of Hodge, Calef & Co., remaining until he had accumulated sufficient capital to organize his own firm, C.H. Woodard & Co. Operating initially at the corner of Front and Alder, the business was forced by fire to relocate at First & Alder. At that time, a Mr. Quiver was admitted to partnership. In 1880, Louis Gaylord Clarke joined the firm, and the name was changed to Woodard, Clarke & Co. Woodard subsequently disposed of his interest in the retail drug business and became a member of, first, Reddington, Woodard & Co. and, later, Snell, Heitshu & Woodard, both wholesale drug companies. Afterwards, he withdrew from the wholesale drug business and opened a surgical instrument store.

SOURCES

Doyle, Patterson & Beach. "Building for Woodard, Clarke & Co." (Working drawings), Nov., 1911. Microfiche Collection, City of Portland Bureau of Buildings.

Gaston, Joseph. *Portland, Oregon; Its History and Builders*. Chicago, 1911.

Oregon Journal, April 3, 1912, sec. 4, p. 5; May 6, 1969, p. 6J.

Oregonian, Jan. 1, 1912, sec. 3, p. 2; Jan. 1, 1913, sec. 3, p. 3; Jan. 1, 1914, p. 4; July 30, 1978, p. G8.

Photographs. (Includes construction photographs and photocopy of rendering.) Collection, Oregon Historical Society.

Schacht & Bergen. "Alterations to Woodlark Building" (Working drawings), 1924. Microfiche Collection, City of Portland Bureau of Buildings.

Vaughan, Thomas and Virginia Guest Ferriday. *Space, Style and Structure; Building in Northwest America*. Portland, 1974.

FIG. III-15.

WOODLARK BUILDING

Northeast corner of Ninth and Alder
1912
Designed by Doyle, Patterson & Beach
Built for Woodard, Clarke & Co.

FIG. III-16.

LIPMAN, WOLFE & CO.

West side of Fifth between Alder and Washington

1912

Designed by Doyle & Patterson

Built for H.W. Corbett Estate & O'Shea Bros., to be occupied by Lipman, Wolfe & Co.

Terra cotta by Gladding, McBean & Co.

This half-block, ten-story building is sheathed entirely in white glazed terra cotta. Its classically-derived ornamental motifs are quite varied: lamb's tongue, bead-and-reel, medallions, egg-and-dart, torus moldings, antefixae, wreaths, and meandering frets. During the 1930s, a terra-cotta lion's head fell from the cornice and, as a result, all cornices in the downtown area were inspected and those found unsafe either removed or repaired. The Lipman, Wolfe & Co. cornice was, fortunately, repaired. Some of the lions were replaced with fiberglass replicas.

The upper, modified-Chicago windows have wood frames and sash. Window and door frames at the lower floors are of decorative cast iron. There were initially cast-iron-and-glass marquees at the main entrances. The original medium-gray granite plinth remains.

The interior was decorated with ornamental plasterwork. Some of the original cast-iron stair railings remain. Fred Baker recalled that the store was lit by carbon arc lamps with gas jets on top. There was originally a grand staircase leading from the main floor to the basement.

There are no light courts. The structure is steel frame with ribbed reinforced concrete slabs formed around integral terra-cotta tiles. The structure was designed to carry an additional four stories.

Spokane Ornamental Ironwork was one of the original subcontractors.

H.W. Corbett (1827-1903) moved to Portland from New York at age 24 to open the H.W. Corbett Co., a general merchandise store at Front and Oak. He was subsequently financially involved in the First National Bank, Oregon Iron Works, Willamette Iron Works, City and Suburban Railway Co., Portland Gas Co., and the Portland Hotel Co., to name a few. By 1870, he had become the largest non-corporate investor in downtown real estate. He was twice elected U.S. Senator, served as County Commissioner, and was appointed to the Water Committee.

The O'Shea Brothers, John F. and James B., are listed in the 1911 City Directory as "capitalists" with offices in the Merchants Trust Building.

Lipman, Wolfe & Co. was founded in 1850 by Solomon Lipman as a small merchandise store in Sacramento. Other branches were subsequently opened in Napa and Virginia City. Adolphe Wolfe (1848-1934), Lipman's nephew, left his native Germany in 1863 for California where he worked for his uncle. In 1880, Lipman sent Wolfe to Portland to establish a store. Wolfe purchased the small store of Clark, Henderson & Cook on First and Washington. Later his uncle joined him, and they relocated in the Dekum Building where they remained until the 1912 move to Fifth. The store has been sold five times: to National Dept. Store, South American Platinum Co., Roberts Bros. Dept. Store, Dayton Hudson, and in 1979 to Frederick & Nelson.

SOURCES

Baker, Fred C. Recorded interview by Janet Charlton, George McMath, and Anne Murphy, 1978. Notes in author's collection.

Doyle & Patterson. "Building for H.W. Corbett Estate and O'Shea Bros." (Working drawings), June, 1910. Microfiche Collection, City of Portland Bureau of Buildings.

Doyle & Patterson. "Lipman, Wolfe & Co." (Working drawings, ink-on-linen and pencil-on-paper). Collection, Oregon Historical Society.

Gladding, McBean & Co. Photographs, Shop Drawings.

Lockley, Fred. *History of the Columbia River Valley, vol. III*. Chicago, 1928.

MacColl, E. Kimbark. *The Shaping of a City, Business and Politics in Portland, Oregon, 1885 to 1915*. Portland, 1976.

Oregon Journal, Feb. 10, 1979, p. 2.

Oregonian, Jan. 1, 1910, sec. 2, p. 2, sec. 3, p. 10; Jan. 1, 1912, sec. 2, p. 2, col. 1; Jan. 1, 1913, sec. 3, p. 3.

The Pacific Coast Architect, vol. 3, no. 6 (Sept., 1912).

Photographs. Oregon Historical Society.

Plamondon, Al J., compiler. "The Plamondon Scrapbooks." Nov., 1955. Collection, Alfred Staehli.

Portland City Directory, 1911.

Roberts, Bill. Unrecorded interview by author, 1980.

Vaughan, Thomas and Virginia Guest Ferriday. *Space, Style and Structure; Building in Northwest America*. Portland, 1974.

The Journal Building was occupied by the *Oregon Journal* until 1948 when the newspaper sold it and moved to a new, larger building on the waterfront. In 1951, the new owners renamed it "Jackson Tower," after C.S. Jackson, publisher of the *Journal*.

The freestanding office tower, unique for Portland's glazed terra-cotta buildings, was a popular form for newspaper buildings throughout the United States at the time. The Reid Brothers firm designed a building similar to the Journal Building for the San Francisco *Call*; it was, however, remodeled beyond recognition in 1938.

The lower floors of the Journal Building are faced with white glazed terra cotta and the upper floors with brick. Terra-cotta ornament includes roof cornice, decorative panels, and lion's head, cartouche, and garlands above the main entrance.

The building is outlined with 1800 light bulbs, which screw into sockets incorporated directly into the terra cotta. During World War II, these lights were turned off to save energy and were not relighted until 1972.

The four large clocks that top the tower originally operated on battery impulses from a master clock in the basement. They were electrified in 1922. While the *Journal* occupied the building, the clocks chimed every 15 minutes.

The building's base, with large arches and heavy rustication, was "modernized" in 1950 and 1953, at the latter date with a four-inch Arizona fieldstone veneer. The original form was restored in 1975, but with stucco rather than terra cotta.

The structure is steel frame.

Dinwiddie Construction Company was the original general contractor.

Charles Samuel Jackson (1860-1924), a Virginian by birth, moved to Portland from Pendleton where he had owned the *East Oregonian*. He purchased the *Evening Journal*, renamed it the *Oregon Daily Journal*, and remained in Portland as its publisher. He was an active supporter of many political and social causes.

SOURCES
Gladding, McBean & Co. Journal Building Shop Drawings, Photographs.
Oregon Journal, April 10, 1972.
Oregonian, Jan. 1914, sec. 4, p. 13.
Page, Charles Hall & Associate, Inc. *Splendid Survivors*. San Francisco, 1979.
Photographs. (Includes construction photographs.) Collection, Oregon Historial Society.
Reid Brothers "Building for the Journal... for C.S. Jackson, Esq." (Working drawings), Oct. 14, 1911.
 Microfiche Collection, City of Portland Bureau of Buildings.
Reid Brothers Watercolor Rendering. Collection, Oregon Historical Society.
Urban Tour Group. Tour Notes (undated and unpublished).
Vaughan, Thomas and Virginia Guest Ferriday. *Space, Style and Structure; Building in Northwest America*.
 Portland, 1974.

FIG. III-17.
JOURNAL BUILDING
Southeast corner of Broadway and Yamhill
1912
Designed by Reid Brothers (San Francisco)
Built for the *Oregon Journal*
Terra cotta by Gladding, McBean & Co.

FIG. III-18.
PLATT BUILDING
Southwest corner of Park and Washington
1913
Designed by Whitehouse & Fouilhoux
Built for Harrison Gray Platt and Robert Treat
Platt

This 50-by-100-foot, six-story building is small compared to other office buildings of the era. Its location on one of the half-size blocks originally intended as a continuation of the South Park Blocks perhaps accounts for this.

The main body of the building is faced with buff-colored brick. The base, which originally had glazed terra-cotta facing at the columns and spandrels, has been extensively remodeled. Early photographs show two semi-circular entrance marquees of metal and glass, also gone. The terra-cotta decoration at the upper story remains, as does the galvanized-iron cornice. Upper-window spandrels are of concrete. A flagpole with gold-leafed ball originally stood at the northeast corner of the roof.

The lobby and vestibule originally had marble floor, scagliola walls, ornamental plaster cornice, brass elevator doors, and wrought-iron railing with oak rail. Only the stair railing and plaster crown molding remain. Office corridors were terrazzo, and each office had a lavatory, chair rail, picture mold, and transom over the corridor door. The working drawings include an unusually clear and attractive drawing of the steam radiator system.

The structure is steel frame, with 13-foot-square bays. Structural designers were the Trussed Concrete Steel Company.

Harrison Gray Platt and Robert Treat Platt were brothers. Harrison, born in 1866 in Milford, Connecticut, received his Bachelor of Arts degree at Yale in 1888 and was enrolled for one year at the Yale Law School. After moving to Portland, he went to work in the law office of George H. Durham. The firm later became Durham & Platt, and Platt married Durham's daughter. He was admitted to the bar in 1890, became an instructor at the University of Oregon, and served as president of the University Club.

Robert was born in New York City in 1868 and spent his early life in Milford, Connecticut. In 1892, he graduated *magna cum laude* from Yale with a Bachelor of Law degree. He then moved to Portland and joined his brother's law firm, Durham & Platt. Robert Platt assisted in the organization of the Bankers & Lumbermen's Bank and in the founding of the Peninsular Bank at St. Johns, of which he was president and director.

SOURCES
Gaston, Joseph. *Portland, Oregon; Its History and Builders*. Chicago, 1911.
Oregon Journal, Dec., 1971.
Oregonian, Jan. 1, 1914, sec. 1, p. 7.
Photographs. Collection, Oregon Historical Society.
Whitehouse & Fouilhoux. "Platt Building" (Working drawings), Dec. 30, 1912. Microfiche Collection, City of Portland Bureau of Buildings.

FIG. III-19.
MORGAN BUILDING
South side of Washington between Broadway and Park
1913
Designed by Doyle, Patterson & Beach
Built for Morgan-Bushong Investment Co.

This half-block building was originally occupied predominantly by physicians. The exterior is faced with red tapestry brick and decorated with cream-colored glazed terra cotta. The bracketed cornice is galvanized iron. Ornamental motifs include dentils, fleur-de-lis, palmettes, egg-and-dart, lamb's tongue, bead-and-reel, acanthus leaves, shells, Neptune's forks, and dolphins. Rusticated terra cotta at the ground-floor columns was removed during an early remodel; the columns were subsequently faced with a ceramic veneer that matches the original terra cotta.

The building lobby initially had a terrazzo floor with marble base, wood crown molding, and ornamental plaster ceiling. A curved marble stair with cast-iron balustrade led to the basement barber shop. Elevators had cast-iron doors, cornices, and grilles. The lobby was remodeled in 1938-39 by Whitehouse & Church, architects. It was at that time that the present bronze entrance was installed.

W.L. Morgan (b. 1856), president of Morgan-Bushong Investment Co., was a native of Tennessee. He came to Portland in 1896. Having worked for insurance companies in Tennessee, New York, and Portland, he graduated in law from the University of Oregon in 1903 and went into business for himself in 1904. An apartment house that he built in 1903 was said to have been the first in Portland. By 1913, when the Morgan Building was constructed, he had built 35 apartment houses and a half-dozen business buildings. He was the senior member of the firm of Morgan, Fliedner and Boyce.

W.A.T. Bushong was formerly of the Bushong Printing Co.

SOURCES
Doyle, Patterson & Beach. "Morgan Building for Morgan-Bushong Inv. Co." (Ink-on-linen working drawings), Oct., 1912. Collection, Oregon Historical Society.
Doyle, Patterson & Beach. "Morgan Building for Morgan-Bushong Inv. Co." (Working drawings), Oct., 1912. Microfiche Collection, City of Portland Bureau of Buildings.
Oregon Brass Works. Photographs (alterations only).
Oregonian, Jan. 1, 1914, sec. 1, p. 1; April 4, 1966; June 3, 1967.
Scrapbook #45, p. 171. Collection, Oregon Historical Society.

As the photograph shows, the Northwestern National Bank Building was constructed directly across Morrison from McKim, Mead & White's 1890 Portland Hotel and backed up to A.E. Doyle's 1910 Selling Building. The three-story building at the right in the photograph was replaced in 1932 by the final segment of the Meier & Frank Co. department store building. In the foreground are the grounds of the 1869 federal (Pioneer) courthouse.

The site of the Northwestern National Bank Building had been occupied previously by the 1891 Richardsonian Romanesque Marquam Building. The Marquam was demolished in 1912 after its east wall collapsed and, upon inspection, other parts were found to be structurally unsound. Henry L. Pittock and his son-in-law Frederick W. Leadbetter, owners of the Marquam at the time of its demise, were organizers of the Northwestern National Bank; they were responsible for construction of the new office building with space for the bank on the first floor. The Northwestern National Bank failed in 1927, as did the two other banks that subsequently occupied the building.

The main shaft of the building is sheathed with smooth-faced buff brick (painted white in 1983). The lower and upper floors are faced with off-white glazed terra cotta. Decorative motifs in terra cotta include urns, egg-and-dart, an acanthus scroll terminated by griffins, and Corinthian column capitals with eagles. A terra-cotta roof balustrade became badly deteriorated and had to be removed. A terra-cotta doorway on Morrison was removed in 1936-37.

Windows at the lower and upper floors are set in cast-iron frames. These were until recently painted a greyish green, simulating weathered bronze. The main building entrance was remodeled in 1936-37 under the direction of A.E. Doyle's office, with Pietro Belluschi as designer. The extruded bronze for this entrance was fabricated by Oregon Brass Works. This entrance was further modified in 1984 when the present marquee was designed and installed.

The main lobby has been totally remodeled, probably at the same time as the entrance. Both the original and the replacement lighting fixtures were provided by Fred C. Baker.

According to the working drawings, the second-floor corridor was finished with cork tile and the upper-floor corridors with terrazzo. Offices had cement-finished floors. Woodwork was mahogany. Each office had a chair rail and picture molding. In spite of the wood doors and moldings, the building was considered "strictly fireproof" and tenants were asked to use as much fireproof furniture as possible.

The basic structure consists of a steel frame with ribbed concrete slabs.

Dinwiddie Construction Co. was the original contractor. Iron stairs were made by City Iron Works.

Henry L. Pittock (1836-1919) arrived in Portland in 1853 to become an assistant on *The Morning Oregonian*, then a struggling weekly. Within seven years he became the paper's owner; the following year he made it a daily. He maintained control of the paper until his death. Following the 1893 marriage of Frederick W. Leadbetter to Pittock's daughter Caroline, Pittock and Leadbetter combined talents to put together a vast timber and paper empire. The two were also extensively involved in real estate and banking.

SOURCES

Baker, Fred C. Recorded interview by Janet Charlton, George McMath, and Anne Murphy, 1978. Notes in author's collection.

Cheney, Charles H. "The Work of Albert E. Doyle, Architect of Portland, Oregon," *The Architect and Engineer*, LVIII, no. 1 (July, 1919) 39-86.

Doyle, Patterson & Beach. "Northwestern Bank Building" (Ink-on-linen working drawings), Feb. 5, 1913. Collection, Oregon Historical Society.

"Northwestern Bank Building" (Working drawings), Feb. 5, 1913. Microfiche Collection, City of Portland Bureau of Buildings.

MacColl, E. Kimbark. *The Growth of a City; Power and Politics in Portland, Oregon, 1915 to 1950*. Portland, 1979.

MacColl, E. Kimbark. *The Shaping of a City; Business and Politics in Portland, Oregon, 1885 to 1915*. Portland, 1976.

Oregonian, Jan. 1, 1913, sec. 3, p. 3; Jan. 1, 1914, p. 13.

Vaughan, Thomas and Virginia Guest Ferriday. *Space, Style and Structure; Building in Northwest America*. Portland, 1974.

FIG. III-20.

NORTHWESTERN NATIONAL BANK BUILDING
North side of Morrison between Sixth and Broadway
1913
Designed by Doyle, Patterson & Beach
Built for Northwestern National Bank
Terra cotta by Gladding, McBean & Co.

FIG. III-21.
OREGON HOTEL
Southwest corner of Broadway and Oak
1913
Designed by Doyle, Patterson & Beach
Built for Simon Benson
Terra cotta by Washington Brick, Lime &
Sewer Pipe Co.
Portland Landmark

This red brick and off-white glazed terra-cotta hotel was renamed for its owner soon after completion. Because it was built adjacent to the existing Oregon Hotel to the south, it was, at the time of construction, often referred to as "The New Oregon Hotel." The older hotel building was demolished to make way for the 1959 addition.

The design of the hotel was inspired by Chicago's famous Blackstone Hotel. The enormous copper-colored mansard roof is actually part copper and part terra cotta glazed the color of weathered copper. (The shingle-like tiles are terra cotta.) Other terra-cotta elements include dormers, consoles, bracketed pediments, and false balustrades. A metal railing, which circled the building atop the cornice, has been removed. The metal-and-glass marquee at the main entrance collapsed in a heavy snow and was also removed. A smaller original marquee remains at the Oak Street façade.

The interior has been refurbished recently, and the ornamental plasterwork and wood paneling cleaned and refinished. The lobby's gilded, coffered, plaster ceiling is especially fine. Lobby paneling is Circassian walnut, the originally planned Pavonazza marble having been eliminated because of its high cost. Fred C. Baker designed the lighting fixtures and had them fabricated in Chicago.

Sound Construction and Engineering Co., Inc. of Portland and Seattle was the general contractor. E.C. McDougall was the plastering contractor; Hanford & Sutthoff of Seattle supplied the mahogany; Washington, Brick, Lime & Sewer Pipe Co. provided the brick (referred to as "mission" brick).

Simon Benson (1852-1942) was born in Norway. After working for a number of years in the Northwest as a farmer and logger, he began to acquire forest land. He built donkey engines, constructed a logging rail line, and rafted logs to southern California. In 1910, he sold his timber holdings for $4.5 million. Benson built his hotel on land that was owned by his close friend John Yeon, who also had made a fortune in the lumber business and was investing in real estate in downtown Portland. When, not long after its opening, the hotel was losing money, Benson assumed management and soon had it operating at a profit. Portlanders know Benson, not only for his hotel, but also for the bronze drinking fountains that he donated to the city and for Benson Polytechnic High School for which he gave $100,000 to construct the initial structure. He was an active supporter of the "Good Roads Movement" in Oregon. He moved to Beverly Hills in 1921.

SOURCES
Baker, Fred C. Recorded interview by Janet Charlton, George McMath, and Anne Murphy, 1978. Notes in author's collection.
Cheney, Charles H. "The Work of Albert E. Doyle, Architect of Portland, Oregon," *The Architect and Engineer*, LVIII, no. 1 (July, 1919) 39-86.
Doyle, Patterson & Beach. "Oregon Hotel for S. Benson" (Working drawings), 1912. Microfiche Collection, City of Portland Bureau of Buildings.
MacColl, E. Kimbark. *The Growth of a City; Power and Politics in Portland, Oregon, 1915 to 1950*. Portland, 1979.
MacColl, E. Kimbark. *The Shaping of a City; Business and Politics in Portland, Oregon 1885 to 1950*. Portland, 1976.
Oregonian, Jan. 1, 1914, sec. 1, p. 1; Jan. 1, 1916, sec. 4, p. 3.
The Pacific Coast Architect, vol. 2, no. 4 (Jan., 1912).
Photographs. Collection, Oregon Historical Society.
Portland Architectural Club Yearbook, 1913.
Vaughan, Thomas and Virginia Guest Ferriday. *Space, Style and Structure; Building in Northwest America*. Portland, 1974.

This 50-by-100-foot office building is nearly identical to the 1911 Wilcox Building, also designed by Whidden & Lewis for Theodore B. Wilcox.

The main body of the building is faced with buff-colored brick and the upper stories with off-white glazed terra cotta. The deep overhanging terra-cotta roof cornice incorporates a dentil course, block modillions, and lions' heads. The original terra cotta at the lower floors has been removed.

The storefronts, which, according to the working drawings, would be "arranged to suit the tenants," had undivided areas of glass below the transoms and transom lights approximately 3-feet-by-6-feet above. An ornate cast-iron, copper, and ribbed wired-glass marquee hung at the building entrance. Marquee chains were attached to cast-iron lions' heads at the spandrel beam. Main entrance doors were also of cast iron. A flagpole with a 16-inch gilded ball stood on the roof at the center of the Washington Street façade.

Each office had a concrete floor, wood base, wood picture mold, and lavatory. There was marble wainscoting in the corridors and in the restrooms, which also had marble tile floors.

The steel-frame and ribbed-concrete-slab structural system was designed by the Trussed Concrete Steel Company. The ribbed slab was noted as a "Floretyle" system on the working drawings.

The Drayton Engineering Co. acted as general contractor.

For information on Theodore B. Wilcox, see data on the Imperial Hotel. (Fig. III-5.)

SOURCES

MacColl, E. Kimbark. *The Growth of a City; Power and Politics in Portland, Oregon, 1915 to 1950*. Portland, 1979.

MacColl, E. Kimbark. *The Shaping of a City; Business and Politics in Portland, Oregon, 1885 to 1915*. Portland, 1976.

Photographs. Collection, Oregon Historical Society.

Vaughan, Thomas and Virginia Guest Ferriday. *Space, Style and Structure; Building in Northwest America*. Portland, 1974.

Whidden & Lewis. "Stevens Building, for Mr. T.B. Wilcox" (Working drawings), 1913. Microfiche Collection, City of Portland Bureau of Buildings.

FIG. III-22.

STEVENS BUILDING

Southeast corner of Ninth and Washington
1914
Designed by Whidden & Lewis
Built for Theodore B. Wilcox

FIG. III-23.

PITTOCK BLOCK

Entire block between Tenth and Eleventh, Washington and Stark

1914-South half, Lower two floors of north half

1923-North half above second floor

Designed by Doyle & Patterson

Built for Pittock Block Inc. (Herbert Fleishhacker)

Terra cotta by N. Clark & Son

The site on which the Pittock Block is located was previously the location of Henry Pittock's house. In 1913, the block was leased by Pittock to Herbert L. Fleishhacker of San Francisco for 99 years. Fleishhacker agreed to construct a building, worth not less than $650,000, to be named "Pittock Building." He formed Pittock Block Inc., in which he maintained a majority interest, for that purpose.

The building is faced with smooth, buff-colored brick. The rather scanty glazed terra-cotta ornament is off-white.

The storefronts, some of which are unaltered, had marble bases with cast-iron grilles. The lobby and interior arcade originally had terrazzo floors with marble borders, marble wainscoting, ornamental plasterwork, and a leaded-glass skylight. The lobby and Washington Street entrance were altered by A.E. Doyle's office in 1939. There have been several subsequent renovations of the interior. Only a bit of egg-and-dart crown molding remains, hidden by a hung ceiling.

The basic structure is reinforced concrete with ribbed concrete slabs. The basement was built to house the electric substation and westside distributing plant for Northwestern Electric Company. For many years it provided both steam and direct current generation to run elevators for downtown buildings.

For information on Henry Pittock, see data on the Northwestern National Bank Building. (Fig. III-20.)

Herbert L. Fleishhacker, one of California's most powerful capitalists and close friend of the Meier family of Meier & Frank, invested in numerous Portland enterprises: Northwestern Electric Power Company, the Northwestern National Bank, and the *Portland Telegram*.

SOURCES

Doyle & Patterson. "Building for the Pittock Block Inc." (Ink-on-linen working drawings), 1913. Collection, Oregon Historical Society.

Doyle & Patterson. "Building for the Pittock Block Inc." (Working drawings), 1913. Microfiche Collection, City of Portland Bureau of Buildings.

Forrester, Steve. "Pittock pegged rent right," *Willamette Week* (week ending Aug. 30, 1976), p. 1.

MacColl, E. Kimbark. *The Growth of a City; Power and Politics in Portland, Oregon, 1915 to 1950*. Portland, 1979.

MacColl, E. Kimbark. *The Shaping of a City; Business and Politics in Portland, Oregon, 1885 to 1915*. Portland, 1976.

Oregon Journal, July 29, 1965.

Oregonian, July 23, 1907, p. 10; Jan. 1, 1914, sec. 1, p. 16.

The Pacific Coast Architect, vol. 5, no. 3 (June, 1913).

Photographs. Collection, Oregon Historical Society.

Vaughan, Thomas and Virginia Guest Ferriday. *Space, Style and Structure; Building in Northwest America*. Portland, 1974.

This is one of the few glazed terra-cotta buildings in Portland with its exterior essentially as it was originally constructed. It was specifically designed to complement the newly erected Oregon Hotel to the west. The lower floors are faced with off-white terra cotta. The upper floors are faced with combed-face red brick and trimmed in terra cotta. The roof balustrade and cornice are galvanized iron, painted to match the terra cotta.

Window and door frames at the lower floors are cast iron. The 1914 half originally had upper windows of wood, but they were replaced with metal frames when the south half was built.

The structure is steel.

SOURCES

Gladding, McBean & Co. Pacific Telephone & Telegraph Co. shop drawings.
Hamrick, James, "National Register of Historic Places Inventory — Nomination Form, Pacific Telephone & Telegraph Co." (Not submitted.)
Oregonian, Jan. 1, 1913, sec. 3, p. 3; Jan. 1, 1914, sec. 1, p. 3.
The Pacific Coast Architect, vol. 2, no. 6 (March, 1912), p. 289.
Pacific Telephone & Telegraph Co. Building Dept.; A.E. Doyle, Supervising Architect. "The Pacific Telephone & Telegraph Co., Additions & Alterations" (Working drawings), Aug. 14, 1926. Microfiche Collection, City of Portland Bureau of Buildings.
Photographs. Collection, Oregon Historical Society.

FIG. III-24.
PACIFIC TELEPHONE & TELEGRAPH CO.
Southeast corner of Park & Oak
1914-North half
1926-South half
Designed by Edwin V. Cobby (San Francisco);
A.E. Doyle & Associates, Associate Architects
Built for Pacific Telephone & Telegraph Co.
Terra cotta by Gladding, McBean & Co.

The lower floors of this delicate little building were covered with brick veneer in 1971. The remaining terra cotta is off-white. Terra-cotta antefixae, lions' heads, consoles, and frieze at the roof cornice are all nicely modeled. The original Chicago windows, relatively rare in Portland, were a logical design element for architect Bennes, who worked in Chicago before moving to Oregon.

In 1936, the first-floor façade was remodeled for Ungar's, a women's specialty clothing store. McClelland & Jones were the architects. Their design was an elegant example of the Moderne. Oregon Brass Works produced the cast bronze. It was probably at the time of this remodel that the original marquee was removed.

SOURCES

Bennes, John V. "Building for Mr. Anton Huth" (Working drawings), 1916. Microfiche Collection, City of Portland Bureau of Buildings.
Oregon Brass Works Photograph.
Photographs. Collection, Oregon Historical Society.

FIG. III-25.
H. LIEBES & CO.
West side of Broadway between Morrison and Alder
1917
Designed by John Virginius Bennes
Built for Anton Huth to be occupied by H. Liebes & Co.

FIG. III-26.

UNITED STATES NATIONAL BANK

North side of Stark between Sixth and Broadway

1917-East half

1925-West half

Designed by A.E. Doyle

Built for United States National Bank

Terra cotta by Gladding, McBean & Co.

Portland Landmark

Modeled on McKim, Mead & White's Knickerbocker Trust Building in New York City (now demolished), this bank temple is very much like the 1907 Bank of California building in San Francisco by Bliss & Faville, which was also inspired by the Knickerbocker. The style is Roman, and the 54-foot-high Corinthian columns are the building's most striking feature. According to a contemporary description, these columns symbolized "the soaring power of finance in a wealthy civilization."

With the exception of the granite plinth, the exterior is sheathed entirely in glazed terra cotta. The light pinkish-gray, matte glaze was developed especially for the project. Decorative terra-cotta features, in addition to the giant columns, include a roof balustrade, lions' heads, palmettes, egg-and-dart, rosettes, rinceau, winged figures, cornucopias, meandering frets, lamb's tongue, beading, acanthus leaves, fish scales, eagles, and urns.

Window frames and spandrels along Stark are of cast iron. Window and door frames, doors, and grilles at the Sixth Avenue and Broadway entrances are of cast bronze. The design for the massive bronze sliding entrance doors was drawn from the Gates of Paradise on the Baptistry in Florence, Italy. Avard Fairbanks, at one time professor of sculpture at the University of Oregon, designed the western doors with panels depicting "Land Transportation" and "Progress by Water," following the theme "The Development of the Oregon Country."

The 30-foot-high main banking space, with mezzanines along its two long sides, occupies the entire street level. Dominated by a beautifully-colored, coffered-plaster ceiling, this room has cast-plaster eagles at column capitals, a marble tile floor (Italian and Hungarian), and marble teller enclosures (Hauteville). Walls of the basement public space are also lined with marble (Tennessee), and the floor of the loggia at the west entrance is a marble mosaic. The bronze lighting fixtures, both inside and out, were designed by Fred C. Baker.

Third- and fourth-floor offices face into an interior light court. The fourth-floor offices were completely redone in 1948, using Oregon myrtle for paneling and desks that follow a design by Pietro Belluschi. The Board Room, in original condition, has a marble fireplace and stained-glass windows by the Povey Brothers.

Terra-cotta flower boxes along the Sixth Avenue façade, flower pots originally in the main banking room, and two fountains for the roof garden were also produced by Gladding, McBean & Co.

In 1919, the Oregon chapter of the A.I.A. named the bank one of the ten most notable examples of architecture in Portland.

The United States National Bank first opened in 1891, at First and Pine. An 1892 fire forced a move to Second and Stark, and, in 1902, the bank moved to Third and Oak. The next move was to the present location. In 1978, the bank was the 39th largest in the United States and had 158 branches. It was the first bank in the world to process checks by computer.

SOURCES

Baker, Fred C. Recorded interview by Janet Charlton, George McMath, and Anne Murphy, 1978. Notes in author's collection.

Cheney, Charles H. "The Work of Albert E. Doyle, Architect, of Portland, Oregon," *The Architect and Engineer*, vol. LVIII, no. 1, (July, 1919), 39-86.

Doyle, A.E. "United States National Bank of Portland, Ore." (Pencil-and ink-on-linen working drawings), 1916. Collection, Oregon Historical Society.

Gladding, McBean & Co. *Shapes of Clay* (Feb., 1926).

Gladding, McBean & Co. Shop Drawings.

Oregon Brass Works. Shop Drawings.

Photographs. Collection, Oregon Historical Society.

United States National Bank. "Beauty in Wood; Some interesting facts about rare Oregon Myrtle and its use in the 4th floor of the United States National Bank of Oregon" (Pamphlet), no date.

United States National Bank. "Bronze Doors, Broadway Entrance, United States National Bank, Portland, Oregon."

United States National Bank News Release (June 21, 1978).

Vaughan, Thomas and Virginia Guest Ferriday. *Space, Style and Structure; Building in Northwest America*. Portland, 1974.

Vaughan, Thomas and George McMath. *A Century of Portland Architecture*. Portland, 1969.

When completed, this was said to be the largest Elks Temple in the country. It was the fourth home for the Portland lodge, which had organized in 1889 with a membership of 25. The lodge was to occupy this building for only 17 years. During the Depression, hundreds of members had to be dropped for non-payment of dues (1,482 at a single meeting in March, 1932); the lodge went bankrupt and lost the building in 1937. It remained vacant until 1939 when the Works Progress Administration took occupancy and set some 1,000 seamstresses to work in the lodge hall, billiard room, and library where they made garments for the poor. During the Second World War, the building was used as a United States Armed Forces Induction Headquarters. Two athletic clubs subsequently occupied the building, the Cosmopolitan Club in 1950 and the Columbia Athletic Club from 1952 to 1958. It stood vacant again from 1959 to 1973, when it was rented to a variety of operations, including the Pussy Cat Theater and the Paddle Palace, a table tennis center operated by the father of Olympic table tennis champion Judi Bochenski. It is presently being renovated for office use.

The design was adapted from the Farnese Palace in Rome. With the exception of the sheet-metal cornice and glass storefronts, the façades are entirely of a pinkish glazed terra cotta. Decorative motifs in terra cotta include an ornamental balustrade, Doric columns, Minoan wave band, triglyphs, metopes, rams' heads, rams' skulls, shields with fleur-de-lis, urns, and bas-relief panels with draped female figures. There are inscriptions in English and Latin at the frieze and above the main entrance: Do Unto Others as You Would Have Them Do Unto You, Elk Living in the Northern Sphere, Truth is Great and Will Prevail, and Love Conquers All.

Interior spaces are richly and variously decorated. Cast-plaster decoration in the lodge hall, ballroom, and ladies' lounge is exceptional. The billiard room is ornamented with plaster snakes, griffins, and parrots. The main lobby and library have coffered plaster ceilings. Ceilings in the banquet room and ballroom-banquet room foyer have painted decoration, somewhat Pompeian in feeling.

The building was lighted by Fred C. Baker. The lodge hall chandeliers are intact and in place. Most of the ballroom chandeliers are in place, but minus their crystals, which were stolen.

There were originally 100 small bedrooms on the upper floors. The basement housed a tiled swimming pool, gymnasium, weight room, handball court, and baths.

The basic structure is steel frame with reinforced-concrete floor systems.

Subcontractors, in addition to the Denny, Renton Clay & Coal Co. and Fred C. Baker's firms (Baker Manufacturing Co. and J.C. English Co.) were numerous: W.F. Blaesing (painting and decorating); Builders Hardware & Supply Co.; Builders Brick Co.; Columbia Wire & Iron Works; Eiseman Hardwood Floor Co.; Grand Sheet Metal Works; Lanning & Hoggan (plasterwork); Nicolai-Neppach Co. (mill work); Otis Elevator Co.; Schanen Marble Works; and Fred W. Wagner (mosaic tile).

SOURCES

"BPOE Temple 142" (Pamphlet). Collection, Multnomah County Library.

Houghtaling & Dougan. "Elks' Club Building" (Ink- and pencil-on-linen working drawings), Nov. 30, 1920. Collection, Don Stastny, architect.

Tess, John M. "National Register of Historic Places Inventory — Nomination Form, Old Elks Temple," no date.

Vaughan, Thomas and Virginia Guest Ferriday. *Space, Style and Structure; Building in Northwest America*. Portland, 1974.

FIG. III-27.

ELKS TEMPLE

Southeast corner of Eleventh and Alder

1920

Designed by Houghtaling & Dougan

Built for Elks Lodge #142

Terra Cotta by Denny, Renton Clay & Coal Co.

Portland Landmark

Listed in National Register

FIG. III-28.

FITZPATRICK BUILDING

West side of Ninth between Oak and Burnside
1922
Designed by Houghtaling & Dougan
Built for T.M. Fitzpatrick

This small office building sits on one of the irregular-shaped blocks created by the juncture of the Portland Plat and Couch's Addition. It is faced with buff-colored brick and has cream-colored glazed terra cotta at the ground floor and over the fourth-floor windows. Baskets and urns in terra cotta terminate pilasters and window mullions. Spiral terra-cotta columns accent the corners. Brickwork features quoining, raised panels, and a diaper pattern. Except for a zigzag motif, the galvanized iron cornice is quite plain.

Upper-story windows and ground-floor transoms were all originally of the awning type. Some upper-story windows have been replaced. Most of the original wood panels and window and doorframes at the first floor are intact.

The structural system combines a reinforced-concrete frame at the exterior walls with a wood floor system.

SOURCES

Houghtaling & Dougan. "Building for T.M. Fitzpatrick" (Working drawings), Jan. 6, 1922. Microfiche Collection, City of Portland Bureau of Buildings.
Photographs. Collection, Oregon Historical Society.

FIG. III-29.

ODD FELLOWS BUILDING

Southwest corner of Tenth and Salmon
1922
Designed by Ernst Kroner
Built for I.O.O.F.
Listed in National Register

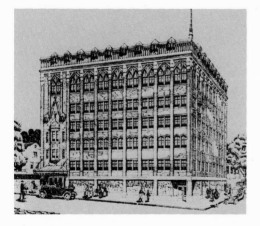

This combination lodge-office-and-retail building was sold by the Odd Fellows and converted in 1980 to federally-subsidized housing. Although extensive alterations were made internally, the exterior remains in its original condition.

The façades are faced with gray, combed-face brick and decorated with cream-colored glazed terra cotta. Along the parapet are terra-cotta, canopy-like features, evidently intended to be baldachins. The incorporation of these and other Gothic motifs with religious associations is explained by the Biblical roots of the Odd Fellows organization. The interiors of the baldachins were originally lighted.

Above the building entrance is a two-story-high glazed terra-cotta oriel window. At the same entrance is Portland's only glazed terra-cotta marquee. It has a cream-colored opalescent glass skirt. Over the entrance marquee is an opalescent stained-glass window that depicts David and Jonathan (personifications of strength and friendship). It is similar to windows by the Povey Brothers.

There were originally two large interior spaces: lodge hall and ballroom. Neither survived the remodeling. The balconied lodge hall was paneled in mahogany and had a decorative plaster ceiling. A series of murals depicted the Biblical scenes from which the Odd Fellow "degrees" are derived. The ballroom was also decorated with cast plaster. It had a large mezzanine.

The original building lobby was retained, along with its marble stairs, plaster "marble" wainscoting, and brass handrails. Some of the original brass doorknobs with the Odd Fellows symbol (three linked rings for friendship, love, and truth) were also retained.

Although original construction commenced in 1922, and that is the date on the cornerstone, the building was not actually completed until 1924 and was not dedicated until 1925.

SOURCES

Bonds, Ainslie, Grand Secretary, I.O.O.F. Unrecorded interview by the author, ca. 1979.
Kroner, Ernst. "Odd Fellows Building" (Working drawings). Microfiche Collection, City of Portland Bureau of Buildings.
Photographs. Collection, Oregon Historical Society.
Williams, James M. and Linda K. Emery. "National Register of Historic Places Inventory — Nomination Form, Odd Fellows Building," April 4, 1980.

When officially opened in February, 1923, this apartment hotel was hailed as the first of its kind in Portland. Designed for the sophisticated urban dweller who did not wish to devote time to housekeeping, each unit came completely furnished and had a living room (with French doors opening onto a tiny balcony), dining alcove, kitchenette, dressing room, bathroom, and Murphy bed. Residents could take their meals at Henry Thiele's Cafe, which occupied the lower floor.

Exterior walls are faced with peach-colored glazed terra cotta at the lower two floors and red tapestry brick at the upper floors. Quoining, parapet facing, and decorative elements are also of terra cotta. Terra-cotta ornamental features are varied: lions' heads, eagles, and the name "Sovereign" at the entrance; balustrades, Doric columns, and segmental-arched pediments at the third floor; bracketed balconies at floors four through eight; and decorative cornice, urns, and broken pediment with Doric columns and crest at the top floor. North and east balconies have the original wrought-iron railings with cast-iron Sovereign crests affixed. The original metal-and-glass entrance marquee no longer remains. The large roof sign with lighted individual letters applied to an open trusswork support, which originally faced northeast, has also been removed.

Fred C. Baker provided lighting fixtures for both the interior and exterior. Bronze fixtures at the Madison entrance (originally the restaurant entrance and now the main building entrance) are in place, as are several fixtures on the main floor.

The main-floor layout has been substantially altered. Some of the interior features, including tilework and wrought-iron stair railings are, however, intact. Original brass hardware has also been retained throughout the building.

In 1973, the apartment units were remodeled and the Murphy beds removed.

SOURCES
Photographs. Collection, Oregon Historical Society.
Portland Historical Landmarks Commission Inventory Form.
Wade, Susan O. "National Register of Historic Places Inventory — Nomination Form, Sovereign Hotel," August 14, 1980.

FIG. III-30.
SOVEREIGN HOTEL
Southwest corner of Broadway and Madison
1922
Designed by Carl Linde
Built for Sovereign Hotel Company (Richard F. Wassell and Claude D. Starr)
Portland Landmark
Listed in National Register

FIG. III-31.

FIRST CHRISTIAN CHURCH

Northeast corner of Park and Columbia
1922
Designed by C.W. Bulgar & Son (Dallas, Texas)
Built for First Christian Church

The First Christian Church (Disciples of Christ) purchased its site facing the South Park Blocks from the Methodist Church in 1880. The double lot had been deeded in 1853 to the Methodists by D.H. Lownsdale as a site for a "Female Seminary of Learning," at the same time that he deeded the Park Blocks to the City and other blocks to the Baptist and Evangelical Churches, Sons of Temperance, and Masons. The present church structure is the congregation's fourth, all on this site; it is the only pioneer church in Portland to have kept its original location.

C.W. Bulgar & Son were specialists in church architecture. Both father and son were members of the Disciples of Christ. In resolving to build a new building, the church board stated in 1919: "Its style of architecture shall be very plain and substantial following straight lines and providing for up-to-date equipment for Bible School and for the general use of religious education." Central in plan, with gables facing Park and Columbia, the church's bulk provides a point of interest as well as an important sense of enclosure for the Park Blocks. Exterior walls are composed of a red tapestry brick base, with grey tapestry brick above laid in a variety of decorative patterns and cream-colored glazed terra-cotta embellishment. A flight of red brick steps spills out from the corner entrance portico. The Doric portico columns and entablature are also of terra cotta. The roof, originally of red tile, has been re-roofed with composition shingles.

Of unusual interest are the art-glass windows produced by the Povey Brothers of Portland. Two sanctuary windows, adapted from Hunt's "Light of the World" and Hoffman's "Jesus in the Garden," are back-lit.

Minor alterations were made to the sanctuary in 1947. In 1952, the basement was extensively remodeled. The north addition dates from ca. 1955.

The congregation, which began with five members in 1879, was, by 1903, the third largest in Portland. Its ministry has included the founding of a Chinese Mission in Portland around 1890, sending aid to San Francisco after the earthquake, establishing the Men's Resort on Skid Road around 1898, and, more recently, sponsoring housing for the low-income elderly and operating a day-care center.

SOURCES
Bulgar, C.W. & Son. "First Christian Church" (Working drawings), March 3, 1921. Microfiche Collection, City of Portland Bureau of Buildings.
First Christian Church. *Seventy-Five Years; A History of First Christian Church, Portland, Oregon*. Portland, 1955.
Oregonian, July 21, 1979, p. A13.
Photographs. Collection, Oregon Historical Society.
Povey Brothers Exhibit. Oregon Historical Society.

FIG. III-32.

PORTLAND TELEGRAM BUILDING

Northwest corner of Eleventh and Washington
1922
Designed by Rasmussen Grace Co., Engineers
Built for J.N. Barde, to be occupied by the *Portland Telegram*

The corner clock tower lends importance to what would otherwise be a rather nondescript structure. The exterior is faced with red brick and trimmed with off-white terra cotta. There has been no alteration to the façades at the upper floors; first-floor windows have been extensively modified.

General contractor was W.D. Andrews Construction Company.

The *Portland Telegram* was founded in 1877 by Henry L. Pittock, E.D. Crandall, and C.M. Elliott. John E. and L.R. Wheeler purchased it in 1914. In 1926, John Wheeler, heavily in debt, tried to sell the paper to the *Oregon Journal*. It was finally rescued in 1927 by Californians Herbert Fleishhacker and Carl Brockhagen. In 1931, it was acquired by the *Portland Daily News* and subsequently published as the *Portland News Telegram*.

Jacob N. (Jack) Barde (1888-1961) was born in St. Paul, Minnesota, and came to Portland with his parents in 1891. He was president of the Barde Wire Rope Co. and the Pacific Steel Warehouse Company. He also headed the Idaho Pacific Steel Warehouse Co. and the Moore Steel Service Co. of Eugene, Medford, and Roseburg.

SOURCES
Andrews, Mrs. John E. Unrecorded interview by the author, ca. 1980.
MacColl, E. Kimbark. *The Growth of a City; Power and Politics in Portland, Oregon, 1915 to 1950*. Portland, 1979.
Oregonian, Dec. 6, 1961.
Photographs. Collection, John E. Andrews.
Rasmussen Grace Company. "*Building for J.N. Barde, Agent*" (Working drawings), 1922. Microfiche Collection, City of Portland Bureau of Buildings.
Turnbull, George Stanley. *History of Oregon Newspapers*. Portland, 1939.
Vital Statistics. Oregon Historical Society.

This 105-room hotel was converted to 56 units of federally-subsidized housing in 1976. Newberry, Schuette & Wheeler were architects for the conversion.

The exterior is in near-original form. It is faced with red tapestry brick and trimmed in off-white terra cotta. Terra-cotta embellishments include decorative roof cornice, belt cornice, and window and door surrounds. Terra cotta at the belt cornice had deteriorated badly and was patched at the time of the 1976 remodel. The original entrance marquee has been replaced, and the restaurant entrance on the north side has undergone numerous changes.

SOURCES

Lofgren, Jean and Shirley Kuse. "Roosevelt Plaza Apartment Block," Urban Tour Group Notebook (Unpublished typescript). Portland, no date.
Oregonian, Dec. 1, 1976, p. D1.
Photographs. Collection, Oregon Historical Society.
Pioneer National Title Insurance. Title Abstract.
Wheeler, Andrew. Unrecorded interview by the author, ca. 1980.

FIG. III-33.
ROOSEVELT HOTEL
Southwest corner of Ninth and Salmon
1924
Designed by Claussen & Claussen
Built for Prudential Finance Corporation
(George Heathman and Dr. Earl Smith)

Bedell's store occupied the lower floors of this building; upper floors were offices. Much of the first floor was originally given over to an atrium lined with display windows. The main entrance to the atrium was through a two-story arched opening in the center of the Sixth Avenue façade. A connecting secondary entrance off Alder created a free-standing display window at the corner. (This is shown on the working drawings, but not the architect's rendering.) Nothing of the atrium or the arch remains, the first floors having been completely enclosed.

Façades are faced entirely with off-white glazed terra cotta. Decorative elements in terra cotta include two-story-high pilasters at the base and cap. Windows are steel.

According to a ca. 1925 promotional brochure, the elevator lobby and corridors were finished in Alabama marble, and doors and trim were mahogany.

It has a steel frame structure.

General contractor was Ross Hammond.

SOURCES

Bedell Building (Promotional pamphlet), ca. 1925. Collection, Multnomah County Library.
Photographs. Collection, Oregon Historical Society.
Schonewald, G.A., A.E. Doyle, Associate Architect. "The Bedell Building" (Working drawings). Microfiche Collection, City of Portland Bureau of Buildings.

FIG. III-34.
BEDELL BUILDING
Northeast corner of Sixth and Alder
1925
Designed by G.A. Schonewald (New York City); A.E. Doyle, Associate Architect.
Built for Bedell Co.

FIG. III-35.

BANK OF CALIFORNIA

Northeast corner of Sixth and Stark
1925
Designed by A.E. Doyle
Built for Bank of California
Terra cotta by N. Clark & Son
Portland Landmark
Listed in National Register

Located directly across Sixth from A.E. Doyle's United States National Bank, designed some ten years previously, this three-story, eighth-block building is a good example of the Italian Renaissance Palatial style popular during the mid-1920s. The exterior is sheathed in rusticated terra cotta, glazed to give the appearance of granite. The decorative cornice is also of terra cotta. Both the plinth and frieze are marble. (The frieze has been plastered over, evidently because of deterioration.) There are bronze grilles at the windows and a bronze pedimented entrance with bronze gates. The roof is red clay tile.

The main banking space was altered in 1977 when the building was acquired by an insurance firm for its own offices. The mezzanine was extended along the east wall and a stair added. The original polychrome plaster ceiling was, however, left intact, as was the marble floor. The original cast-plaster "travertine" interior wall finish is also in place, though it had been painted prior to 1977.

The Bank of California was founded in San Francisco in 1864. In 1905, it purchased the London & San Francisco Bank Ltd., thereby gaining offices in Portland, Tacoma, and Seattle. The London & San Francisco Bank Ltd. had established its first West Coast agency in San Francisco eight months after the Bank of California was founded. Its Portland office, established in 1882 in order to finance grain shipments, was first located at Third and Oak. It moved two years later to First Avenue and shortly thereafter to Third and Stark, where it was located when acquired by the Bank of California. The Bank of California remained at Third and Stark until its move to this structure. In 1970, it relocated to its own newly-constructed office tower one block to the southwest.

SOURCES
The Bank of California. *A Native of Oregon Since 1882* (Promotional brochure), 1982.
Doyle, A.E. "Bank of California" (Ink-on-linen working drawings), 1924. Collection, Oregon Historical Society.
Finch, H. Curtis. "National Register of Historic Places Inventory — Nomination Form, Bank of California Building (Old)," Dec. 5, 1977.
Photographs. Collection, Oregon Historical Society.
Vaughan, Thomas and Virginia Guest Ferriday. *Space, Style and Structure; Building in Northwest America*. Portland, 1974.
Vaughan, Thomas and George McMath. *A Century of Portland Architecture*, 2nd edition. Portland, 1969.

FIG. III-36.

MAYER BUILDING

Southeast corner of Twelfth and Morrison
1926
Designed by Schacht & Bergen
Built for Mark A. Mayer

The tile roof and decorative galvanized-iron cornice have been removed from this building. The ground-floor façades, which had undergone extensive alterations, have recently been restored to their near-original condition. The main entrance, with its large glazed terra-cotta consoles, door surround, and cast-iron balconet, is in place. Some serious deterioration of the terra cotta where the balconet posts are attached has been repaired. Terra-cotta belt cornices and decorative panels at the upper stories appear to be in good condition. Brick is a pale yellow.

According to the working drawings, the lobby was originally decorated with ornamental plasterwork, marble panels, bronze grilles, and a terrazzo floor with ceramic tile border. Fred C. Baker recalled lighting the building's offices with blown-glass units suspended on chains.

The basic structure is reinforced concrete.

SOURCES
Baker, Fred C. Recorded interview by Janet Charlton, George McMath, and Anne Murphy, 1978. Notes in author's collection.
Photographs. Collection, Oregon Historical Society.
Schacht & Bergen. "Store & Office Building for Mark A. Mayer" (Working drawings). Microfiche Collection, City of Portland Bureau of Buildings.

This is one of three downtown buildings designed by the A.E. Doyle firm in the Italian Renaissance Palatial mode. Its glazed terra-cotta cornice is identical to the one on the earlier Bank of California, which also had rusticated terra cotta, steel sash, and a red clay tile roof.

The upper floors of the Pacific Building are faced with buff-colored brick. Plinths and storefront bulkheads were originally marble. Spindles at the transom lights are cast iron.

The main lobby, entered through a two-story round arch, is essentially in its original condition. Lobby floors and walls are faced with marble. Doors, frames, lighting fixtures, grilles, etc. are of cast bronze. There is a coffered, barrel-vaulted ceiling with indirect lighting placed above a coved plaster molding.

Office corridor floors were terrazzo with marble bases. Offices had cement-finished floors. Each office had a lavatory.

There were two penthouse studios on the south wings, one for Mrs. Corbett and one for A.E. Doyle's architectural firm. Doyle's two-story office had a walnut-paneled library and marble fireplace. Mrs. Corbett's studio included a loggia, now enclosed with glass.

Design of the Pacific Building is attributed to Charles K. Greene. Greene, who had worked in Doyle's office since 1908, was placed in charge of design prior to this project. An avowed homosexual, he was, reportedly, not long after the building was completed, run out of town and later died of starvation in San Francisco.

For information on H.W. Corbett, see data on Lipman, Wolfe & Co. (Fig. III-16.)

SOURCES
Doyle, A.E. "Pacific Building for the H.W. Corbett Estate" (Pencil and ink-on-linen working drawings), June, 1925. Collection, Oregon Historical Society.
"Pacific Building for the H.W. Corbett Estate" (Working drawings), June, 1925. Microfiche Collection, City of Portland Bureau of Buildings.
MacColl, E. Kimbark. *The Shaping of a City; Business and Politics in Portland, Oregon, 1885 to 1915*. Portland, 1976.
Musick, Felicity. "The Development of the Pacific Building and the Public Service Building" (Unpublished thesis). Oregon Historical Society, 1976.
Oregon Brass Works. Pacific Building Shop Drawings.
"Pacific Building" (Promotional brochure distributed by Strong & MacNaughton Trust Company). Collection, Oregon Historical Society.
Photographs. Collection, Oregon Historical Society.
Vaughan, Thomas and Virginia Guest Ferriday. *Space, Style and Structure; Building in Northwest America*. Portland, 1974.

FIG. III-37.
PACIFIC BUILDING
South side of Yamhill between Fifth and Sixth
1926
Designed by A.E. Doyle
Built for H.W. Corbett Estate

S.H. Kress & Co. took great pride in its store buildings, many of which were faced with glazed terra cotta. At about the time this one was constructed, Kress, and architect Hoffman, abandoned classical motifs for Art Deco.

The Portland Kress building is faced entirely with cream-colored glazed terra cotta. Between the ground-floor pilasters, there were originally large transoms and recessed display windows. The traditional red-and-gold Kress sign ran along both street façades just above the transoms. Porcelain enamel panels now cover the area where the signs were. The ornament is relatively spare: cartouche over the corner pilasters, a modified wave scroll along the belt course, rosettes at the spandrel panels, a bracketed cornice with dentil course, and the name "Kress" in the two parapets. With the exception of the first-floor corner column, all terra cotta is in place.

A later two-story addition to the east was carried out in a similar style, using ceramic veneer and some pressed terra cotta for ornamental units. The interior was completely remodeled in 1975.

Pacific States Construction Company was the general contractor for the 1928 building.

SOURCES
Card Files, City of Portland Bureau of Buildings.
Gladding, McBean & Co. Photographs, Job List.
Photographs. Collection, Oregon Historical Society.
"Walking Tour of Downtown Asheville" (Includes Art Deco Kress building by E.J.T. Hoffman). The Preservation Society, Asheville, North Carolina, no date.

FIG. III-38.
S.H. KRESS & CO.
North side of Morrison between Fourth and Fifth
1928
Designed by E.J.T. Hoffman, S.H. Kress & Co.
Built for S.H. Kress & Co.

FIG. III-39.

Public Service Building

East side of Sixth between Salmon & Taylor
1928
Designed by A.E. Doyle
Built for Pacific Power & Light Co.
Terra cotta by N. Clark & Son

Originally occupied by the Portland Gas & Coke Co. and the Northwestern Electric Co., as well as the Pacific Power & Light Co., this was for 30 years the tallest building in Portland. Though a part of the original design, the present twelve-story wings were, for economic reasons, initially only two-stories high. They were increased to five stories in 1947-48 and to their full height in 1957.

It is said that the design was inspired by the Pacific Gas & Electric Co. building on Market Street in San Francisco. The buildings are certainly very similar. Charles K. Greene, in charge of design in A.E. Doyle's office, was initially responsible for design of the Public Service Building. He left Portland before design work was completed, however, and Pietro Belluschi, also at the time a designer in the Doyle office, was put in charge. (See data for Fig. III-37.) The original lobby (later completely remodeled by Skidmore, Owings & Merrill with Edgar Smith in charge) is said to have been Belluschi's work alone. A.E. Doyle died soon after construction was complete, and Belluschi's office produced plans for ensuing additions and alterations. Original structural design was by James Beach, son-in-law of Simon Benson and at one time a partner in the Doyle office.

General contractor was L.H. Hoffman.

The main body of the building is faced with gray brick. The lower two floors are faced with rusticated terra cotta, with a gray, granite-like glaze. A terra-cotta belt course with an enlarged and flattened wave scroll runs above the base. The corbeled cornice, loggia columns, and dentil course at the building's cap are also terra cotta.

The tower roof was originally red tile with a story-high sign on top. Individual letters outlined in neon on the sign spelled GAS, POWER, HEAT, and LIGHT on the four sides. The sign and tile roof were replaced with a metal roof in 1973.

Upper windows are steel frame. Windows at the base are cast iron painted a weathered bronze.

When it first opened, the Public Service Building was described as the latest word in efficiency. It had an elevator that could travel at 500 feet per minute, thermostatically-controlled heat and ventilation, and a garage in the basement. There were displays of appliances on the first floors. Six upper floors were rented to non-utility tenants.

SOURCES

Clark, N. and Son. "Public Service Building, Preliminary Jointing Plan" (Blueprint), Feb., 1927. Collection, Oregon Historical Society.

Dierdorff, John. *How Edison's Lamp Helped Light the West; The Story of Pacific Power & Light Company and Its Pioneer Forebears*. Portland, 1971.

Doyle, A.E. "Public Service Building" (Ink-on-linen and pencil-on-paper working drawings), 1926, 1927. Collection, Oregon Historical Society.

McMath, George. Talk on A.E. Doyle at A.I.A. Meeting. Portland, Jan. 17, 1983.

Musick, Felicity. "The Development of the Pacific Building and the Public Service Building" (Unpublished thesis). Oregon Historical Society, 1976.

Oregonian, Aug. 17, 1947.

Page, Charles Hall & Associates, Inc. *Splendid Survivors*. San Francisco, 1979.

Photographs. Collection, Oregon Historical Society.

Schlieman, Bonnie. Portland Historical Landmarks Commission Inventory Form, Pacific Building, undated.

Vaughan, Thomas and Virginia Guest Ferriday. *Space, Style and Structure; Building in Northwest America*. Portland, 1974.

This is Portland's only example of Art Deco, glazed terra cotta and one of   city's few examples of polychrome work. The façade was applied to the 1902 Dolph Building when the entire structure was remodeled. The basic color is black with textured gold ("real gold of 18 karat fineness" according to the 1930 newspaper account of the opening) which emphasizes the streamlined pilasters. The third-floor spandrels are decorated with peacocks and an abstract sunburst in cream-colored terra cotta. Directly above the third-story windows are spirals in cream-colored terra cotta. Above these panels are rain clouds and more sunbursts in dark greenish-blue terra cotta and along the roof a zigzag pattern. There are metal grilles over the first-floor windows. A similar grille with the store name in metal letters was originally located over the center entrance. The letters, which were for a time placed on the spandrel above after the grille was removed, are now in their original position, but with a new, simplified grille. The exterior metal fire escape dates from the 1930 remodel, as does the steel sash.

In Portland in 1930, this façade was considered rather extreme; it was, in fact, rare nation-wide. At the time, there were only two other buildings in the United States with 18-karat gold decoration: the American Radiator skyscraper in New York City and the twelve-story Richfield Oil Building in Los Angeles.

The Grand Rapids Store Equipment Corp. owned a subsidiary in Portland, the Portland Case Building Co., and this no doubt explains how the Michigan firm happened to be designer for the project. At the time, Grand Rapids was somewhat of a center for avant-garde design, much of it even more modern, though no more artistic, than the Berg building.

The ground floor of the remodeled building featured a large atrium with a free-standing shoe display window in the center. This atrium was completely enclosed in 1975 to create more selling-floor area. The first floor has recently been partially opened up to the basement, as a part of the building's conversion to lower-level retail and upper-level office space.

A description of the 1930 interior (none of which remains) is mouthwatering: elevator doors finished in a silver-stippled lacquer with black enameled columns; elevator cab designed by Tiffany with chromium-plated fixtures; lighting fixtures of bronze or satin silver with frosted glass; woodwork enameled in brown, jade green, or light orchid and silver; draperies with silver threads; and carpets in a large diagonal pattern grading from light violet to full mauve. In the ladies' lounge, decorator George A. Mansfield recreated the effect of the Submarine Gardens of the Catalina Islands, with blue walls, a mauve velvet divan, furniture finished in coral and silver, and a window covered in translucent hand-colored paper depicting a submarine scene with tropical fish.

Ross B. Hammond was general contractor; English Baker Company (Fred C. Baker) supplied the lighting fixtures; Shearer & Sons did the plasterwork; the Oregon Door Company supplied the millwork; Grand Sheet Metal Works produced metal work; and Columbia Wire & Iron Works fabricated the ornamental iron work.

Charles F. Berg (1871-1932) was born in San Francisco. His merchandising experience began at age ten when his father died and his mother started a store with the life insurance proceeds. Later he worked for Newman & Levinson on Kearney Street and, at age 19, took charge of a glove store in San Francisco. In 1907, he joined the Lennon Corporation as a full partner and opened a store on Morrison Street in Portland. In 1921, he dissolved the partnership but retained the Portland store, changing its name to Charles F. Berg, Inc. The following year, his son Forrest Berg came to Portland from San Francisco to join the enterprise. After his father's death, Forrest remained as manager, continuing until 1975 when the store merged with Rusan's, an eleven-unit chain.

SOURCES
Downtowner, Portland, June 23, 1975.
Gladding, McBean & Co. *Shapes of Clay*, 1930.
Gladding, McBean & Co. Job List.
The Grand Rapids Designing Service, Grand Rapids Store Equipment Corporation. "Alterations to Store for Charles F. Berg" (Working drawings), Oct. 30, 1929. Microfiche Collection, City of Portland Bureau of Buildings.
Moody's Manual of Investments, American and Foreign Industrial Securities, New York, 1930.
Oregonian, Jan. 31, 1930, sec. 3 (Entirely devoted to Charles F. Berg opening).
Photographs. Collection, Oregon Historical Society.
Tess, John. "National Register of Historic Places, Inventory — Nomination Form, Dolph Building," March 31, 1982.

FIG. III-40.
CHARLES F. BERG
West side of Broadway between Morrison and Alder
1930
Designed by The Grand Rapids Designing Service, Grand Rapids Store Equipment Corp.
Built for Charles F. Berg, Inc.
Terra cotta by Gladding, McBean & Co.
Listed in National Register

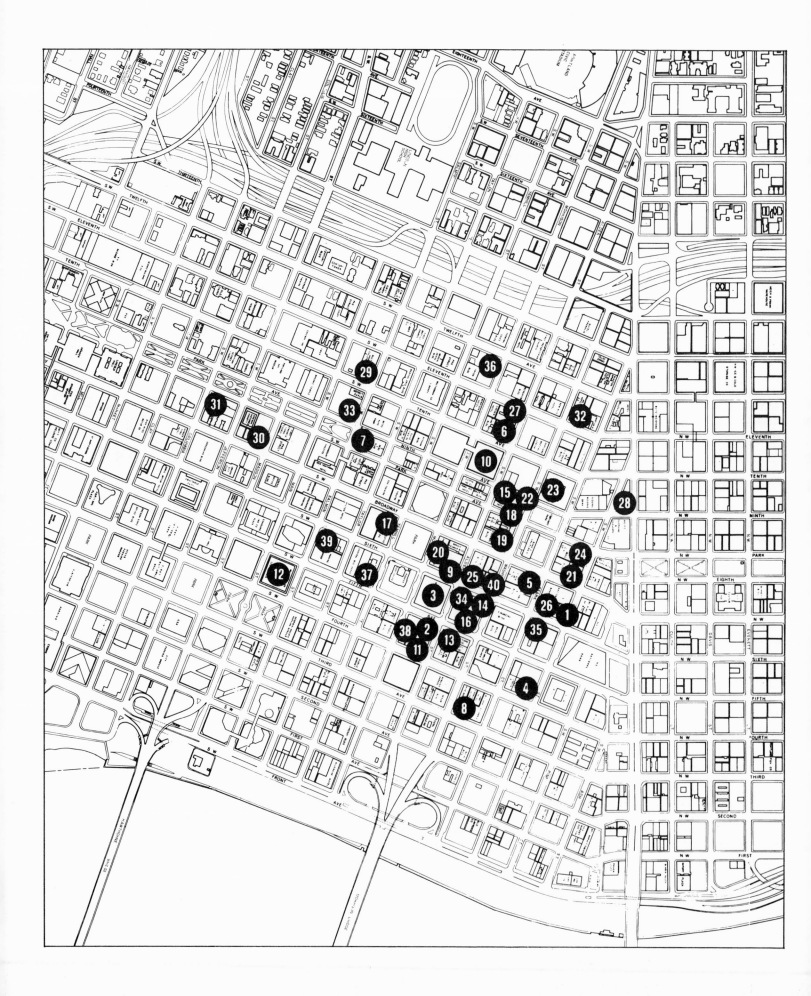

ALPHABETICAL LIST

ORIGINAL NAME	PRESENT NAME	MAP AND PART III ILLUSTRATION NUMBERS
Arlington Club	Unchanged	7
Bank of California	Durham & Bates	35
Bedell Building	Cascade Building	34
Charles F. Berg	Unchanged	40
Elks Temple	Unchanged	27
Failing Building	620 Building	2
First Christian Church	Unchanged	31
Fitzpatrick Building	North Pacific Building	28
Graves Music Company	Vacant	11
Henry Building	Unchanged	4
Imperial Hotel	Unchanged	5
Journal Building	Jackson Tower	17
S.H. Kress & Co.	Vacant	38
H. Liebes & Co.	Continental Crossroads	25
Lipman, Wolfe & Co.	Frederick & Nelson	16
Mayer Building	Unchanged	36
Meier & Frank Co.	Unchanged	3
Morgan Building	Unchanged	19
Multnomah County Courthouse	Unchanged	12
Northwestern Bank Building	American Bank Building	20
Odd Fellows Building	Chaucer Court	29
Olds, Wortman & King	Galleria	10
Oregon Hotel	Benson Hotel	21
Pacific Building	Unchanged	37
Pacific Telephone & Telegraph Co.	Capitol Building, Pacific Northwest Bell Building	24
Pittock Block	Unchanged	23
Platt Building	Park/Washington Building	18
Portland Telegram Building	Telegram Building	32
Public Service Building	Unchanged	39
Roosevelt Hotel	Roosevelt Plaza Apartments	33
Selling Building	Oregon National Building	9
Seward Hotel	Governor Hotel	6
Sovereign Hotel	Sovereign Apartments	30
Spalding Building	Oregon Bank Building	8
Stevens Building	Farwest Assurance Building	22
United States National Bank	Unchanged	26
Wells Fargo Building	United States National Bank Building	1
Wilcox Building	Unchanged	14
Woodlark Building	Unchanged	15
Yeon Building	Unchanged	13

Notes on the Architects

JOHN VIRGINIUS BENNES (1867-1943) was born in Peru, Illinois, but moved to Chicago with his family at age one. His father, John Virginius Benes, (spelling changed by his son) was uncle of Edward Benes, president of Chechoslovakia. Bennes attended the School of Fine Arts in Prague, Bohemia, for one year and also studied at Chicago University. He worked in his father's office and in his early twenties had his own office in Chicago. In 1900 he moved with his family to Baker, Oregon, and in 1906 to Portland. He was architect for Oregon State University for over 30 years and also a member of the Oregon State Board of Architect Examiners. he formed various partnerships during his career: Bennes, Hendricks & Tobey (1908-1909); Bennes, Hendricks & Thompson (1909); Bennes & Hendricks (1909-1913 and 1925); and Bennes & Herzog (1924-1928). In 1943 he moved to Los Angeles because of poor health.

SOURCES
Author's file containing miscellaneous clippings, photocopies, unpublished typescripts, correspondence, etc.

LEIGH L. DOUGAN (1883-1983) was born in Princeton, Indiana. He studied architecture at the Armour Institute of Technology in Chicago, withdrawing at the end of his junior year to obtain practical experience in Tulsa, Oklahoma. He remained in Tulsa for two years, moving to Portland in 1911. In 1914 he formed a partnership with Chester A. Houghtaling, which he maintained until 1925. He then practiced alone until 1950, after which he formed partnerships with Bernard A. Heims and Morton Caine. He retired in 1965.

SOURCES
Carey, Charles H. *A General History of Oregon*. Portland, 1935.
Ritz, Richard E. "Luther Lee Dougan," *Architalk*. December, 1983.
Tess, John. "National Register of Historic Places Inventory — Nomination Form, Old Elks Temple," no date.

ALBERT E. DOYLE (1877-1928) was born in Santa Cruz, California, but moved to Portland at an early age. Upon completion of the eighth grade he apprenticed with Whidden & Lewis. After twelve years Doyle went to New York where he studied design and engineering at Columbia University and worked in the office of Henry Bacon. In 1906 he was awarded a traveling scholarship and spent most of the year in Europe. Early in 1907, after returning to Portland, Doyle opened an office with construction supervisor William B. Patterson. Within months Doyle was hired to design the 1909 Meier & Frank Co. building and by 1910 he had the largest and most prestigious architectural practice in Portland. James George Beach, an engineer, joined the firm for brief periods in 1912 and 1920. Doyle's practice was carried on after his death by Pietro Belluschi, who had joined the firm in 1925.

SOURCES
McMath, George. "National Register of Historic Places Inventory — Nomination Form, Meier & Frank Building," 1981.

Placzek, Adolf K., ed. *Macmillan Encyclopedia of Architects,* 4 vols. New York, 1982.
Withey, Henry F. and Elsie Rathburn. *Biographical Dictionary of American Architects (Deceased)*. Los Angeles, 1956.

JACQUES ANDRE FOUILHOUX (1879-1945), a native of Paris, studied at the Sorbonne and graduated as a mechanical engineer from the Ecole Centrale des Arts et Manufactures. He came to the United States in 1904 and worked for Albert Kahn in Detroit. In 1905 he moved to Portland where he practiced with Morris H. Whitehouse until 1917. After World War I (during which he received the French Legion of Honor) he practiced in New York. He joined Raymond Hood in 1921 just prior to the Chicago Tribune competition. In 1927 the firm name was changed to Hood, Godley & Fouilhoux and in 1931 to Hood & Fouilhoux. At the time of his death Fouilhoux was a member of the firm of Harrison, Fouilhoux & Abramovitz.

SOURCES
Contemporary American Architects, Raymond M. Hood. New York, 1931.
Placzek, Adolf K., ed. *Macmillan Encyclopedia of Architects,* 4 vols. New York, 1982.
Withey, Henry F. and Elsie Rathburn. *Biographical Dictionary of American Architects (Deceased)*. Los Angeles, 1956.

CASS GILBERT (1859-1934) was born in Zanesville, Ohio, but moved to St. Paul, Minnesota with his family in 1868. He began his architectural training in an office in St. Paul in 1876. In 1879, following a year of architectural studies at M.I.T., he traveled in Europe. After working from 1880 to 1882 in the New York office of McKim, Mead & White, Gilbert returned to St. Paul, where he opened an office with James Knox Taylor (architect for Portland's 1900 custom house). After Taylor left St. Paul for Philadelphia in 1892, Gilbert continued the practice alone. In 1895 he won the competition for the Minnesota State Capitol Building, which was completed in 1903. Around 1900 he moved his office to New York City. Two of his best known buildings are the Woolworth Building and the United States Custom House in New York City. He also designed the Supreme Court Building in Washington, D.C.

SOURCES
Murphy, Patricia Anne. *Cass Gilbert, Minnesota Master Architect* (Catalogue). University of Minnesota Gallery, no date (ca. 1980).
Placzek, Adolf K., ed. *Macmillan Encyclopedia of Architects,* 4 vols. New York, 1982.
Randolph, Thomas. "National Register of Historic Places Inventory — Nomination Form, Spalding Building," 1982.
Withey, Henry F. and Elsie Rathburn. *Biographical Dictionary of American Architects (Deceased)*. Los Angeles, 1956.

CHESTER A. HOUGHTALING (1882-1940) was born in Cleveland, Ohio. He studied construction engineering at the Lewis Institute of Chicago. After working in various projects in Chicago he moved in 1903 to Saskatoon, Canada. Three years later he moved to Spokane, Washington, where he worked for Cutter & Malmgren. He subsequently worked in Twin Falls, Idaho and Canada. In 1913 he opened an office in Portland and in 1914 formed a partnership with L. L. Dougan. Houghtaling was design engineer for the Burnside and Ross Island bridges in Portland.

SOURCES
Carey, Charles H. *A General History of Oregon.* Portland, 1935.
Tess, John. "National Register of Historic Places Inventory — Nomination Form, Old Elks Temple," no date.
Withey, Henry F. and Elsie Rathburn. *Biographical Dictionary of American Architects (Deceased)*. Los Angeles, 1956.

WILLIAM C. KNIGHTON (1867-1938) was born in Indianapolis, Indiana. He moved to Salem, Oregon, where he practiced from 1893 to 1896. He then spent several years in Birmingham, Alabama, moving to Portland in 1902. He was State Architect from 1912 to 1917 and first president of the Oregon Board of Architectural Examiners, appointed in 1919. As State Architect he designed the Oregon Supreme Court building. In 1922 he formed a partnership with L.D. Howell, which continued until his death.

SOURCES
Duniway, David C. "National Register of Historic Places Inventory — Nomination Form, Bayne Building, Salem, Oregon," 1982.
Withey, Henry F. and Elsie Rathburn. *Biographical Dictionary of American Architects (Deceased).* Los Angeles, 1956.

ERNST KRONER (1866-1955) was born in Germany and received his training in Stuttgart. In 1882 he immigrated to the United States, where he worked as a draftsman, contractor and architect. He moved to Portland in 1889 and for the next eight years was involved in politics, at the same time operating a construction firm. He established his architectural practice in 1897. His specialty was the design of churches and schools.

SOURCES
Williams, James M. and Linda K. Emery. "National Register of Historic Places Inventory — Nomination Form, Oddfellows Building," 1980.

ION LEWIS (1858-1933) was born and educated in Lynn, Massachusetts. He studied architecture at M.I.T. and, after graduating in 1880, worked in the Boston office of Peabody & Stearns. In 1882 he formed a partnership with Henry Paston Clark. In 1889 he came to Portland and formed a partnership with his friend and classmate, William M. Whidden. Their firm designed many prominent Portland buildings, including the 1895 City Hall.

SOURCES
McMath, George. "National Register of Historic Places Inventory — Nomination Form, Concord Building," 1977.
McMath, George. Notes for the author, 1984.
Placzek, Adolf K., ed. *Macmillan Encyclopedia of Architects,* 4 vols. New York, 1984.
Withey, Henry F. and Elsie Rathburn, *Biographical Dictionary of American Architects (Deceased).* Los Angeles, 1956.

CARL L. LINDE (1864-1945) was born in Germany and settled in Wisconsin in 1870. His architectural training was evidently obtained exclusively through apprenticeship in Milwaukee, Wisconsin, Chicago, and New York. After moving to Oregon in 1906, Linde worked in the offices of Edgar M. Lazarus, Whidden & Lewis, David C. Lewis, A.E. Doyle and Whitehouse & Fouilhoux. From 1921, when he obtained his architect's license, until 1940 he maintained his own practice in Portland. From 1941 until 1945 he was associated with the army engineers at Vancouver, Washington.

SOURCES
Jacobs, Martin L. "Portland Historical Landmarks Inventory Form, Holman Gardens," (attachment), no date.
Wade, Susan O. "National Register of Historic Places Inventory — Nomination Form, Sovereign Hotel," 1980.

BENJAMIN WISTAR MORRIS III (1870-1944), son of Oregon Bishop Benjamin Wistar Morris II, was born in Portland and educated at St. Paul's in Concord, New Hampshire. He received his architectural training at Columbia University, where he graduated in 1894, and at the Ecole des Beaux Arts. On his return to New York he worked for Carrere and Hastings, assisting with plans for the New York Public Library. He started his own practice around 1900 with Butter and Morgan, but soon withdrew and practiced alone until 1910. From 1910 to 1915 he was associated with Grant LaFarge and from 1915 to his death with Robert O'Connor.

SOURCES
Withey, Henry F. and Elsie Rathburn. *Biographical Dictionary of American Architects (Deceased).* Los Angeles, 1956.

JAMES AND MERRITT REID (Reid Brothers) maintained one of the leading architectural offices in San Francisco for nearly half a century. James (1851-1943) and Merritt (d. 1932) were born in New Brunswick, Canada. James was educated at McGill University and studied architecture at M.I.T. and the Ecole des Beaux Arts. He worked in Evansville, Indiana, as a draftsman with the Evansville & Terre Haute Railroad, leaving in 1886 to design the Hotel del Coronado in California. In 1888 he joined his brother Merritt's architectural office in San Francisco. Many of the firm's buildings were faced with glazed terra cotta. Two notable surviving buildings in downtown San Francisco are the Fairmont Hotel and the Hale Bros. Dept. Store building. One of their best works in San Francisco, the Fitzhugh Building on Union Square, was demolished in 1979.

SOURCES
Page, Charles Hall & Associates, Inc. *Splendid Survivors*. San Francisco, 1979.
Placzek, Adolf K., ed., *Macmillan Encyclopedia of Architects*, 4 vols., New York, 1982
Withey, Henry F. and Elsie Rathburn, *Biographical Dictionary of American Architects (Deceased)*. Los Angeles, 1956.

GEORGE A. SCHONEWALD (1888-1939) was born and educated in New York. He attended New York City University and completed his architectural studies in Paris, France. For several years he had an office in the Grand Central Terminal Building. His practice was of a general nature including business and commercial structures.

SOURCES
Withey, Henry F. and Elsie Rathburn. *Biographical Dictionary of American Architects (Deceased)*. Los Angeles, 1956.

WILLIAM M. WHIDDEN (1857-1929) was born in Boston, Massachusetts. He received his architectural training at M.I.T. and at the Ecole des Beaux Arts, where he spent four years. In January, 1882, he entered the office of McKim, Mead & White. He came from New York to Portland in May, 1882 to supervise construction of the Portland Hotel for McKim, Mead & White. In 1883 work on the hotel ceased and Whidden returned to Boston, where he formed a partnership with classmate William E. Chamberlain. He came back to Portland in 1888 when construction resumed. In 1889 he was joined by his friend and classmate Ion Lewis and the two established an office. The firm designed many prominent Portland buildings, including the 1895 City Hall.

SOURCES
Corning, Howard M. ed. Dictionary of Oregon History, Portland 1956.
McMath, George. "National Register of Historic Places Inventory — Nomination Form, Concord Building," 1977.
McMath, George. Notes for the author, 1984.
Placzek, Adolf K., ed. *Macmillan Encyclopedia of Architects*, 4 vols. New York, 1982.
Withey, Henry F. and Elsie Rathburn. *Biographical Dictionary of American Architects (Deceased)*. Los Angeles, 1956.

MORRIS H. WHITEHOUSE (1878-1944), a native and life-long resident of Portland, began his architectural training in local offices. At age 20 he entered M.I.T. where he remained for post-graduate work. In 1908, after 18 months of travel abroad, he opened an office in Portland in association with Bruce Honeyman. A year later he formed a partnership with Edgar M. Lazarus and Jacques Andre Fouilhoux. Lazarus subsequently left and the firm remained Whitehouse & Fouilhoux until 1917, when Whitehouse began practicing alone. Glenn Stanton, Earl Newberry and Walter Church were all at one time associated with Whitehouse. In 1936 the firm name was changed to Whitehouse & Church.

SOURCES
Placzek, Adolf K., ed. *Macmillan Encyclopedia of Architects*, 4 vols. New York, 1982.
Withey, Henry F. and Elsie Rathburn, *Biographical Dictionary of American Architects (Deceased)*. Los Angeles, 1956.

ILLUSTRATION CREDITS

Fig. I-1. *Oregonian*, Jan. 1, 1896.

Fig. I-2. Brubaker Aerial Survey. Oregon Historical Society Neg. #47392

Fig. I-3. Author and Corinna Campbell.

Fig. I-4. Author and Corinna Campbell.

Fig. I-5. *Oregonian*, Jan. 1, 1916.

Fig. I-6. Portland Association of Building Owners and Managers. Oregon Historical Society Neg. #56832

Fig. I-7. Benjamin Gifford photo. Oregon Historical Society Neg. #Gi 7786

Fig. I-8. Oregon Historical Society Neg. #53729

Fig. I-9. *Oregonian*, Jan. 1, 1907, p.1.

Fig. I-10. Microfiche Collection, City of Portland Bureau of Buildings.

Fig. I-11. Oregon Historical Society Neg. #56825

Fig. I-12. *Pacific Coast Architect*, Jan. 1912, p. 169. Oregon Historical Society Neg. #64468

Fig. I-13. *The Spalding Building* (Promotional brochure). Collection Miller/Cook, Architects. Oregon Historical Society Neg. #64492

Fig. I-14. Oregon Historical Society MSS. 3076-8

Fig. I-15. Oregon Historical Society MSS. 3075-4, Neg. #62500

Fig. I-16. Oregon Historical Society Neg. #35352-a

Fig. I-17. Oregon Historical Society Neg. #53448

Fig. I-18. Oregon Historical Society MSS. 3022-78, Neg. #62501

Fig. I-19. *Pacific Coast Architect*, vol. 2, no. 4 (Jan. 1912) 164. Oregon Historical Society Neg. #47201

Fig. I-20. Al Edelman photo.

Fig. I-21. Al Edelman photo.

Fig. I-22. Al Edelman photo.

Fig. I-23. Al Edelman photo.

Fig. I-24. Oregon Historical Society MSS. 3076-9, Neg. #62499

Fig. I-25. Oregon Historical Society Neg. #57251

Fig. I-26. Oregon Historical Society Neg. #57250

Fig. I-27. Gladding, McBean & Co.

Fig. I-28. Gladding, McBean & Co.

Fig. I-29. Gladding, McBean & Co.

Fig. I-30. Photo by author.

Fig. I-31. Gladding, McBean & Co.

Fig. I-32. Gladding, McBean & Co.

Fig. I-33. Gladding, McBean & Co.

Fig. I-34. Don Wilson photo.

Fig. I-35. Photo by author.

Fig. I-36. Gladding, McBean & Co.

Fig. I-37. Gladding, McBean & Co.

Fig. I-38. Photo by author.

Fig. I-39. Oregon Historical Society Neg. #55697

Fig. I-40. Oregon Historical Society MSS. 3022-78, Neg. #62497

Fig. I-41. Oregon Historical Society, McMath/Doyle Collection.

Fig. I-42. Oregon Historical Society MSS. 3076-9, Neg. #57248

Fig. I-43. Photo by author.

Fig. I-44. Oregon Historical Society Neg. #45433

Fig. I-45. Angelus Studio. Oregon Historical Society Neg. #53450

Fig. I-46. Photo by author.

Fig. I-47. Corinna Campbell.

Fig. I-48. Oregon Historical Society Neg. #55700

Fig. I-49. Oregon Historical Society, McMath/Doyle Collection.

Fig. I-50. Oregon Historical Society, Baker Collection.

Fig. I-51. Author's Collection.

Fig. I-52. Gladding, McBean & Co. Oregon Historical Society Neg. #57253

Fig. I-53. Gladding, McBean & Co. Oregon Historical Society Neg. #57252

Fig. I-54. Microfiche Collection, City of Portland Bureau of Buildings.

Fig. I-55. Sowell Studio. Oregon Historical Society Neg. #64467

Fig. II-1. Portland Bureau of Planning. *Planning Guidelines, Portland Downtown Plan*, (1972).

Fig. II-2. Author and Corinna Campbell, from information provided by Steve Iwata, Portland Bureau of Planning.

Fig. II-3. Author and Corinna Campbell, from information provided by Portland Bureau of Planning.

Fig. II-4. Author and Corinna Campbell, from information provided by Portland Bureau of Planning.

Fig. II-5. Author and Corinna Campbell, from information provided by Portland Bureau of Planning.

Fig. II-6. Author and Corinna Campbell.

Fig. II-7. Ed Hershberger photo. Collection Sheldon, Eggleston, Riddick, Aanderud.

Fig. II-8. Photo by author.

Fig. II-9. Photo by author.

Fig. II-10. Al Edelman photo.

Fig. II-11. Al Edelman photo.

Fig. III-1. Oregon Historical Society Neg. #51414

Fig. III-2. Watercolor by Wilding. Oregon Historical Society Neg. #56877

Fig. III-3. Walter Boychuk photo. Oregon Historical Society Neg. #43189

Fig. III-4. Oregon Historical Society Neg. #27912

Fig. III-5. Oregon Historical Society Neg. #52604

Fig. III-6. Oregon Historical Society Neg. #39256

Fig. III-7. Oregon Historical Society Neg. #Oreg. 4572

Fig. III-8. Oregon Historical Society Neg. #56845

Fig. III-9. Oregon Historical Society Neg. #56829

Fig. III-10. Oregon Historical Society Neg. #Oreg. 4371

Fig. III-11. Photo by author.

Fig. III-12. Oregon Historical Society Neg. #42125

Fig. III-13. Oregon Historical Society Neg. #Oreg. 4842

Fig. III-14. Oregon Historical Society Neg. #52605

Fig. III-15. Oregon Historical Society Neg. #56844

Fig. III-16. Oregon Historical Society Neg. #12973

Fig. III-17. Oregon Historical Society Neg. #50379

Fig. III-18. Oregon Historical Society Neg. #56847

Fig. III-19. Oregon Historical Society Neg. #50921

Fig. III-20. Oregon Historical Society Neg. #56842

Fig. III-21. Angelus Collection, Univ. of Oregon. Oregon Historical Society Neg. #51693

Fig. III-22. Oregon Historical Society Neg. #56828

Fig. III-23. Oregon Historical Society Neg. #50411

Fig. III-24. Oregon Historical Society Neg. #56826

Fig. III-25. Oregon Historical Society Neg. #36331

Fig. III-26. Oregon Historical Society Neg. #12974

Fig. III-27. Oregon Historical Society Neg. #54827

Fig. III-28. Oregon Historical Society Neg. #56850

Fig. III-29. Oregon Historical Society Neg. #55702

Fig. III-30. Weber Collection. Oregon Historical Society Neg. #51769

Fig. III-31. Oregon Historical Society Neg. #56849

Fig. III-32. John E. Andrews Collection.
Fig. III-33. Oregon Historical Society Neg. #56827
Fig. III-34. Oregon Historical Society Neg. #53401
Fig. III-35. Oregon Historical Society Neg. #53449
Fig. III-36. Oregon Historical Society Neg. #56846
Fig. III-37. Oregon Historical Society Neg. #56848
Fig. III-38. Oregon Historical Society Neg. #55703
Fig. III-39. Postcard, Steve Dotterrer Collection.
Fig. III-40. Oregon Historical Society, McMath/Doyle Collection.
Fig. III-41. Author and Corinna Campbell.

SELECTED BIBLIOGRAPHY

Sources of information for individual buildings and architects can be found in Part III.

The serious researcher should also consult three bibliographies that contain entries not listed in this publication:

Prudon, Theodore H.M. "Terra Cotta as a Building Material," The Association for Preservation Technology, Incorporated, *Communique*, vol. V (June, 1976).

Tindall, Susan and James Hamrick. *American Architectural Terra Cotta: A Bibliography*, Vance Bibliographies. Monticello, Illinois.

Wilson, Hewitt. "Monograph and Bibliography on Terra Cotta," *American Ceramic Society Journal (Bulletin)*, IX (Feb., 1926), 94-136.

The Wilson monograph is also the best single reference document for technical information on the production of terra cotta.

BOOKS

Berryman, Nancy D. and Susan M. Tindall. Terra Cotta; *Preservation and Maintenance of an Historic Building Material*. Landmarks Preservation Council of Illinois, 1984.

Bragdon, Claude Fayette. *Architecture and Democracy*. New York, 1926.

Dalton, Byron Wm. *Practical Plastering, Cement Finishing and Related Subjects*. Chicago, 1937.

Gayle, Margot, David W. Look, and John G. Waite. *Metals in America's Historic Buildings; Uses and Preservation Treatments*. U.S. Department of the Interior, 1980.

Hamlin, Talbot Faulkner. *The American Spirit in Architecture*. New Haven, 1926.

Harbeson, John F. *The Study of Architectural Design*. New York, 1927.

Harrison, Michael. *Downtown Design Standards*, City of Portland, Oregon. Bureau of Planning, July, 1980.

International Library of Technology. 9 vols. Scranton, Pa.: International Textbook Company, 1922.

Jordy, William H. *American Buildings and their Architects*, vol. 3. Garden City, N.Y., 1972.

Labbe, John T. *Fares Please! Those Portland Trolley Years*. Caldwell, Idaho, 1980.

Laurence, F.S. *Color in Architecture*. New York: National Terra Cotta Society, 1924.

Lowndes, William S. *Brickwork, Terra Cotta and Concrete*. Scranton, Pa: International Library of Technology, 1920.

MacColl, E. Kimbark. *The Growth of a City; Power and Politics in Portland, Oregon, 1915 to 1950*. Portland, 1979.

MacColl, E. Kimbark. *The Shaping of a City; Business and Politics in Portland, Oregon, 1885 to 1915*. Portland, 1976.

Meyer, Franz Sales. *A Handbook of Ornament*. 3rd English ed. London, 1924.

National Association of Sheet Metal Contractors of the U.S. *Standard Practice in Sheet Metal Work*. Pittsburgh, Pa., 1929.

National Terra Cotta Society. *Architectural Terra Cotta, Standard Construction*. New York, N.Y., 1914.

National Terra Cotta Society. *Architectural Terra Cotta, Standard Construction*. Rev. ed. Chicago, 1927.

National Terra Cotta Society. *Terra Cotta of the Italian Renaissance*. New York, 1925.

Page, Charles Hall & Associates, Inc. *Splendid Survivors*. San Francisco, 1979.

Portland Architectural Club Yearbook. Portland, 1908, 1909, 1910, 1913.

Portland Bureau of Planning. *Planning Guidelines/Portland Downtown Plan as adopted by City Council*. December, 1972.

Portland Bureau of Planning. *Downtown Plan Handbook, Portland, Oregon*. June, 1981.

Ross, Marion Dean. *A Century of Architecture in Oregon, 1859-1959*. Portland, 1959.

The San Francisco Earthquake and Fire of April 18, 1906 and Their Effects on Structures and Structural Materials. U.S. Geological Survey Bulletin No. 324.

Staehli, Alfred M. "John Staehli: A Note on the Independent Artisan and Architectural Ornament." *Festschrift; A Collection of Essays on Architectural History*. Northern Coast Chapter, Society of Architectural Historians, 1978.

Tallmadge, Thomas E. *The Story of Architecture in America*. New York, 1927.

Vaughan, Thomas and Virginia Guest Ferriday. *Space, Style and Structure; Building in Northwest America*. Portland, 1974.

Vaughan, Thomas and George McMath. *A Century of Portland Architecture*. 2nd ed. Portland, 1969.

Voss, Walter C. and Ralph Coolidge Henry. *Architectural Construction*, vol. I. New York, 1925.

Weese, Harry & Associates. *Four Landmark Buildings in Chicago's Loop; A Study of Historic Conservation Options*. Chicago, 1978.

MISCELLANEOUS

Baker, Fred C. Recorded interview by Janet Charlton, George McMath, and Anne Murphy, 1978. Notes in author's collection.

Fredericks, Herb. "Whidden & Lewis Job List" (Typescript). Collection, Oregon Historical Society.

Hamrick, James Marshall, Jr. "A Survey of the Use of Architectural Terra Cotta in American Commercial Architecture: 1870-1930" (Master's thesis). Univ. of Oregon, 1979.

Keefe, Lloyd T. "History of Zoning in Portland, 1918 to 1959" (Typescript). Portland Planning Bureau, 1975.

Musick, Felicity. "The Development of the Pacific Building and the Public Service Building" (Thesis). Oregon Historical Society, 1976.

Plamondon, Al J., compiler. "The Plamondon Scrapbooks" Nov., 1955. Collection, Alfred Staehli.

Rutherford, Janice. "Richardsonian Romanesque Architecture in Portland, Oregon, 1889-95" (Typescript), 1980.

Thomasen, Sven E., Wiss, Janney, Elstner and Associates, Inc. "Inspecting, Testing and Analyzing Terra Cotta" (Typescript), no date.

Weiss, Norman R. "Exterior Cleaning of Historic Masonry Buildings, Draft," United States Department of the Interior, Heritage Conservation and Recreation Service, Office of Archaeology and Historic Preservation, 1976.

PERIODICALS

Alberry, D.F. "Grog for Terra Cotta," *American Ceramic Society Journal (Bulletin)*, IX (July, 1926), 316-19.

Anderegg, F.O. "Water-tight Terra Cotta Masonry," *American Ceramic Society Journal*, XVI (Dec., 1933), 634-9.

The Architect and Engineer, vol. LVI (March, 1919). Entire issue devoted to Portland architecture and planning.

Berryman, Nancy D. "Architectural Terra Cotta; History of Architectural Terra Cotta," *NCECA Journal* (1981).

Cheney, Charles H. "The Work of Albert E. Doyle, Architect of Portland, Oregon," *The Architect and Engineer*, LVIII, no. 1 (July, 1919), 39-86.

Clare, R.L. and R.N. Long. "Value of Ageing the Terra Cotta Body," *American Ceramic Society Journal*, IV, no. 6 (June, 1921), 453-58.

Croly, Herbert D. "The Advantages of Terra Cotta," *Architectural Record*, XVIII, no. 4 (Oct., 1905), 315-23.

Croly, Herbert D. "Portland, Oregon, The Transformation of the City from an Architectural & Social Viewpoint," *Architectural Record*, XXI (June, 1912), 591-607.

Croly, Herbert D. "The Proper Use of Terra Cotta," *Architectural Record* (Jan., 1906), pp. 73-81.

Croly, Herbert D. "The Use of Terra Cotta in the United States, How It Has Increased," *Architectural Record*, XVIII, no. 1 (July, 1905), 86-94.

Deemer, Charles. "The Draftsman as Artist," (Fred C. Baker) *Oregonian Northwest Magazine*, November 19, 1978, p. 14.

"Development of Inland Empire Clay Industries," *Pacific Builder and Engineer* (March 18, 1911).

Eskesen, Eckardt V. "Investigation of Terra Cotta Work at the Bureau of Standards," *American Ceramic Society Journal (Bulletin)*, VII (May, 1924), 158-61.

Eskesen, Eckardt V. "Water-tight Terra Cotta Construction," *American Ceramic Society (Bulletin)*, XIII (June, 1934), 154-62.

Fitch, Dr. James Marston. "Renovation of Alwyn Court, New York City: Restoring the Façades & Improving Public Spaces," *Technology & Conservation* (Summer, 1980), pp. 24-27.

Floyd, Margaret Henderson. "A Terra-Cotta Cornerstone for Copley Square," *Journal of the Society of Architectural Historians*, XXXII (May, 1973), 83-103.

"Fred C. Baker, King of Ornamental Light Fixtures,"*Business Success*, II, no. 5 (May, 1979), 6, 7, 36; II, no. 6 (June, 1979), 6-8.

Friends of Terra Cotta Newsletter, vols. 1, 2, 3 (1982 to 1984).

"From Backyard Shop to World's Best: St. Louis Terra Cotta Co. Plant,"*Brick and Clay Record*, LXVIII (April 27, 1926), 698-702.

Fryer, William F. Jr. "Skeleton Construction — The New Method of Constructing High Buildings,"*Architectural Record*, I (July, 1891), 228-35.

Geijsbeek, S. "Architectural Terra Cotta,"*The Pacific Coast Architect* (April, 1912), pp. 312-13; (May, 1912), pp. 360-61.

Gladding, McBean & Co., *Shapes of Clay* (Feb., 1926); (July, 1927); (Jan., 1928); (June, 1930).

"Gladding, McBean & Co. and Denny-Renton Clay & Coal Consolidate,"*Brick and Clay Record* (March 15, 1925), p. 459.

Grimmer, Anne E. "Dangers of Abrasive Cleaning to Historic Buildings,"*Preservation Brief*, No. 6, Heritage Conservation and Recreation Service (1979).

Hemp, Paul. "Cleaning Those Grime-Encrusted Façades,"*New York Times*, Jan. 22, 1984.

Hill, George. "Some Practical Limiting Conditions in the Design of the Modern Office Building,"*Architectural Record*, II, no. 4 (June, 1893), 445-68.

Hottinger, A. "Looking Backward in the Terra Cotta Field," *American Ceramic Society Journal*, VI (Jan., 1923), 306-8.

Hottinger, A. "Soluble Salts and their Application to Terra Cotta,"*American Ceramic Society Journal (Bulletin)*, X (Nov., 1927), 341-2.

Klinefelter, T.A. and F.C. Parsons. "Good and Bad Practice in the Pressing Department,"*American Ceramic Society Journal*, V (Sept., 1922), 632-42.

Laurence, F.S. "Color in Architecture, Part III," *The American Architect*, CXXII, 311-18.

"Lock-keyed Terra Cotta; Interview with J.R. Gwynn,"*Brick and Clay Record*, LXXVII (Oct. 21, 1930), 469-70.

Lucas, James L. "Causes and Cures for Deteriorating Masonry," *The Construction Specifier* (March, 1983), pp. 60-70.

Mack, Robert C. "The Cleaning and Waterproof Coating of Masonry Buildings,"*Preservation Brief*, No. 1, National Park Service (no date).

Mack, Robert C. "Repointing Mortar Joints in Historic Brick Buildings,"*Preservation Brief*, No. 2, National Park Service (1976).

"Making of Terra Cotta; A Pictorial Review,"*Architecture* (New York), LXVII (April, 1933), 207-10.

Matthews, Mary J. "Kansas City Experiments with Tera Cotta Replacement,"*Friends of Terra Cotta Newsletter* (Fall, 1983), pp. 3, 4.

Musselman, J.F. "Notes on Illumination,"*Architectural Review* (June, 1919), pp. 177-78.

New York Building Congress, "Standard Specification for the Manufacture and Finishing of Terra Cotta, Part B,"*American Architecture and Building News*, CXXXV, no. 2570 (June 5, 1929), 767-70.

New York Building Congress, "Standard Specification for Setting of Terra Cotta, Part B," *The American Architect* (June 20, 1929), 837-39.

Ortman, F.B. "Terra Cotta Cracking,"*American Ceramic Society Journal*, XVI (Dec., 1933), 639-42.

Peterson, Harold L. "Conservation of Metals,"*Technical Leaflet*, 10, American Association for State and Local History (1968).

"Popularity of Terra Cotta," *The Pacific Coast Architect* (June, 1913), p. 133.

Prudon, Theodore H.M. "Architectural Terra Cotta: Analyzing the Deterioration Problems & Restoration Approaches,"*Technology & Conservation*, III, no. 3 (Fall, 1978), 30-38.

Ross, Marion Dean. "One Hundred Twenty-Five Years of Building,"*AIA Journal*, XLIX (June, 1968), 120-26, 172, 178-86.

"Scaffolds allow workers to range; Terra cotta tiles inspected one by one," *Engineering News Record* (February 16, 1984), pp. 24-25.

"Setting Terra Cotta," *The American Architect*, CXXIII (May 9, 1923), 425-6.

"6 Plants Now Under McBean Control,"*Brick and Clay Record* (Feb. 16, 1926), p. 283.

Stockbridge, J.G. "Evaluation of Terra Cotta on In-Service Structures,"*Special Technical Publication*, 691, American Society for Testing and Materials (1980).

Sturgis, John H. "Terra Cotta and Its Uses,"*American Institute of Architects Proceedings* (1871), pp. 39-43.

Taylor, James. "Terra-Cotta — Some of Its Characteristics,"*Architectural Record*, I (July-Sept., 1891), 63-68.

"Terra Cotta" (Pre-cast panels for Reading & Bates Mid-Continent Tower), *Progressive Architecture* (June, 1983), pp. 96-97.

Thomasen, Sven E. "Inspecting, Testing and Analyzing Terra Cotta," *Friends of Terra Cotta Newsletter* (Summer 1982), pp. 1, 3, 4.

Tiller, de Teel Patterson. "The Preservation of Historic Glazed Architectural Terra-Cotta,"*Preservation Brief*, No. 7, Heritage Conservation and Recreation Service (1979).

de Teel Patterson Tiller, and James S. Askins. "Repointing Joints in Historic Brick Buildings; A Procedural guide," *The Construction Specifier* (June, 1980), pp. 35-41.

Timmerman, W. "Polychrome Terra Cotta,"*American Ceramic Society (Bulletin)*, XII (Sept., 1933), 276-80.

Tindall, Susan M. "Architectural Terra Cotta Restoration,"*NCECA Journal* (1981), pp. 37-39.

United States Gypsum Company, "Classic elegance at a bargain price; Glass-reinforced gypsum recreates the authentic look of traditional plaster craft,"*form & function*, Issue 1 (1984), 9-11.

United States Gypsum Company, "Plasterers Add 100 Years to Landmark's Life," *form & function*, Issue 1 (1983), 11-14.

Van Court, D.P. "Guide to Maintenance Caulking," *Plant Engineering* (April 28, 1977), p. 249.

Weeks, Christopher. "Preserving An Old-World Heritage" (Ornamental Plaster), *Historic Preservation* (November/December, 1981), pp. 30-35.

Weiss, Norman R. "Cleaning of Building Exteriors: Problems and Procedures of Dirt Removal," *Technology & Conservation*, 2/76, (Fall 1976), pp. 8-13.

Wilmson, H. Robert. "Old Fred," (Fred C. Baker) *Symposia*, XIII, no. 4 (Dec.-Jan., 1978-79) 16-17.

Wilson, H., "Notes on Terra Cotta Slips with Reference to the Use of Asbestos and Chlorite Mica," *American Ceramic Society Journal*, III (Feb., 1920), 114-33.

CORRESPONDENCE

Edward Burkhalter, former officer of Washington Brick, Lime & Sewer Pipe Co., Nov. 3, 1979.

George Dickson Clark, Jr., formerly of N. Clark & Son, Aug. 21, 1979.

Neal R. Fosseen, former president of Washington Brick, Lime & Sewer Pipe Co., Sept. 25, 1979.

Scanlan, Robert D., Coldwell Banker, Sept. 23, 1983.

Thomas J. Usher, Cushman & Wakefield of Oregon, Inc., Oct. 10, 1983.

UNRECORDED INTERVIEWS

John Clark, 1978.

Dick Durland, 1984.

Sheila Finch-Tepper, 1984.

Lewis McArthur, 1982, 1983.

Bill Roberts, 1980.

INDEX